Matteo Legrenzi is Associate Professor at the School of International Relations of Ca' Foscari University of Venice, and is President of the Italian Association for Middle Eastern Studies (SeSaMO).

'Matteo Legrenzi has written the essential guide to the history and politics of the Gulf Cooperation Council. As the centre of political and economic gravity in the Arab world shifts decisively towards the Gulf, professionals and analysts will find in Legrenzi's brilliantly concise book a reliable guide to this complex and misunderstood corner of the globe. His many years of personal experience in the Gulf, and the deep connections he has established with policy makers in the region, make Legrenzi one of the most authoritative Western authors on the Arab states of the Gulf at work today.'
— Eugene Rogan, The Middle East Centre, St Antony's College, Oxford University

'There are few serious books on the Gulf Cooperation Council, and even fewer that take a critical look at what the organization has and has not accomplished. Matteo Legrenzi has written a balanced, well-researched and comprehensive overview of this little-understood and frequently over-hyped regional international organization. It is the best book on the topic.'
— F. Gregory Gause, III, Professor of Political Science, University of Vermont

'This book could not be more timely. The Gulf Cooperation Council, which many have seen as a mere "shaikhly" club, is exercising real muscle as never before. The GCC is playing a direct role not only in the politics and economics of Gulf affairs, but also in security developments. Matteo Legrenzi provides the essential context to understand these transformations in this smoothly written and meticulously researched account. For anyone interested in the evolution of the Gulf since the British withdrawal, this book is an indispensable resource.'
— Gary Sick, Senior Research Scholar and Director of the Gulf/2000 Project, Columbia University

THE GCC AND THE INTERNATIONAL RELATIONS OF THE GULF

Diplomacy, Security and Economic Coordination in a Changing Middle East

MATTEO LEGRENZI

I.B. TAURIS
LONDON · NEW YORK

New paperback edition published in 2015 by
I.B.Tauris & Co Ltd
London • New York
www.ibtauris.com

First published in hardback in 2011 by I.B.Tauris & Co Ltd

Copyright © 2011, 2015 Matteo Legrenzi

The right of Matteo Legrenzi to be identified as the author of this work has been asserted by the author in accordance with the Copyright, Designs and Patents Act 1988.

All rights reserved. Except for brief quotations in a review, this book, or any part thereof, may not be reproduced, stored in or introduced into a retrieval system, or transmitted, in any form or by any means, electronic, mechanical, photocopying, recording or otherwise, without the prior written permission of the publisher.

Every attempt has been made to gain permission for the use of the images in this book.
Any omissions will be rectified in future editions.

References to websites were correct at the time of writing.

ISBN: 978 1 78453 236 9
eISBN: 978 0 85773 386 3

A full CIP record for this book is available from the British Library
A full CIP record is available from the Library of Congress

Library of Congress Catalog Card Number: available

Typeset in Garamond Three by OKS Prepress Services, Chennai, India

To St Antony's

TABLE OF CONTENTS

Note on Transliteration   ix
Maps   x

INTRODUCTION   1

1   THE CREATION OF THE UNITED ARAB EMIRATES AND THE FIRST INTEGRATION EXPERIMENTS OF THE ARAB STATES OF THE GULF   11

2   CREATION, STRUCTURE AND ORGANIZATION OF THE GCC   27

3   THE GCC IN LIGHT OF INTERNATIONAL RELATIONS THEORY   41

4   GCC ECONOMIC INTEGRATION: DISAPPOINTING REGIONALISM AND ENCOURAGING REGIONALISATION   57

5   GCC DEFENSE COOPERATION: BEYOND SYMBOLISM?   73

6   GCC DIPLOMATIC COORDINATION: THE LIMITED ROLE OF INSTITUTIONS   87

7   THE GCC, IRAN AND NUCLEAR PROLIFERATION IN THE GULF   113

8	THE GCC, NATO AND THE GULF SECURITY COMPLEX	139
	CONCLUSION	149
	Notes	157
	Appendix	185
	Bibliography	189
	Index	201

NOTE ON TRANSLITERATION

After pondering the question for a fairly long time the author has decided to spare the reader the inconvenience of diacritical marks over and under Arabic words and names. This has not been an easy decision for someone who has spent a long time sweating over Arabic texts at the Oxford Faculty of Oriental Studies, but it is believed to be in line with the International Relations character of the work. Otherwise, words and names are transliterated as in the *Dictionary of Modern Written Arabic* by Hans Wehr. Some additional leeway has been given for names of leaders who appear frequently in the news media so as not to confuse further the odd generalist who may come to read this work.

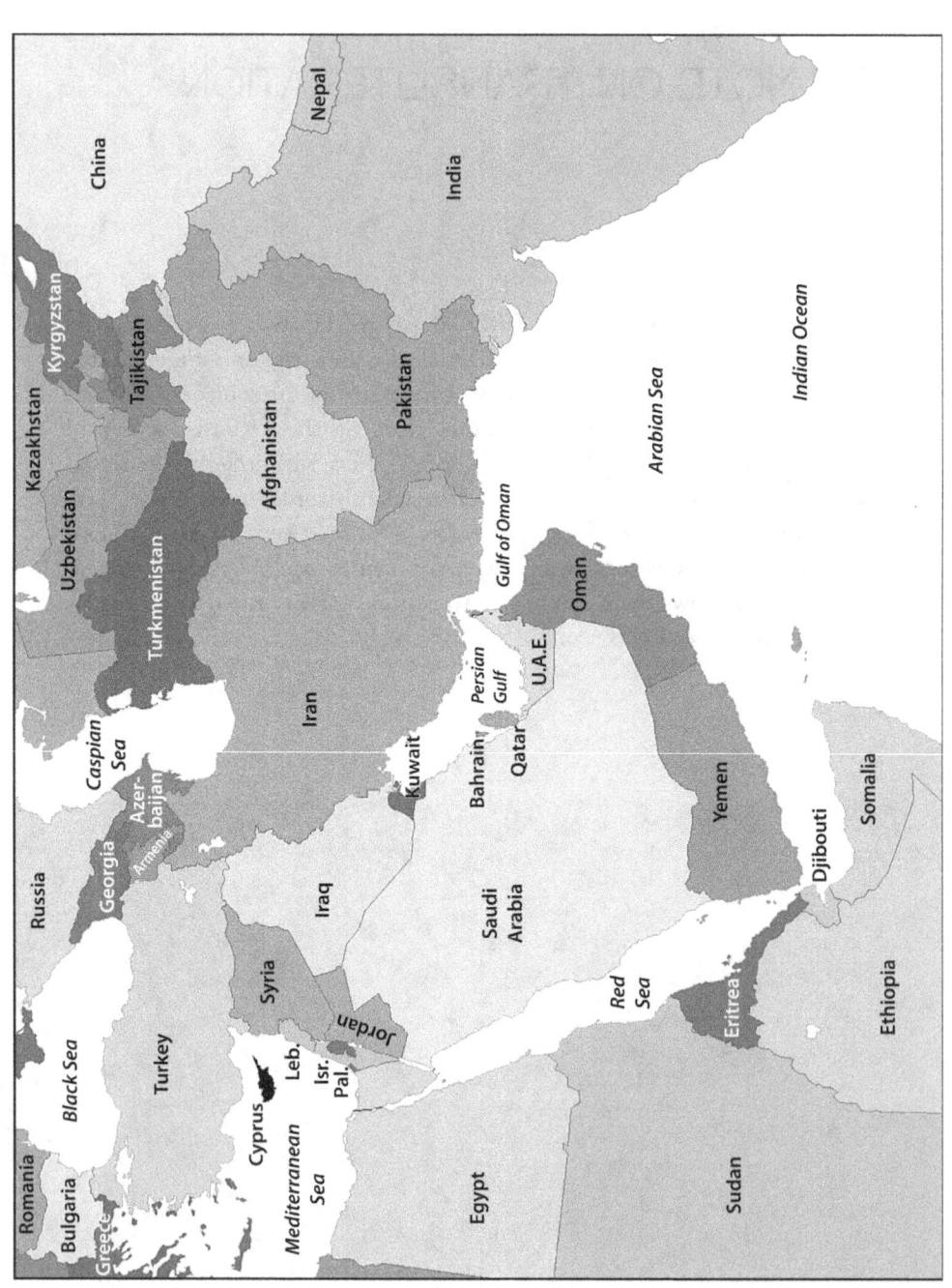

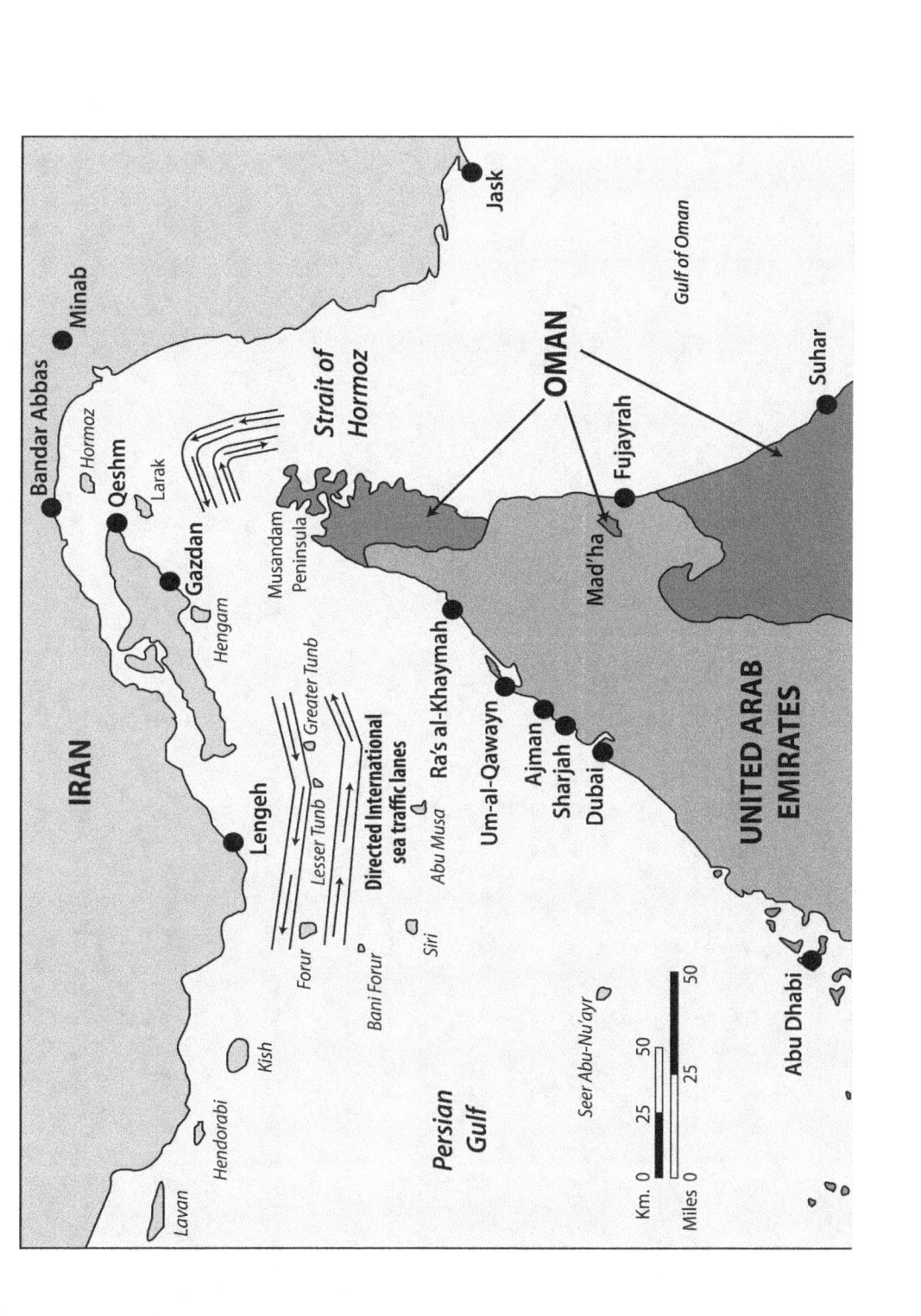

INTRODUCTION

We have not yet set up a unified military force that deters enemies and supports friends. We have not reached a common market, nor formulated a unified political position on political crises ... objectivity and frankness require us to declare that all that has been achieved is too little and it reminds us of the bigger part that has yet to be accomplished. ... We are still moving at a slow pace that does not conform with the modern one.[1]

King Abdullah of Saudi Arabia

The purpose of this work is to study the origins and the evolution of the Cooperation Council for the Arab States of the Gulf, better known in the English-speaking world as the Gulf Cooperation Council (GCC). The GCC is the most resilient sub-regional organization in the Arab world. I will argue that in the years since its founding the GCC has achieved several results in enhancing the level of cooperation among its six member states: Saudi Arabia, Bahrain, Kuwait, Oman, Qatar and the United Arab Emirates (UAE). However, the organization falls far short of the goals set out in its founding charter.[2] I will submit that, from its onset, the GCC was not created to serve a regional institutional purpose, but rather, was deliberately made hollow and served primarily to project a semblance of unity. As in previous cases in the history of the Arab state system,[3] the smaller member states fear the interdependence that such an institution was ostensibly designed to promote. Nonetheless, the six member states achieved a high level of cooperation in a field such as internal security. This is strictly linked to the issue of regime survival, an issue in which all six royal families share an overriding interest. Joint cultural initiatives are often planned too, and in the long run, as will be seen, they may indeed have an impact. In any case these are areas that are difficult to exploit by any single state *vis-à-vis* the others.

In my work I explore the reasons for this difficulty in approaching the level of integration set out in ambitious communiqués and in the founding charter.

The first puzzle in which I am interested is how to explain the gap between the rhetoric of integration and the actual results achieved by the organization. A lack of integration that has continued in spite of plentiful resources and the creation of a fairly large and articulated bureaucracy modelled after that of the European Union. On the other hand, I will also strive to explain why the GCC proved to be the most resilient sub-regional organization in the Arab world. It is true that up until now the GCC has behaved more as a council of rulers than as a truly regional organization such as the European Union. However, Gulf press reports and other primary sources indicate that 28 years after its founding, something is stirring at the societal level. The notion of a 'GCC' popular identity, introduced by local rulers at the beginning of the 1980s, at a time when it did not represent any substantive reality, is working its way into the political and economic landscape of the six Gulf monarchies.[4] Therefore, the second puzzle I intend to explore is whether the mere resilience of the GCC has led to a possible 'spillover' at the societal level and a *de facto* regionalism akin to that observed by scholars of 'new regionalism' in other parts of the world.[5] Therefore, while after a sober assessment the reservations of more sceptical scholars seem justified,[6] they risk overlooking an interesting trend within the societies of these states. I chart how the establishment of the GCC led to various societal groups starting to think in regional terms. On the other hand, I try to refute the enthusiastic assessments of what I would call the 'apologetic' strand of literature on the GCC. This is constituted by those authors who take an exceedingly enthusiastic attitude towards the study of this organization.[7] The latter, more often than not, couch their study of the GCC in legalistic terms and display a tendency to accept the fact that any project that has been agreed upon on paper will eventually materialize. Unfortunately, most books that deal specifically with the GCC as a regional organization tend to fall in this category. These authors do a very good job in gathering a large quantity of record material. However, to find out about the actual problems faced by the organization one is better off referring to the works of scholars who touch on the GCC while dealing with the wider questions of Gulf politics, economics or security.[8] The fact that policymakers and scholars of the region who do not work on the GCC *per se* pay scant attention to the workings of the organization may serve as a signal that the latter has so far failed to achieve considerable influence in coordinating the policies of the member states.

I purport to steer a middle course between those who consider the GCC nothing more than a council of rulers and those who believe that the establishment of the organization heralded a shift in the organization of the international politics of the Gulf. I will look closely and critically at the level of integration achieved in the fields covered by the founding charter and the subsequent agreements entered into by the six constituent states. I will also focus on how the GCC reacted *as an organization* to the major international crises that it had to confront from its inception. On the other hand, I will outline how the formation of the GCC affected a partial shift in the identity of various constituents at the societal level.

In the first chapter I provide the geographical and historical background for the formation of the GCC. My point of departure will be the announcement in 1968 by the British government that it was going to withdraw British military forces from east of Suez by 1971. As will be shown, the initial responses by the Gulf rulers were permeated by fear and disbelief. However, when it became clear that the British really intended to leave, discussions about the possibility of some future form of sub-regional cooperation started in earnest. For the purpose of this work I will focus on the numerous functional organizations set up in the economic field by the six member states before the establishment of the GCC in May 1981. I will argue that these ventures at regional cooperation were purely functional in character, and while they cannot be seen as laying the foundation for the future establishment of the GCC they certainly provide an insight in how the bureaucracy of the organization functioned in the last 20 years.[9]

Very significant to an understanding of the genesis of the GCC are the security agreements entered into by Saudi Arabia and its conservative neighbours between 1976 and 1979. They provide a useful hint to what the GCC would become, namely an organization constituted chiefly to help shaikhly regimes maintain their grip on power through security and economic means. The GCC expounds the language of regionalism, thereby conforming to what has become an authoritative norm in international politics.[10] In fact, the organization symbolizes an affirmation of statist identities. Its purpose is more to exclude other entities, be they incipient regional powers (Iran and, even more so, Iraq) or poor neighbours (Yemen), than to work towards the integration of the policies of the six member states.

In this context the GCC represents a qualitative and quantitative leap over previous cooperation initiatives. In the second chapter I take a close look at the theory and practice of decision-making throughout the life of the organization. I look at how joint decisions are arrived at and what is the role of the permanent bureaucracy in the life of the organization. I make an effort to distinguish between the juridical and the 'material' constitution of the organization. In other words, between what was envisaged in the founding charter and how things go on in practice. Based on the evidence, I will also try to define in theoretical terms the true nature of the organization.[11] I examine whether after all the years from its inception the GCC has evolved into a regional organization whose existence is taken into account by individual governments when setting their national policies. This view would contrast with the more 'cynical' accounts of the life of the organization. These narratives, often couched in realist terms, stress how the existence of common enemies and common internal security problems are what really binds the six member states together and how collaboration is of a purely functional character.[12] To make sense of these conflicting interpretations, I will examine the subtle but recognizable changes at the societal level that took place in the six member countries in relation to the establishment of the organization. I will argue that there is evidence that various societal groups have begun to think in regional terms. Increasingly pressure groups join forces and try and influence the policies of the six member states from a regional perspective. In particular, intellectual and business groups from different states have often banded together to lobby for specific issues related to political and economic liberalization. In other words, the campaign by GCC states to drum up the importance of the organization for presentational purposes may have had an unexpected effect. A discourse centred on Gulf identity has emerged throughout the region. While not by any means hegemonic, it has certainly worked its way in the political and social agenda of the region.[13]

In the next three thematic chapters, I will carry out an empirical study of the level of integration achieved by the organization in the fields of economics, diplomacy, and internal and external security. In the chapter devoted to economics, I will stress how GCC officials and sympathetic analysts like to portray the problem of economic integration in the GCC as more than anything else an issue of coordination, if not outright integration, of the various national schemes for development. As the former GCC Associate Secretary General for Economic Affairs, Abdullah Al-Kuwaiz – an economist educated in the United States – once wrote, 'the GCC member states are more or less trading in one line of production',[14] i.e. the export of oil and petrochemical products. The economic dependence on a single depletable resource does characterize the economies of all member states with the exception of Bahrain. In this context, it can be argued that free trade agreements are less important than when entered into by countries with diversified, sustainable economies such as the member states of the European Union. Little trade complementarity exists among the six countries. The GCC economies are similar and produce essentially competitive rather than complementary goods.[15] GCC states import virtually all their industrial and consumer goods and a great part of their labour from outside the region. However, it must also be noted that other economic analysts argue that 'complementarity grows in line with international specialization engendered by trade. It should be the objective rather than the precondition of trade liberalization'.[16] Therefore, the situation is more complex than it is portrayed by many observers.

Given these peculiarities, the issue of economic integration can be approached by the analyst in at least three ways. It should be ascertained to what extent the GCC states have been able to implement and formulate a common GCC oil policy. Such a development would clearly give all six member states increased leverage in the world oil market. Furthermore, as mentioned previously, the issue of joint development becomes very important. I will look at how successful GCC members have been at coordinating, and sometimes integrating, their national development schemes. Finally, I will devote special attention to the thorny issue of a customs union that has beset the economic life of the organization almost from its inception in May 1981. This can be considered a bellweather to gauge the seriousness of GCC efforts at economic integration.

A customs union gives greatly improved leverage to the GCC in its trade negotiations with the United States, Japan and the European Union. The latter, in particular, is the biggest market for GCC petrochemical products. A customs union of the GCC states is a precondition for a free trade agreement with the European Union that would open European markets to the products of the GCC petrochemical industries, by far the biggest industrial sector in the GCC states. I explore the reasons for the delay in reaching such a union despite the great incentives. The issue was first raised at a GCC meeting in 1982. I will explain the historical reasons why the hypothesis of a customs union is particularly troublesome for these states. The relationship with merchants was the mainstay of the shaikhly regimes before the discovery of oil. Customs were the main source of revenue for them and an important source of patronage. The abolition of the right to set external tariffs is felt not only as a major abdication of sovereignty, but also as the weakening of the link to an extremely important constituency. Any analysis of the issue must take into consideration this important historical factor. However, in light of this chequered history, other ideas that came up for discussion at subsequent meetings, such as the establishment of a single currency, appear futuristic.

Thus, it does not come as a surprise that individual governments have consistently flouted even the more modest free trade area provisions of the Unified Economic Agreement, signed in 1981. Lack of progress is due also to the absence of a supranational authority of any kind in the GCC organizational structure that can push for the implementation of the agreements decided upon by the Supreme Council. Jealousy of their domestic schemes and fear of alienating influential domestic constituencies have thus prevented substantial achievements, particularly at those times when conditions in the oil market were not bright. Overall, I will illustrate how, in the economic field, as in other areas, GCC member states, many years after the organization was established, are still short of their self-declared goals.

In the realm of defense, cooperation and coordination are also limited. This in spite of the formation of a token collective rapid deployment force under the name of Peninsula Shield, finally disbanded for all intents and purposes in 2006, and numerous joint manoeuvres by the armed forces of the six member states.[17] The reasons for this lack of integration, though, are more complex than in the economic field. The armed forces of the six member states will always be inherently weak *vis-à-vis* the two regional powers: Iran and Iraq. These states will always lack the necessary manpower. It is no wonder that census statistics are treated with the outmost confidentiality. If they were made public they would probably reveal that the number of foreign workers is even higher than what is believed to be the case today (over 50% of residents in the UAE, Qatar and Kuwait slightly less in the other three states).[18] Additionally, it is unlikely that many citizens of these rentier states will rush to enlist in a well-disciplined, fully functional modern army.[19]

The prospect of armies fully staffed by mercenaries and without members of the royal families in key positions of responsibility is very sensitive for rulers of the Arabian Peninsula. In spite of a long tradition of utilizing foreign personnel for technical posts and, in the case of the UAE, even in fighting positions, Gulf rulers remain wary of the role armies can play in their societies. They are well aware that monarchical regimes in the Arab Middle East have always been toppled by army coups in the decades since independence. Additionally, they worry about the presence of large contingents from other Arab countries on their territories. They know that in the past arrangements of this kind have spelled trouble for the hosting countries and, as in the case of the Syrian presence in Lebanon, they have often become a permanent feature on the political scene. Such worries go a long way in explaining why agreements such as the Damascus declaration did not produce the desired results and why GCC rulers prefer the presence of British and American troops to the establishment of a regional peace-keeping force.[20] This in spite of the friction that a non-Muslim military presence on the Arabian Peninsula is bound to provoke, particularly for the government of Saudi Arabia.

GCC leaders clearly pride themselves in ruling the only 'revolution-free' part of Eurasia in the last 70 years. Internal stability is clearly preferred to the prospect of maximizing the fighting capability of the armed forces. Finally, one area in which integration would make a lot of military sense, but which is politically unpalatable, is arms procurement. The six member states spend around 37% of the developing world total on weapons.[21] However, efforts at standardization, which have been endorsed by the GCC since 1982, have so far yielded meagre results. The reluctance of the United States to make certain high-technology items sold to Saudi Arabia available to smaller GCC states, as well as the fear of coming to rely exclusively on the United States for arms supplies, are often cited as reasons by GCC officials.[22]

However, the most important reason for the lack of a unified procurements policy remains the six states' diplomatic strategy of involving as many influential countries as possible in support of their defense, including China and Russia. GCC states continue to prefer utilizing arms procurement as a tool of foreign policy, a sort of 'insurance policy' aimed at securing the support of the external powers, chiefly the United States, in case of a threat from the two regional powers. Arms procurement complements and integrates a strategy of carefully balanced foreign investments aimed at forging interdependence with external powers. This role is then of course supplemented by important domestic purposes in terms of patronage and consensus building. The management of individual arms procurement programmes is often assigned to members of the royal families and their key allies. The lucrative commissions deriving from these contracts serve as rewards for services rendered to the rulers. Such a strategy that, it must be added, proved all its worth at the time of the Gulf conflict of 1990–91 gives GCC rulers a powerful tool in the conduct of both foreign and domestic policies. It is therefore unlikely to be modified by GCC rulers anytime soon.

In the sphere of internal security, though, integration is more advanced. It builds on informal patterns of behaviour predating the establishment of institutionalized cooperation. From the beginning, member states cooperated extensively in a field where they perceive to be sharing similar threats and goals. Therefore, the GCC has achieved a good record in coordinating and sometime unifying the response of its member states to internal threats. Obviously, this is a difficult area to research thoroughly because of the requirements of national security. I will focus on the external face of internal security by highlighting how frequent are meetings of the interior ministers as opposed to other officials from GCC countries and how often individuals suspected of crimes against national security are extradited from one GCC state to another.

In the third of my thematic chapters, I will focus on cooperation and integration in the diplomatic sphere. The GCC has proved to be quite a useful forum for the six member states to debate and formulate common diplomatic positions. It is doubtful, though, whether it has been effective at mediating the numerous border disputes among member states. The latter have been dealt with more often than not by bilateral negotiations or the referral to other international forms of mediation.[23] It is a fact that member states throughout the life of the organization were able to adopt common foreign policy stances on important regional issues. Additionally, smaller member states were able, under the collective cloak provided by the organization, to undertake diplomatic initiatives that they could not have sustained individually. In particular, the UAE was able to behave more assertively in its long running dispute with Iran as the GCC collectively supported its position. In this chapter I also outline how the GCC, as a sub-regional organization, reacts to crises. The three detailed case studies examine theorganization's reaction to the Iran–Iraq War; its dealings with the internal border dispute between Bahrain and Qatar; and the aforementioned long-running dispute of one of the member states, the UAE, with a prominent regional power, Iran, over the Abu Musa and Tunbs islands. I purport to show that, while having made significant strides since its establishment, the GCC is still far short from reaching the goals set out in the founding charter.

This leads me to the last part of my work. In the last two chapters I situate the GCC in the wider context of the international relations of the region and I focus specifically on the role that the GCC states fulfil in the Gulf security complex. Firstly I chart the attitudes of the GCC states *vis-à-vis* Iran in the dispute about the latter's nuclear programme. I come to the conclusion that GCC states increasingly see the issue as being global in character and they accordingly strive to keep a low profile since they, correctly, conclude that there is little they can do to influence the final output of the dispute. This new reality of a 'globalized Gulf' also makes the smaller GCC states increasingly less deferent in their dealings with Saudi Arabia. I then go on to consider what are the chances that GCC states will follow in the path of nuclear and weapons of mass destruction (WMD) proliferation and I come to the conclusion that for a variety of reasons there is little chance that they will ever come to embark on such a course. In the final chapter I critique current Western and North Atlantic Treaty Organization (NATO) attempts to nudge GCC states in the direction of reforming their security sectors. I argue that these attempts are conceptualized as offers that cannot be refused by most GCC states. And while this reformist agenda has certainly not been internalized, it has the potential of upsetting the domestic stability of these states while adding very little to their autonomy in the realm of external defense.

I conclude by drawing attention to some of the new challenges that the GCC and its member states have to face as they chart their course in the twenty-first century. As new challenges emerge and new external powers try to bring their influence to bear, the GCC and its constituent states have to navigate the perilous political currents of the Gulf at least as skilfully as they have done in recent decades.

This work is based on a variety of sources in multiple languages. The consultation of a wealth of primary and secondary sources was very important to set the stage for this research. However, it was the interviews I conducted in the Gulf with GCC staff, local decision-makers and also with members of the business community, the majority of which regrettably were strictly off the record, that proved essential. This is because they were key in understanding the gap between charter provisions, as well as other regulations, and the way decisions are taken on a daily basis. It would have been impossible to gain a full picture of how the GCC and other local governments operate on a daily basis without spending time in the region. This is actually the principal shortcoming from which a number of studies of the international relations of the region suffer: taking at face value the provisions contained in the charter of the GCC and in the regulations of other Gulf institutions. When the output does not match the lofty goals propounded in those documents, scepticism, if not outright cynicism, arises.

This attitude is misplaced as such a superficial analysis misses both the wealth of interaction and the results that are achieved outside the public eye. It is only by spending time there that a fuller, richer picture emerges of how the business of these organizations is conducted. I am therefore grateful to the many institutions that hosted me and to the countless individuals who helped me to understand how decisions are reached and how policies are implemented in this part of the world.

Above all I hope this study helps to bridge the gap between area studies and international relations; the strictly enforced separation between the two has traditionally obfuscated rather than illuminated new developments in the Gulf. It is my contention that theoretically informed area studies are the best approach and that in these circumstances judicious hybridity should be embraced rather than feared.

1

THE CREATION OF THE UNITED ARAB EMIRATES AND THE FIRST INTEGRATION EXPERIMENTS OF THE ARAB STATES OF THE GULF

> The trouble as always, is that each state imagines that a proposal of any sort from any other is motivated by self-interest. Generally speaking, this is true.[1]
>
> Ronald H. M. Boyle

Sir William Luce and the Peninsula Solidarity Project

The idea of cooperation among the Arab monarchies of the Gulf predates the independence of a majority of them. Sir William Luce, who was British Political Resident in the Gulf between 1960 and 1966, identified in Nasserism the prime threat to the survival of the shaikhly system of government.[2] Sir William tried to promote a cooperative arrangement between the nine protected states and Saudi Arabia based on what he saw as their fundamentally shared interests and their common hostility to Nasserism. It was a belief widely held by foreign observers in the 1950s and 1960s that the shaikhly regimes of the nine protected states would find it extremely difficult to survive the departure of the British. Nasserism had made inroads among the populations of these states, particularly Bahrain. Both the rulers and the British saw Nasserism as the gravest danger to traditional systems of rule. The project could not take off then as too many border disputes remained unresolved.[3] Additionally, the rulers of the nine protected states felt secure under British protection and feared the predominance of Saudi Arabia.[4]

However, it is striking to observe the similarities between Sir William's blueprint for Gulf cooperation elaborated in the early 1960s and what became the Gulf Cooperation Council (GCC) two decades later. Cooperation followed by integration in the economic, cultural and, most crucially, internal and external security fields were all envisaged. Saudi Arabia was to play a leading role in the new organization that could then present a common front on the international scene. This cohesion on the Arab side of the Gulf was in turn to be coupled with an understanding between the Saudis and the Shah of Iran to set up and preserve a security regime in the waterway of the Gulf. The importance of this second element was recognized in London and a dialogue was encouraged between Saudi Arabia and Iran. On the other hand, 15 years had to elapse after the departure of Sir William from his post as Political Resident before the now fully independent Gulf Arab monarchies were in a position to give birth to the GCC.

The purpose of this chapter is twofold. On the one hand, the historical background to the creation of the GCC is illustrated by discussing the relevant material. On the other hand, GCC integration can best be understood by looking at the previous experiments in political integration and administrative cooperation.

The United Arab Emirates (UAE) as a precursor of the GCC: myths and realities

Along with the independence of Kuwait in 1961, the establishment of the UAE in 1971 is widely seen as one of the two crucial junctures in the modern history of the Gulf. The founding of the UAE is moreover viewed within the literature as proof that Arab states can indeed experiment with novel forms of integration, leading, in the case of the seven Arab emirates, even to the formation of a federation.[5] I will argue that the UAE, in addition to having been throughout its history a *sui generis* federation, in fact owes its origins more to a concerted diplomatic effort orchestrated by outside forces than to the genuine will of the peoples of the seven emirates or indeed their rulers. In fact, after the initial thrust the constituent emirates could not agree on a replacement for the provisional constitution that was originally intended to elapse in 1976. After several rounds of negotiation to replace it, the provisional constitution, a woolly and deliberately vague document, was declared permanent on the 25th anniversary of independence in December

1996. This episode illustrates the painstaking search for compromise and incessant negotiations that characterize the workings of the federation.[6] From the start the seven leaders deliberately eschewed a clear institutional structure for fear that it would encroach on the prerogatives of the individual rulers. Leadership is still very much a personal affair.

My argument on the origins of the federation is founded on documentation released in 1998 by the British Foreign and Commonwealth Office. British diplomats were players throughout the negotiations leading to the establishment of the UAE. They could also count on the assistance of their colleagues posted in Jeddah, Washington and, crucially, Teheran. They also continuously monitored the local press and included the most important articles in their dispatches. Therefore, they seem to be the best source to follow the complex processes leading to the establishment of the federation. While a number of good memoirs by some of the key local players have appeared, the archives of the Gulf emirates are still closed. Therefore, we are still short of documentation on some key meetings that took place without any British representative present.

By debunking the myth of a federation freely entered into by the seven emirates, it is possible to demonstrate how fallacious is the ancillary argument, made in some of the most partisan literature, that the GCC is bound to thrive and succeed in its integrative efforts on the strength of this precedent. Indeed, the formation of the UAE may well provide insights into the subsequent creation of the GCC. The parallels, though, have more to do with the continuous quarrels between the rulers up to the very eve of British departure and subsequently each emir's desire to retain as much sovereignty as possible than with the creation of a truly federal state.

Other less ambitious and purely functional forms of cooperation, which began in the 1970s, shed much more light on the origins and development of the GCC. These will be analysed in the second part of the chapter.

The official narrative and the myth of 'free will'

Traditional accounts of the founding of the UAE correctly emphasize the feeling of insecurity and estrangement that gripped the rulers of the nine protected states in 1968. That was the year when Britain, following a severe domestic economic crisis, announced its intention to withdraw from commitments east of Suez by the end of 1971.[7] It is worth reviewing the accepted historical account of the establishment of the UAE.[8] As this chapter will show, the conventional account consistently underplays the role of external powers such as Iran and Britain and the disagreements between the rulers of the nine protected states.

Following the announcement by Prime Minister Harold Wilson on 16 January 1968 that the British withdrawal from east of Suez would be completed by 1971, the rulers of the nine protected states of the Gulf started searching for the political means to secure their small, vulnerable entities in what was, and is even more today, a turbulent regional environment.[9] The idea of forming a federation became the subject of frequent meetings and discussions. It built on the existence of the Trucial States Council of rulers, a consultative council that had been established by Britain in 1952 to further the development of the seven Trucial states, which held 30 sessions between 1952 and 1968.[10] The workings of the council offer a good insight into elite interaction and administrative practice in the protected states. Meetings were very long and there was a tendency, according to British representatives, to drift into somewhat sterile abstract arguments. The strenuous search for compromise caused severe delay in reaching important decisions. The same decision-making approach continues in the new federation where the situation is aggravated by the absence of the British arbiter.

The first concrete initiative on the tortuous path of establishing a federation came from Abu Dhabi and Dubai. Their rulers met in Simayh on 18 February 1968 and announced the decision to federate the two emirates and devolve responsibility for the areas of foreign affairs, defense, citizenship, health and education to the future federal government.[11] At the end of the joint declaration the two rulers extended an invitation to the other five Trucial emirates to join the incipient union. They also extended a more cautious invitation to the rulers of Qatar and Bahrain to discuss the future of the region with a view to forming a federation of all nine protected states.

In fact the union of the nine never materialized. After a first enthusiastic meeting held in Dubai between 25 and 27 February 1968, differences began to appear between the nine rulers over many aspects of the future federation. A draft prepared by the Government of Qatar provided the basis of the discussions between the nine delegations. Much of the text of this draft was actually incorporated in the first agreement between the nine.[12] The Dubai proposals dominated negotiations between the nine rulers for the next three years. The framework was loose enough to serve as the launching pad for extended negotiations which centred on the need to reconcile the traditional privileges of the ruling families with the institutions required to establish a modern state.[13] Ultimately, a dilemma surfaced that would come back to haunt the GCC repeatedly. The ruling families of the Gulf shaikhly regimes find it difficult to relinquish some of their sovereignty to a supranational entity when they refuse, with the partial exception of Kuwait, to hand over much of the same sovereignty to their own citizens. Admittedly, it is easier for a Shaikh to defer to a fellow ruler than to public opinion. However, a number of prerogatives are closely guarded by the rulers of the region. First and foremost of these is control over the distribution of the wealth derived from the exploitation of mineral resources.[14] This fundamental question is supplemented by other factors such as the long-running dynastic rivalries between the ruling families of the Gulf and the vexed question of border disputes.

The failure of the federation of the nine is generally attributed to Qatar and Bahrain mainly due to their territorial disputes and the historical rift between the two ruling families.[15] It is certainly true that the federation of the rest of the emirates proved to be more practical. However, even in the case of the remaining emirates, at the end of three years of argument and negotiation, only six out of seven were in a position to promulgate even a provisional constitution. The exception was Ra's al Khaimah.

Ra's al Khaimah joined the federation only on 10 February 1972 when its ruler realized that continuation as an independent entity would not be viable. It is possible to identify three reasons why Ra's al Khaimah did not join the UAE until three months after its formation.[16] These are worth discussing as they epitomize general issues that would continue to hamper integration efforts between Gulf states for the coming decades.

Firstly, Ra's al Khaimah's ruler, Shaikh Saqr bin Muhammad Al Qasimi, resented the fact that throughout negotiations between the nine states it did not rank equally with Bahrain, Qatar, Abu Dhabi and Dubai in such matters as the number of delegates and voting rights. Issues such as prestige and reputation will prove considerable stumbling blocks throughout the life of the UAE and later of the GCC. Underlying these issues is a concrete fear on the part of the smaller members that their bigger brethren would assume a hegemonic role. This concern is indeed the cause of continuous tensions between Dubai and Abu Dhabi within the UAE and, to a lesser extent, between Saudi Arabia and the other GCC states. In the context of associations of states with great power disparities between their members, what may seem *prima facie* trivial gestures, such as the venue of a particular meeting or the arrangement of the national flags, may hold important symbolic meaning for both constituents and the outside world.[17] This phenomenon is particularly relevant in the Arab Middle East for reasons that will be scrutinized later in this thesis. Symbols and rhetorical discourse have played a prominent part in intra-Arab relations in the past 40 years. The symbolic drive towards some form of unity, however hesitant in practice, remains a defining characteristic in the international relations of the Arab Middle East.[18]

The second reason for Ra's al Khaimah reluctance to join the UAE was that explorations were underway at the time for oil off the coast of the emirate. Shaikh Saqr hoped that Ra's al Khaimah would be able to join the UAE on the wave of a successful oil strike. This would have enabled him to negotiate much better representation on both the Union Council and the cabinet. Unfortunately for both the people and the ruler of the shaikhdom, when the results of the strike were revealed it transpired that oil had not been found in sufficient quantities and the ruler had to resign himself to joining the union as a relatively oil-poor member. The difference in wealth of the constituent emirates of the UAE and, later, the member states of the GCC has constituted a persistent problem. If a budgetary structure is adopted whereby wealthier members contribute the most, such as in the UAE, the power asymmetry is institutionalized and eventually one member assumes a leading position in relation to the others. This creates recurrent crises as poorer members try to resist further integration as the frequent Dubai/Abu Dhabi quarrels within the UAE demonstrate. If, on the other hand, members are required to contribute an equal share to the budget, as is the case in the GCC, the organization will always be limited in its activities since poorer members such as Bahrain or Oman will not be able to contribute enough to establish a regional organization able to assume some of the sovereign prerogatives of its members.[19] These preliminary considerations will be further examined later in this work.

Finally, the thorny issue of the Abu Musa and Tunbs islands has its origins in this turbulent period. The issue, which remains high on the UAE's political agenda today, has influenced the international relations of the Gulf for a considerable time and will form the subject of a separate discussion. Suffice it to say here that the three islands, two of which are sparsely inhabited, had belonged to the two shaikhdoms of Sharjah and Ra's al Khaimah for the past century or so.[20]

The Shah of Iran who had surrendered his long-standing claim to Bahrain in 1970 was in no mood to compromise about the two islands. After a series of fruitless negotiations with the British, who were managing the external relations of the Trucial states, he decided to issue an ultimatum by which Iran would gain a military presence on the strategic islands while letting the Arab inhabitants continue with their lives free from interference. Sharjah eventually accepted the Iranian diktat regarding Abu Musa, but Ra's al Khaimah held out. On 29 November 1971, shortly before Britain was to relinquish its obligations, Iranian forces seized the two Tunbs killing four Arab policemen and expelling all the inhabitants. The invasion put the issue of the islands on the agenda of relations between the two sides of the Gulf for a long time to come. Ra's al Khaimah did not agree to join the UAE until the other emirates decided to adopt the question of Iranian occupation of the islands. The other six rulers agreed to consider the issue a federal one.

The dispute over the islands highlights the vexing question of security dependency of the Gulf states. Ra's al Khaimah had long relied on Britain for external defense; when British assistance was not forthcoming there was nothing it could do. Its appeals to fellow Arab states were met with muted responses and a call for moderation in its dealings with Iran.[21] This impotence *vis-à-vis* one of the two regional powers, Iran and Iraq, will be a recurrent theme for the six states of the GCC. The need to resort to external powers to guarantee their external defense informs the foreign policies of the six monarchies despite the public protestations of neutrality expressed in the early 1980s.

The role of outside powers in the formation of the UAE

The documents declassified a decade ago cast a fresh light on the bargaining process that led to the formation of the UAE.[22] These documents indicate how the global and the regional level of analysis must be the focus of attention when one looks at the genesis of the UAE. In other words, the interplay of the great powers and their interaction with the main regional powers had a much greater influence on the genesis of the UAE than had previously been realized.

This is in contrast to the unit level of analysis that we identify here with the bargaining and interplay between different Shaikhs. It is apparent that the ruling families of the protected states had no wish to pursue independence for their shaikhdoms and that the idea of forming a federation was greatly encouraged by the British. Additionally, it surfaces that the influence of the Shah of Iran was decisive in excluding Bahrain from the federation. Regarding the wish of most rulers to preserve their protected status and the necessity of British prompting, the evidence seems overwhelming. British officials on the ground and at the Arabian department of the Foreign Office had to work against a strict deadline with little support from ministers. The latter wanted the matter of the union settled as soon as possible without prejudice to British relations with the two dominant regional powers, Saudi Arabia and Iran. They failed to grasp the complexity of the situation and often surprised diplomats with impromptu pronouncements that caused a stir among the rulers, leaving it to British officials on the ground to smooth ruffled feathers.[23]

The enthusiasm of a few rulers for the establishment of a federation, notably Shaikh Saqr, ruler of Ra's al Khaimah, is repeatedly attributed by British diplomats to their financial plight. It is understandable therefore that Shaikh Zayid, ruler of oil-rich Abu Dhabi, at first resisted the idea of a tight federation. It would have been more prudent for him to dispense financial assistance from a less formal setting so as to make the other rulers completely dependent on his largesse. This haggling about financial resources further sets the UAE experience apart from the GCC where all expenses are divided equally between poor and rich member states. In general, the possibility that the rulers of the seven Trucial States, not to mention Bahrain and Qatar, would integrate without significant prodding was discounted by Sir Stewart Crawford, British Political Resident in Bahrain.[24]

Crawford and the other British diplomats in the Gulf recognized that while the rulers of these states did indeed realize the risk of falling under the influence of powerful neighbours such as Saudi Arabia if they remained independently separate, they loathed even more the idea of surrendering their national prerogatives to a federal government structure. In a dispatch dated 28 December 1967 Crawford goes as far as to say:

> For various reasons, organic association of the four principal protected states [Abu Dhabi, Dubai, Qatar, Oman] is impracticable. On the other hand, there is a chance of another rulers' meeting, and continuing scope for functional cooperation between pairs or groups of states. We should encourage this.

He went on to say, 'However logical it may seem to expect these small States to coalesce and to form a larger and more durable unit, this is not the way their rulers think.'

Eventually, Sir Stewart was proven wrong. As the deadline for the withdrawal of British protection approached, the vulnerability of the single emirates became clear even to their rulers and a somewhat uneasy union could be forced on seven of the nine protected states. However, the point here is that such a union did not come about voluntarily or at the initiative of the rulers, but had to be gradually imposed by the departing British. As Sir Stewart remarked, the rulers were extremely jealous of their sovereign prerogatives. It is significant that even in the UAE the merger of the armed forces of all the constituent emirates was completed only in 1998 when the separate force that Abu Dhabi had retained was finally incorporated after long negotiations. A careful balance had to be maintained in the officer corps between representatives of the various emirates. This occurred in spite of British pressure as early as 1968 to effect a merger of the Abu Dhabi Defense Forces with the Trucial Oman Scouts.[25] This points to the importance that Gulf leaders attach to military forces as directly underpinning their rule. Border disputes are still active among the constitutive states of the UAE. Furthermore, their union was greatly facilitated by the perception that the Gulf micro-states would have difficulty surviving in such a turbulent regional environment without falling under the influence of the major regional powers. In the case of the GCC, all member states are confident that the bilateral agreements negotiated with the United States after the Second Gulf War will provide a reliable security guarantee for the foreseeable future.

In a letter from the Foreign Office to Gulf political agents dated 1 February 1968, Michael Weir, a senior official in the Arabian department at the Foreign Office, remarked that the whole machine of the UAE

> would no doubt function no more as an effective unit than say the central government of the UAR did between 1958 and 1961.[26] But the advantage would be that its recognition as an international entity would make it more difficult for outsiders, whether Iran or Egypt (or Saudi Arabia working through Dubai), to justify intervention in the affairs of the seven.[27]

This passage illuminates the vulnerability of the entities and underlines the difficulties of fostering the union of a number of patriarchal Gulf states.

With regard to the regional environment, the need for a cooperative security regime among the countries surrounding the Gulf was already recognized by British officials on the eve of the withdrawal. However, most of these same officials also seemed very sceptical about the possibility of achieving it. Three decades later the prospects for such a regime seem not to have improved and in many ways have actually worsened.[28] The scepticism at the time centred mainly on the hostile attitude taken by the Shah of Iran to the inclusion of Bahrain into a possible federation of all nine protected states. It transpires that the attitude of the Shah towards Bahrain was much more uncompromising than what has hitherto been believed.[29]

For Iran to renounce its claim over Bahrain, the Shah insisted that Bahrain would not become part of the new federation. Iran clearly considered Bahrain's mini-statehood the lesser of two evils compared to the disadvantages of its membership in the UAE. In the words of C. D. Wiggin, a Foreign Office official writing to the Arabian department on 25 July 1968, 'if Bahrain goes it alone, the Iranians have a much better chance of "limiting" their quarrel to Bahrain and ourselves and maintaining good relations with other

Arabs.'[30] If Bahrain were to be incorporated into the UAE, it would be impossible for Iran to recognize the new federation and this 'would therefore greatly complicate their relations with the other protected states and Saudi Arabia and Kuwait as well'. The Shah, recognizing that he did not enjoy enough support for his claim to Bahrain in the international community and, crucially, from Saudi Arabia, indicated that he would be prepared to drop his claim to the island if a 'suitable face-saving device could be found'.[31] An appeal for arbitration by the International Court of Justice was hastily arranged by Iran and Britain and Iran dropped its claim to Bahrain. The other Trucial shaikhs for fear of antagonizing Iran subsequently refused to hold constitutive meetings of the UAE in Bahrain.[32] The ruler of Bahrain refused to meet elsewhere and eventually withdrew from the organization. Iran, a regional power, and Britain, a global actor, were instrumental in defining the boundaries and the nature of the new federation. In fact, as will be shown later, the Trucial shaikhs were very keen for the British to stay and even made financial offers to persuade them to do so.[33]

Functional cooperation in the 1970s as a precursor to the establishment of the GCC

It is my contention that, contrary to the official rhetoric, experiments in functional cooperation entertained by the six Gulf states in the 1970s are much more a source of GCC practice than processes of 'high politics' such as the foundation of the UAE which were in large part orchestrated by outside powers.[34] A considerable number of ministerial meetings, joint working groups, and bilateral and multilateral treaties were completed in the 1970s.[35] These usually encompass matters that would later be incorporated by the GCC charter and the Unified Economic Agreement signed by the six constituent states in the 1980s. I will discuss them briefly by issue areas. This will allow a more direct comparison to be made with the various sections of the GCC charter.

The most numerous contacts and functional cooperation experiments fall within the realm of economics and planning. The agreements and understandings in the economic sphere usually reflect prior agreements that had been reached in the 1950s and 1960s among members of the League of Arab States (LAS) but had never been implemented. The charter of the LAS explicitly authorizes member states 'to establish closer cooperation and stronger bonds than are provided by this pact'.[36] Given the moribund status of the LAS economic cooperation, it was not very difficult to improve on the record of that organization. Additionally, the explicit mention of the possibility of closer cooperation in the charter of the LAS gave all Gulf rulers an ideological cover by making it a legitimate field of cooperation. Sub-regional cooperation by oil-rich states was regarded with suspicion in the Arab world at the time. In the rest of the Arab world it was feared that sub-regional cooperation may lead to a growing spirit of isolation and an organization of international activity based on geography rather than on shared identity.[37] By cooperating in the economic sector the Gulf rulers did not risk violating the norms of Arabism. As will become increasingly clear with a discussion of the formation of the GCC, this is a very important factor in the international relations of the Arab Middle East. There has always been strong pressure on Gulf Arab leaders not to violate the norms of Arabism.

The emphasis at the time was on joint planning and development. Economic integration was seen as an issue of integrated development in the industrial and agricultural fields. Only much later, after the establishment of the GCC, in line with new thinking in International Political Economy, the emphasis was shifted to free markets. It has always been clear, however, that the fact that GCC member states are more or less trading in one line of production, e.g. the export of oil and petroleum products, makes economic integration qualitatively different from the kind pursued by industrialized countries.[38] Thus, throughout the 1970s the 'six'[39] and Iraq, sometime joined by Iran, started building joint institutions, working groups, and harmonizing laws and regulations. The idea was to create a joint productive capacity in many areas that would promote integration by building up economies of scale. The main obstacle here, as in other issue areas, was the obligatory inclusion of Iraq in most multilateral ventures. The 'six' did not trust the Ba'athist regime in Baghdad but the ideological climate of the 1970s made it impossible to exclude this important Arab regional power from multilateral projects and working groups.[40] This made the resulting institutions necessarily weak. The problem was solved only with the creation of the GCC in 1981 after the outbreak of the Iran–Iraq War when Iraq could conveniently be excluded as a belligerent. The 'six' had a possibility to form an organization that would deliberately exclude the two regional powers that were at the time embroiled in a military conflict.

More specifically in the economic field, Gulf efforts at closer integration throughout the 1970s were aimed at a number of goals. They included harmonizing development plans to promote integration; working towards a common oil policy; coordinating industrial policy, particularly with respect to petroleum-based products; adopting a common legal framework for regional trade and investment; and linking transportation networks.[41] These goals remained the same when bilateral and multilateral institutions came under the GCC umbrella in the 1980s, even if their scope was expanded and other objectives were added.

The rationale behind the functional experiments of the 1970s was the same one behind all GCC activities in the economic sector. Industrial diversification is regarded as an antidote to excessive reliance on a single depletable commodity and its upstream and downstream industries. However, formidable obstacles lay in the way of industrial diversification in the Gulf states. Small internal markets and limited domestic labour forces inhibit industrial development and largely preclude regional import–substitution strategies. Additionally, all intermediate goods with the exception of oil, gas and sand must be imported.[42] Water must also be purchased abroad or desalinized at substantial cost.[43] Therefore, effective joint committees to coordinate industrial development and institutions such as the Gulf Investment Corporation would actually play a crucial role, at the very least in preventing industrial duplication.

The main obstacle to the development of these institutions at the time was the perceived need to include Iraq and sometimes Iran in all joint efforts. This hindered effective integration and coordination in the fields described above. As will be shown, after the GCC was set up new obstacles emerged and the process of economic integration proceeded by fits and starts. The achievements after 18 years are meagre if compared with what has been achieved by regional organizations such as the European Union and the North American Free Trade Agreement (NAFTA). On the other hand, results are significant when judged against those obtained in this field by the LAS and its associated agencies.

In the cultural sphere contacts and experiments in the 1970s fared better as the participating states deemed this area as less threatening to their sovereignty. Most agreements in this field were reached within the framework of the Cultural Treaty of the LAS. The latter called upon the Arab states to encourage the exchange of students, teachers and scholars; harmonize educational syllabi; and the establishment of contacts between libraries, museums and the like.[44] The future GCC states were already importing a large number of Arab teachers from countries such as Egypt, Iraq, Jordan and Sudan. Additionally, many students were studying in the rest of the Arab world.

These ties were expanded. Bilateral treaties among the future GCC states were formulated with reference to the Cultural Treaty of the LAS. These agreements involved cooperation between libraries and schools, the standardization of curricula and educational objectives, and the exchange of teachers. On the other hand, mutual projects and institutions were often the result of bilateral and multilateral meetings between Gulf ministers of culture, education and information. They invariably included Iraq and concerned the development of higher education and vocational training, as well as joint projects in broadcasting and news dissemination. Permission was given to newspapers, magazines and other publications of the signatory countries to be sold throughout the Gulf. This step was taken only after adequate measures were taken to prevent criticism of the policies of the other signatory states in the national media. Projects in the information and broadcasting field include the Gulf News Agency, 1976; Gulf States Joint Programming Production Company, 1976; Gulf Center for Broadcast and Television Training, 1979; and the Gulf Television Bureau, 1977. Most of these bodies continued their work after the establishment of the GCC when Iraqi delegates stopped attending the meetings.

As in the case of economic projects these multilateral ventures were hampered by the presence of Iraq. The University of the Gulf, for example, was established only after the creation of the GCC and the exclusion of Iraq from the project. This area blossomed after the creation of the GCC. Cultural policies highlighting the distinctiveness of the Gulf are positively encouraged by the six member states. As in the other areas many of the activities that started in the 1970s continued under the umbrella of the newly founded organization.

The areas of internal security and defense are the most difficult to research. The discussion of their evolution in the 1970s is therefore limited to process rather than to content. With regard to internal security there is reason to believe that contacts were widespread among the security apparatuses and this was the one area where Iran and Iraq could wilfully be excluded. According to officials from the six states there were many meetings and a good cooperation network was established.[45] However, no public record is available for most of these meetings given their extremely sensitive nature. Interviews with officials active at the time also do not yield much. The latter are more than happy to elaborate on the successes and failures in the economic and cultural fields, but are extremely tight-lipped when it comes to internal and external security. Cooperation in this area was institutionalized only after the founding of the GCC with the signing of the Security and Extradition treaty. Thus discussion of the evolution in these areas is necessarily limited to process rather than to content.

In the case of external defense the presence of other international and regional actors complicated multilateral efforts. Cooperation in this area during the 1970s can be divided in three periods: the period from 1971 to 1976; the Muscat conference of 1976; and the period leading to the formation of the GCC in 1981. In the first half of the decade bilateral agreements and ministerial meetings dominated the agenda. Then, in November 1976, the ruler of Oman, Sultan Qabus, organized a major conference in Muscat that was attended by the foreign ministries of the 'six' plus Iran and Iraq. This was the first attempt to set up a comprehensive security regime for the Gulf. No concrete progress was made as the result of this conference as the parties left pledging nothing more than to meet again in the future. However, the Muscat conference must still be regarded as a milestone in Gulf cooperation, since for the first time the idea of a multilateral security regime was discussed in a formal setting. The rest of the decade, leading to the creation of the GCC in 1981, was spent trying unsuccessfully to jumpstart a multilateral regime based on the discussion held in Muscat in November 1976.

From 1971 to 1976 discussion of security matters was confined to bilateral meetings. These usually took place as part of 'tours' of the Gulf region undertaken by the various leaders. One of the most active leaders on the diplomatic scene was Shaikh Jabar Al Sabah, then Prime Minister and Crown Prince of Kuwait. He was the first leader publicly to acknowledge the desirability of a multilateral organization that would cover a number of fields. In May 1976 he called for 'the establishment of a Gulf Union, with the object of realizing cooperation in all economic, political, educational and informational spheres, to serve the interests of the region'.[46] His invitation was taken up by Sultan Qabus of Oman who organized a conference in Muscat in November 1976 with the explicit aim of reaching a collective agreement regarding security and defining areas of cooperation among all Gulf countries.

Sultan Qabus was a keen advocate of cooperation in the fields of internal security and defense. His speech at the conference reflected Oman's recent experience of war in the southern region of Dhufar and its important strategic position as the gateway of the Straits of Hormuz.[47] Then, as in future years, Oman was trying to set up a comprehensive security regime that would cover the lower Gulf. Sultan Qabus remains well aware that the strategic position of Oman exposes it to turbulence in the area and threats to freedom of navigation.

The Shah of Iran was also an enthusiast for regional cooperation at the time. He saw his role as the natural successor to Britain's hegemony in the Gulf, acting as protector of security in the area. Iran was hostile to forms of cooperation limited to the Arab states of the Gulf. In particular, Iran continuously objected to Arab governments referring to the Gulf as an 'Arab' Gulf. Iran considered the security of the Gulf its responsibility with or without cooperation from the Arab states of the region. This position was clearly unacceptable to the future GCC states as was Iraq's insistence at the conference that it acted as the champion of Arab littoral states. The conference deadlocked and it transpired that the problem for the Gulf monarchies was how to exclude Iran and Iraq from cooperative efforts in the field of security without antagonizing them.

The Muscat conference made it clear that security cooperation had to be limited to the exchange of information if Iran and Iraq were to be included. Consequently, in the next two years efforts were limited to the economic and the cultural spheres. In December 1978 the new Kuwaiti Crown Prince and Prime Minister, Shaikh Saad Al Sabah, undertook a tour of Saudi Arabia, Bahrain, Qatar, the UAE and Oman. The final communiqués of the various meetings all indicate the desire to set up some sort of formal cooperation. However the tone is extremely vague and cautious.[48] The inauguration of formal multilateral cooperation in security matters as well as in other fields had to await the radical changes that affected the region in the following months.

Experiments in administrative cooperation throughout the 1970s are a much better guide to the later functioning of the GCC than the creation of the UAE earlier in the decade. The latter is too often cited as proof that successful political integration is possible in the Arab Middle East. In fact, traditional accounts underestimate the role of external powers in bringing about the federation of the seven emirates.

The administrative practices that informed the bilateral and multilateral joint initiatives of the 1970s in the Gulf characterize the workings of the GCC in the first 20 years of its existence. The peculiar nature of decision-making and leadership in the Gulf Arab monarchies lend the GCC its unique character as a regional organization. The next chapter describes the specific circumstances surrounding the formation of the GCC and the negotiations that led to its formal establishment in 1981 as well as its structure and organization.

2

CREATION, STRUCTURE AND ORGANIZATION OF THE GCC

Rules are there to serve a purpose. If a particular purpose is better served by ignoring the rules [of the Gulf Cooperation Council (GCC)] they will be ignored.[1]

GCC Secretary General Abdullah Bishara

Changed security conditions in the Gulf

At the beginning of the 1980s, two factors turned all of the Gulf's previous experiments in sub-regional integration into reality. Without these intervening factors, discussions on the type and membership of a future gulf organization would have probably continued for much longer. The Iranian Revolution and the outbreak of the Iran–Iraq War go a long way toward explaining the timing of the establishment of the Gulf Cooperation Council (GCC).

In 1979 the Shah of Iran was overthrown in a popular revolution. The establishment of a revolutionary regime under Ayatollah Khomeini caused much anxiety among the elites of the six oil-producing shaikhdoms of the Gulf. The Shah had always been perceived as a supercilious rival, but at least he shared a commitment to the preservation of the shaikhly system of government on the Arab side of the Gulf.[2] Iran's help in bringing to an end the Communist-inspired insurrection in the southern Omani province of Dhufar had been appreciated, and economic ties between the two shores of the Gulf fostered good relations. The displacement of the Iranian monarch by a revolutionary Islamic regime transformed the security situation in the region. Commercial contacts continued, particularly those with Dubai, as they had for centuries, but Iran came to be viewed not only as a rival, but also as a potential threat to the survival of the ruling families. The establishment of 'the first state in modern times to allegedly use Islam as its sole constitutional and social foundations'[3] appealed to many people in the Gulf among the Shi'ah populations of Bahrain, Kuwait and the Eastern Province of Saudi Arabia. The initial foreign policy thrust of the new Iranian regime was aimed at exporting the Islamic revolutionary model. This greatly increased the threat of subversion by indigenous forces in the eyes of the Gulf Arab rulers.

The Iran–Iraq War thus provided 'a perfect excuse for excluding Iraq from membership in the GCC'.[4] The Ba'athist regime would certainly have insisted, as it had done in the past, on being included in any security arrangement set up by the Arab littoral states. The war gave the six Gulf shaikhdoms the possibility of setting up an alliance that professed neutrality. The inclusion of Iraq would have led to a widening of the conflict, the rulers of the six states said, and this was to be avoided at the cost of excluding Iraq from the new organization. In fact, the prospect of including Iraq in the GCC was never seriously considered. The revisionist politics of the Ba'athist regime were the very antithesis of the conservative approach championed by the Gulf shaikhdoms.

After the start of the Iran–Iraq War, the six Arab shaikhdoms that would eventually join together to form the GCC were finally free to discuss the shape of the future organization without regional constraints. Even among the six, however, there were considerable differences of opinion about the shape the future organization should take. It is therefore useful to review the preparatory contacts that followed the failure of the Muscat conference of 1976 discussed in the previous chapter.

In 1978 Kuwait tried again to table the idea of Gulf cooperation after the failure of the Muscat conference, but yet again the impossibility of reaching an understanding with the two regional powers, Iran and Iraq, made even this foray fruitless. All that was achieved was the establishment of a bilateral ministerial council with the United Arab Emirates (UAE) that committed the two countries to regular meetings at the prime ministerial level.[5] The other four states that would one day form the GCC – Saudi Arabia, Bahrain, Qatar and Oman – officially endorsed the concept of a Gulf union and consultations continued over the next few years. It was during these consultations, deliberately kept at the junior level so as not to irk the two regional powers, that the different ideas of what the GCC should become were first aired.

The obstacles that lay in the path of formal Gulf cooperation before the outbreak of the Iran–Iraq War are well illustrated by the fact that the Kuwaiti overture was immediately countered by Iraq, which was keen to reserve for itself the role of leader of at least the 'Arab' side of the Gulf. In September 1979 Saddam Hussein formally offered to send troops to Bahrain and Kuwait in the event of either an internal uprising or an external attack. He also unveiled the idea of an Arab Deterrent Force for the Gulf with an independent budget and the contribution of contingents from all the Arab states of the Gulf. Not surprisingly, the offer was not embraced by any of the future GCC states. Iraq then drew up an even more ambitious eight-point 'Arab National Charter' that called for the termination of all foreign military presence in the Arab world and unity among its members. The Charter was announced with great fanfare on 8 February 1980, with Iraqi Foreign Minister Saadoun Hammadi being sent to Kuwait, Bahrain, Qatar, the UAE and North Yemen to shore up support for this new idea. At the same time the more senior Vice Chairman of the Iraqi Revolutionary Command Ezzat Ibrahim, a veteran collaborator of Saddam Hussein, visited Jordan and Saudi Arabia.[6] None of the prospective partners was interested. Nevertheless, these Iraqi diplomatic overtures shed light on the formation of the GCC in two important respects. First, they illustrate the difficult circumstances that the six shaikhdoms had to negotiate in the regional political climate of the time. All Iraq's initiatives had to be given token consideration even if it was clear from the start that the six would never actually agree to form strong links with a revisionist state such as Iraq. There was strong pressure from the other Arab countries to be seen as playing the role of the cooperative Arab states. This pressure was particularly acute following the signature by Egypt's President Sadat of the Camp David accords, an event that had caused great turmoil in the Arab world. This is a clear illustration of the normative pressures discussed at length by Michael Barnett in his book on the constructive nature of international relations in the Middle East.[7]

Second, and perhaps more importantly, an Omani proposal that came in response to the first of these Iraqi initiatives later formed the backbone of the Omani concept of what the GCC should constitute first and foremost: the organizer of a joint military force. In September 1979 while Iraq was offering bilateral security arrangements to any interested state, Oman floated the idea of raising US$100 million to bolster the defense of the Gulf. The money was to be spent on the purchase of minesweepers and radar equipment to protect the Strait of Hormuz.[8] More worryingly for Iraq, the Omani proposal also envisaged the creation of a naval taskforce to be drawn from the United

States, Britain and West Germany to ensure continued freedom of navigation through the strait. The proposal was openly criticized by Iraq, which interpreted it as a bid to create a renewed Baghdad Pact. This treaty had been signed by the Hashemite monarchy in 1955 and had been reviled ever since as one of the most flagrant infringements of the norms of Arab nationalism.[9] Oman denied that it wanted to set up a military alliance with these Western powers, but stressed that Iraqi objections should not influence the decision of the other Arab states of the Gulf to set up a collective security effort.[10] This was a noteworthy moment in the history of collaboration among Gulf states because it was the first time that the exclusion of Iraq from a prospective security regime was explicitly contemplated.

The Omani proposal was discussed in Ta'if, Saudi Arabia, on 16 October 1979 at a meeting that would become pivotal in the establishment of the GCC. This special meeting had been convened to assess the domestic risks posed by the Iranian call to export its revolution. The foreign ministers of the six participated at the meeting, from which both Iran and more significantly Iraq were excluded. While the Omani preoccupation with freedom of passage in the Straits of Hormuz was recognized, the focus of the meeting shifted to the threat of domestic uprisings stemming from Iranian calls to 'export the revolution' to the Arab shaikhdoms of the Gulf.[11] This preoccupation with internal security would prove to be one of the principal characteristics of the future organization. Internal security is a field in which the interests of the six GCC states coincide, and, unlike external defense, it is also an area where a lot can be achieved without external assistance. While the first Ta'if meeting did not lead to any concrete results, the exclusion of Iraq from a multilateral effort focusing on internal and external security in and of itself constituted a significant break with a previously held taboo.

The seizure of the Great Mosque of Mecca in November 1979 by Islamists under the leadership of Juhayman bin Muhammad bin Sayf al-Utaybi, a member of the powerful Utayba tribe, followed by Iranian-inspired disturbances in the predominantly Shi'ah oil-producing Eastern Province, helped convince the House of Saud of the need for further collaboration, particularly in the sphere of internal security. The insurgents were protesting the religious laxity prevailing in the Kingdom and accused the Saudi royal family of having betrayed the tenets of Wahhabism. What was particularly disturbing to the ruling family was that the Saudi National Guard was unable to regain control of the Mosque for two weeks. French special forces had to lend their assistance and the insurgents surrendered after running out of ammunition in the aftermath of a bloody battle.[12] The Shi'ah riots in the

Eastern Province were also controlled with difficulty and resulted in the deaths of at least 17 people.

With the outbreak of the Iran–Iraq War in September 1980, all hesitations about forming an organization that would bring together the Arab shaikhdoms of the Gulf were laid to rest. Iraq, as a combatant, could be safely excluded. The summit of Organization of the Islamic Conference that took place in the Saudi resort of Ta'if in January 1981 proved an ideal forum for the leaders of the Gulf shaikhdoms to consult informally on the future shape of the organization. From the start it was clear that while all six governments agreed on the need to establish a regional organization, there were differences regarding its structure and aims. The first meeting of the foreign ministers of the six countries to pave the way for the establishment of the GCC took place in Kuwait on 4 February 1981. Three different drafts were put forward that envisaged very different models of cooperation.

Kuwait, at that time the only one of the six countries to have diplomatic relations with the Union of Socialist Soviet Republics (USSR), stressed cooperation in the economic and cultural fields. This was partly because of the desire that the new organization should not be seen as a defensive alliance aligned with the United States.[13] The Kuwaiti government actively sought the diplomatic approval of the USSR for the creation of the GCC and never tired of stressing the 'neutrality' of the new organization *vis-à-vis* the two blocs. According to Kuwait, security cooperation should be confined to the exchange of information, something that was already occurring on an informal basis. Saudi Arabia, still reeling from the recent internal disturbances in Mecca and the Eastern Province, stressed the need for formal cooperation in the realm of internal security and a commitment to military intervention to preserve and restore order and stability. As a close ally of the United States, the Kingdom was not encumbered by reservations concerning neutrality and was less concerned about the GCC being seen as too close to the United States. Finally, Oman pushed for the creation of a fully fledged military alliance embodied in the creation of a joint military force. This proposal was based on the idea it had put forward a year earlier. Muscat stressed the importance of ensuring free passage through the Straits of Hormuz as well as preserving internal stability. If doing so required the direct assistance of the United States, so be it.

The three drafts that were discussed reflected very different approaches to the nature of regional cooperation in the Gulf. Eventually, as so often happens in the dealings of the Arab shaikhdoms, a unanimous compromise was reached. After two additional meetings of a panel of experts from the six governments, composed of diplomats and lawyers from the six member states, in Riyadh on 24 February and then in Muscat on 4 March, the foreign ministers were ready to meet again on 9 March in Muscat to approve the basic structure of the organization and the draft charter. Specifically, the ministers approved three documents setting out the by-laws for the Cooperation Council, the Supreme Council and the Ministerial Council.[14] Additionally, it was decided that the meetings of the Supreme Council would take place twice a year in May and November, the latter being the more formal of the two gatherings. Finally, it was decided in principle that the first Secretary General of the GCC would be from Kuwait. This decision was taken to project the idea that the new organization would steer a neutral course between the two superpowers. This despite the fact that of the six member states only Kuwait had diplomatic relations with the Soviet Union at the time. This paved the way for Abdullah Bishara to become the first Secretary General. Bishara, then Kuwait's permanent representative at the United Nations, had been sent the previous month to the Soviet Union to convince Moscow to give its blessing to the new organization.

A shrewd and intelligent negotiator, Bishara had been behind Kuwait's insistence on the social, economic and political aspects of cooperation, foregoing any mention of collaboration in the internal and external security fields. He was convinced that this was the key to obtaining Soviet assent to the formation of the organization, something he considered vital to avoid giving the impression that the new organization was a re-enactment of the Baghdad Pact. His view, and the Kuwaiti version of cooperation, won the day even if the foreign ministers who met on 23 May in Abu Dhabi to finalize plans for the establishment of the GCC did not rule out the adoption of the Omani and Saudi perspectives at a later date. In other words, the door was left open for further cooperation in the internal and external security fields, elements which member states eventually implemented.

However, the controversy over the three draft plans lingered on until the last moment. There were tense exchanges when Oman warned that 'economic cooperation is not enough' and that the Soviet threat should be taken into consideration. The possibility of excluding Oman because of its insistence in explicitly recognizing cooperation in the security realm was aired.[15] This happened despite the fact that the first summit of the Supreme Council was to be held in just a few days. The host of the summit, Shaikh Zayid, stated that there were significant differences between the Omani and the Kuwaiti positions regarding security issues, even if he hastened to add, 'our viewpoints may differ but our goals are identical'.[16] The fact that this disagreement came to the surface underlined the vibrancy of the debate. Disputes at such a high level are usually kept carefully under wraps. Ultimately, the six states emphasized the primacy of cooperation in the economic and social fields, something that was reflected in the wording of the charter of the organization.

The foreign ministers also prepared the agenda for the first summit meeting of the new organization, approved the by-laws and officially nominated Bishara as Secretary General, a post he would hold for ten years despite the limit of two three year terms laid out in the GCC Charter.

The first GCC summit was finally held on 25–26 May 1981 in Abu Dhabi. Each delegation from the six states included the head of state, a special advisor, the foreign minister, the finance minister and numerous bureaucrats. This impressive line-up underlined the importance of the occasion. The summit culminated in the establishment of the GCC.

An analysis of the Charter of the GCC

The Charter of the GCC consists of a preamble and 22 articles.[17] The 22 articles are divided into six topics:

- Basic Information (Articles 1–3).
- Objectives (Article 4).
- Membership (Article 5).
- Functions of the Main Bodies (Articles 6–16).
- Privileges and Immunities (Article 17).
- Charter implementation, Amendment and Deposition (Articles 18–22).

While Articles 1–3 and 5 are straightforward stipulations of the name of the organization, the location of the headquarters and other practical matters, it is significant that while none of the member states is explicitly mentioned by name, Article 5 states that 'the Cooperation Council shall be formed of the six states that participated in the Foreign Ministers' meeting held at Riyadh on 4 February 1981'. This meant that the admission of new states would actually require an amendment to the Charter. This sort of legalistic device is one of the many utilized to fend off the ever-more pressing requests by Yemen to be admitted as a full member. This idea of a closed grouping recurs even in the preamble, where the GCC is defined as a grouping of 'similar regimes', a clear reference to the hereditary shaikhly political systems of the member states.

Article 4 sets out the basic objectives of the Charter. The collaboration envisaged is wide ranging, encompassing commerce, economics and finance, customs and communication, education and culture, legislation and administration among others. It is difficult to think of an issue or area that has been left out. Moreover, the end result of the proposed cooperation is spelt out and it is very ambitious: cooperation in all fields is seen as a prelude to unity. However, this is certainly a concession to the spirit of the times. The principle of unity is lionized yet there does not seem to be a clear indication of how unity will actually be achieved.

The most conspicuous exception to the above is internal and external security. This omission is a direct result of the lengthy and often heated negotiations leading up to the creation of the GCC. Yet security was in many ways the organization's animating spirit, infusing most of the its activities without ever being explicitly mentioned. It is among the top priorities of GCC decision-makers even now, and it has been discussed at every single meeting of the Supreme and Ministerial Councils. However, it was never formally mentioned in the Charter, and until the creation of the token Peninsula Shield force in 1986, cooperation in the realm of security was never institutionalized. The six rulers decided instead to establish five technical committees at their first meeting. These cover social and economic planning, economic and financial cooperation, industrial cooperation, oil, and social and cultural affairs. As will be shown, the efficacy of these committees varies widely. Some, such as the social and cultural committee, have been very active throughout the life of the organization, whereas others are less visible or have had their functions addressed by other organizations. For example, oil matters have been dealt with in the context of the Organization of Arab Petroleum Exporting Countries (OAPEC) and the Organization of the Petroleum Exporting Countries (OPEC), and they do not figure in the final deliberations of GCC Supreme Councils – which does not mean, of course, that oil matters are not discussed informally by GCC rulers during the summits of the Supreme Council.

Articles 9 and 13 stipulate that unanimity is required when voting on substantive matters in both the Supreme Council and the Ministerial Council, whereas only a majority is required for procedural matters. The lack of majority voting on substantive issues further highlights the fundamentally different nature of the GCC compared with organizations such as the European Union. To this must be added the lack of supranational powers on the part of the General Secretariat, a provision that has caused constant complaints on the part of the bureaucrats charged with implementing the decisions of the Supreme and Ministerial Councils.[18]

Article 7 stipulates that the Supreme Council should meet once a year and that its chairmanship is to be held by each member country rotating in alphabetical order (in Arabic) for one year. The meeting of the Supreme Council usually takes place in November or December. A decision was taken in 1998 to add an informal session halfway through the year so that rulers now meet every six months. The functions of the Supreme Council are laid out in the Charter, but at the end of the day it exercises, political, judicial and legislative control over all decisions taken by the organization. This makes the GCC stand out among modern international organizations.[19] Even the GCC's proposed Commission for the Settlement of Disputes would submit its recommendations or opinions to the Supreme Council for ratification by a unanimous vote, since it would not have the power to issue verdicts on its own. There are no well-defined liability rules within the organization.[20] Therefore, in some ways the decision-making structure of the GCC reflects the domestic forms of government prevailing among member states; final authority resides with the rulers even if extensive processes of consultation are envisaged and carried out. The requirement of unanimity and the fact that all member states are treated equally also explains the reluctance on the part of member states to grant supranational powers to the General Secretariat. Saudi Arabia, the leading state within the GCC, is not in a position to devolve sovereignty to the Secretariat General if its smaller neighbour Bahrain has the same influence over what decisions are taken.

In other international organizations such as the International Monetary Fund (IMF) and The World Bank, the number of votes is proportional to the financial contributions of the member states. This makes these organizations agile and effective while preserving their multilateral character as even major players such as the United States know that they have a bigger say in the decisions that are ultimately taken. In a different context, it is worth noting how even in the UAE each emirate has an influence that is roughly equivalent to its contribution to the federal budget.[21] It is difficult to envisage the Secretariat General acquiring supranational powers so long as all countries have the same voting rights and contribute equally to the budget.

Articles 11 and 12 of the Charter set the functions of the Ministerial Council, the grouping of foreign ministers of the member states. Meetings of the Ministerial Council take place every three months, unless an extraordinary session is convened at the request of any member and seconded by another member. The presidency of the Ministerial Council goes to the member state that presided over the last ordinary session of the Supreme Council. The Ministerial Council is the main decision-making organ of the GCC. Most decisions taken at the level of the Supreme Council have been negotiated and agreed upon by the Ministerial Council. More often than not the Supreme Council in its biannual meetings ratifies what the Ministerial Council has decided upon.

Article 12 assigns the Ministerial Council 11 major functions:

- To propose policies and recommendations for further cooperation among the member states.
- To encourage cooperation among the member states in all fields and to recommend related policies to the Supreme Council for approval.
- To submit recommendations to the appropriate Ministries for implementation.
- To encourage cooperation among all segments within the member states, particularly the private sector, to expand cooperation among the member states' chambers of commerce and industry, and to facilitate the movement of indigenous workers among the member states.
- To refer any issue pertaining to cooperation to one or more technical and/or specialized committees for further study.
- To review any proposal related to amending the Charter and to refer such a proposal to the Supreme Council for action.
- To approve its own by-laws as well as the by-laws of the Secretariat.
- To appoint, upon the recommendation of the Secretary General, the Assistant Secretary Generals for renewable three-year terms.
- To approve periodic reports and regulations relating to financial, monetary and administrative affairs proposed by the Secretary General, and to submit the budget of the Secretariat to the Supreme Council for action.
- To arrange for the Supreme Council's meetings and prepare their agendas.
- To review the matters referred to it by the Supreme Council.

It must be noted how some of these functions have been superseded during the life of the organization. For example, ministers from member countries, particularly those for defense, interior and finance, now meet routinely to coordinate their policies without the need of the GCC Ministerial Council to act as a filter. From this point of view, the GCC has evolved as an organization and spurred collaboration between member countries even at a technical level. It is now common for directors general of ministries from the member states to meet to share information and best practice in their respective fields.

Article 10 of the Charter also envisages the creation of a Commission for the Settlement of Disputes. The Supreme Council is supposed to set up the Commission on an ad hoc basis when disputes arise among member states regarding the interpretation of the Charter that cannot be solved by the Supreme or the Ministerial Councils. Originally, the Commission for the Settlement of Disputes was also supposed to help defuse disputes among member states regarding borders and other such issues. In fact, the Commission has never been constituted. Saudi Arabia has usually taken upon itself unilaterally to diffuse border tensions between member states and possible disputes about the interpretation of the Charter have never surfaced having been solved through informal negotiations. This is consistent with the domestic style of decision-making in the six GCC states. Open confrontation is eschewed as much as possible and the accommodation of disputes is sought on an informal basis.

Articles 15 and 16 of the Charter regulate the functions of the Secretariat General, the permanent bureaucracy of the GCC. This includes around 300 employees drawn from the six member states, predominantly from Saudi Arabia.[22] However, all member states contribute equally to the budget. This is another characteristic that distinguishes the GCC from most other International Organizations. Article 15 assigns nine tasks to the Secretariat General:

- To prepare studies related to cooperation and coordination.
- To prepare periodic reports on the work of the GCC.
- To follow up the implementation by the member states of the resolutions and recommendations of the Supreme and Ministerial Councils.
- Prepare reports and studies requested by the Supreme and Ministerial Council.
- Draft administrative and financial regulations for the GCC.
- Prepare the budgets and closing accounts of the GCC.
- Make preparations for meetings and prepare agendas and draft resolutions for the Ministerial Council.
- Recommend to the Chairman of the Ministerial Council the convening of an extraordinary session of the Council.
- Any other tasks entrusted to it by the Supreme or Ministerial Council.

It is interesting to note how the formulation of Article 15 leaves the door open for a future expansion of the role of the Secretariat General. The task of following up the implementation by the member states of the resolutions and recommendations of the Supreme and Ministerial Council is the most crucial and also the most difficult to carry out lacking supranational powers. Former General Secretariat officials have complained that all they have at their disposal is an inadequate faculty of moral suasion *vis-à-vis* member states.[23] As will be shown, the number of decisions taken at the level of the Supreme and Ministerial Councils that have not been adequately implemented, particularly in the economic realm, is vast. Notwithstanding its numerous achievements, as long as a mechanism to nudge member states into compliance is not found, the GCC will find it impossible to evolve into a truly functional regional organization.

From an organizational point of view, the General Secretariat is divided into five Directorates and an Information Center. Two Associate Secretary Generals head the two most important Directorates, one for Political Affairs and the other for Economic Affairs. The Directorate of Environment and Human Resources, the Directorate of Legal Affairs and the General Directorate of Financial and Administrative Affairs as well as an Information Center complete the structure of the General Secretariat. Each of the Directorates is divided into a number of departments. Among the most active are the Department of Cultural Affairs and the Department of Education. Article 17 states that all the staff of the General Secretariat must carry out their duties independently from the particular interests of their country of origin and for the joint benefit of the member states. In practice, every senior appointment is the result of negotiations between the member states, whereas the lower ranking staff are predominantly Saudi.

The GCC Charter is a document inspired by the founding treaties of other international organizations, particularly the European Union. However, decision-making within the organization is highly personalized and ad hoc. This approach reflects traditional administrative practices inspired by the bureaucratic culture predominant within member states. At a senior level, deals are struck between the ruling families and are then implemented by the permanent bureaucracies. Given this milieu it is not surprising to discover that institutional rules can be flouted if a particular goal is seen as being more easily reached by doing so.

The adverse consequence of this flexible approach to rules and regulations is that over the years the GCC as an institution risked losing credibility in the international arena. The GCC came to be seen by many observers as a club where the ruling families of the six member states meet to strike their deals.[24] The achievements of the organization in both the diplomatic and the economic fields are consequently overlooked. The fact that internal and external security cooperation is not mentioned in the Charter, as a consequence of the negotiations outlined above, must also be seen as anomalous. This is because one of the fields where cooperation is more active is pursued entirely outside the formal structure of the organization. The General Secretariat is assigned no formal staff except a liaison officer. Institutionalization of cooperation in the internal and external security fields would certainly lend credibility to the organization. This in time could also lead to the conclusion of multilateral agreements in this sphere with the United States. The latter has sought in the past to reach a multilateral framework of cooperation in the defense field with GCC states.[25] However, partly as a result of the lack of a single voice on defense matters on the part of the GCC, it has had to confine itself to bilateral agreements with each member state. This is a situation reminiscent of that predominant in Asia where the United States has pursued bilateral agreements with allied countries in the wake of the Second World War. If GCC countries were to move beyond a symbolic joint force towards integration in their command structure similar to that of the North Atlantic Treaty Organization (NATO), the United States would find it easier to absolve its security commitments in the Gulf to the advantage of all parties.

In this chapter I looked at the run up to the formation of the GCC, the constitutive meetings and some of the factors that led the six future member states to set up the organization at this particular moment in time. I also offered a brief analysis of the Charter of the GCC highlighting its strengths and weaknesses. In the next chapter I look at the genesis of the GCC in light of International Relations theory. More specifically, I ascertain how the current debate on the usefulness of institutions in the international arena sheds light on the origins and effectiveness of the GCC.

3

THE GCC IN LIGHT OF INTERNATIONAL RELATIONS THEORY

The choice for practitioners is not between being influenced by theory or examining each case 'on its merits': it is rather between being aware of the theoretical basis for one's interpretation and action and being unaware of it.[1]

No single approach can capture all the complexity of contemporary world politics. Therefore, we are better off with a diverse array of competing ideas rather than a single theoretical orthodoxy. Competition between theories helps reveal their strengths and weaknesses and spurs subsequent refinements, while revealing flaws in conventional wisdom.[2]

Robert O. Keohane

Introduction

The Gulf Cooperation Council (GCC) is an unusual international organization as it aims at furthering integration in both the security and economic realms. This has led to a fair degree of confusion among analysts who have tried to apply analytical tools drawn from either Security Studies or International Political Economy. The result has been that while some scholars have emphasized the lofty but unfulfilled promises made by GCC leaders in the security sphere,[3] others have tried to derive some satisfaction from the slightly more encouraging results achieved in the sphere of economic coordination and integration.[4] In fact, the GCC is a peculiar organization, in many respects a unique one, and its hybrid nature resists full explanation when the organization is treated only as a regional economic institution or as an alliance.[5] The decision-making within the organization differs quite radically from any other international organization.[6] The search for consensus is painstaking, but the top-down structure and absence of checks and balances makes it easier to implement some types of decisions once these are arrived at by the Supreme Council. When it is viewed in its entirety the GCC involves cooperation, or more often purported cooperation, in external and internal security, foreign policy, trade, finance and monetary issues.[7] It is a hybrid organization that needs to be analysed comprehensively.

In this chapter I intend to demonstrate the hybrid nature of the GCC. I will then conduct a brief review of the debate on regionalism within International Relations Theory. I will then analyse the GCC from the point of view of alliance theory. I will purport to prove that traditional Neorealist concern with power is fundamental in understanding the creation of the GCC. However, cultural variables have to be taken into account to comprehend the particular timing of the formation of the organization as well as its durability. From this point of view a Neoclassical Realist approach, which borrows heavily from the current wave of constructivist work in International Relations Theory, may have the most explanatory power as we fully try to comprehend the history of the organization. I will then argue that to understand a hybrid organization such as the GCC we have to take a step back and try to explore the more general question of whether institutions have an independent effect on state behaviour. To do this I will first try to understand how the GCC fares with regard to the five analytical categories devised by Andrew Hurrell to break up the overtly broad notion of 'regionalism'.[8] I will finally argue that the loose nature of the organization should encourage us to arrive at the conclusion that the most relevant theoretical discussion with regards to the nature of the GCC is the one on international institutions and cooperation conducted by scholars such as Joseph Nye and John Mearsheimer.

I will start by exposing briefly the connection between the analysis of contemporary regionalism and three mainstream traditional currents in the study of International Relations. This will help to clarify the subsequent discussion on the nature of the GCC.

The concept of 'regionalism' in International Relations Theory

Most prominent scholars of International Relations Theory have something to say about regionalism and, more specifically, sub-regional integration. It is useful to adopt as a starting point Nye's classic definition of a region in International Relations as 'a limited number of states linked together by a geographical relationship and by a degree of mutual interdependence'.[9] This interdependence in the case of the GCC, as will be shown, is more geopolitical than economic. We can then define regionalism simply as the formation of interstate groupings on the basis of a region. If we stand by this broad definition there is a long history of regionalism.

It is safe to say, though, that most theoretical thinking about the subject was inspired by two major phenomena: European integration since the Second World War and the proliferation of regionalist efforts in the Third World in the 1960s (e.g. the Organization of African Unity founded in 1963, the Arab Free trade area established in 1964, etc.).[10] Major theoreticians of International Relations reacted to the challenge that these experiments posed to the traditional concept of the state. They started speculating about the nature and motives of states that decided to join together in some form or another. However, the peculiar history and decision-making structure of the six founding states of the GCC render much of this traditional work on regionalism superfluous for the needs of our analysis. The political systems of the constituent states are very different from those found in regional groupings of Western industrialized democracies. The differences at the domestic level inform the workings and the nature of the organization.

For example, one of the main characteristics of Western European integration was the strict separation of external security issues from politico-economic ones.[11] This separation, which is explicitly rejected by the states that gave birth to the GCC, informs most of the work done on European integration processes. Furthermore, leaders of organizations such as the Organization of American States or the Organization of African Unity never enjoyed the close personal relationship that the leaders of the six GCC states shared. Abdullah Bishara, former Secretary General, has dubbed the Supreme Council 'a club of elderly gentlemen'.[12] One can legitimately disagree with such a characterization, but the fact remains that these leaders are in close consultation throughout the year and their contacts are certainly not confined to their formal meetings. This makes a comparison with the regional organizations that flourished in the 1960s and 1970s not very pertinent.

If we look at the major theoretical paradigms in International Relations, Neorealism remains the most influential. As of today a plurality of scholars of International Relations still conduct their work according to the assumption that we can fruitfully conceive of state behaviour as the product of a 'rational, unitary actor', to use Graham Allison's famous phrase.[13] Moreover, in sprite of rhetorical statements to the contrary, a number of influential decision-makers seem to share this assumption, which consequently holds a significant amount of sway in the 'corridors of power'.[14] Indeed, such an assumption has proved beneficial and many insights have been gained in numerous subfields of International Relations by adopting this premise. Some exponents of the influential school of Neorealism have taken this assumption even further arguing that, given the systemic constraints inherent to the international system, most states tend to behave in the same way when facing an identical situation.[15] For most Neorealist thinkers the politics of regionalism have much in common with the politics of alliance formation. Kenneth Waltz, the leading proponent of the Neorealist paradigm, spends little time differentiating between economic and political regionalism.[16] Sub-regional integration is seen as the response of weak states to potential hegemonic powers in accordance with the belief that states will tend to balance power rather than bandwagon. Furthermore, the presence of a 'core' power, which in the GCC case would be Saudi Arabia, is often emphasized. Regional awareness and other cultural constructs are accorded little importance. The Neorealists have the merit of focusing our attention on the centrality of power in international relations. Indeed, it would be difficult to envisage the creation of an organization such as the GCC without the need of the six constituent states to adapt their behaviour to the presence of two regional powers such as Iraq and Iran. Their behaviour has been perceived as menacing by the six member states throughout the last 30 years. As we will see, though, the definition of 'threat' is essential to understanding the international politics of the Gulf in recent years. It is against threat that the six member states tend to balance, not against power. Therefore, it becomes important to understand which are the threats that the rulers of these countries consider menacing at any given time to their regimes. These may well include internal threats that only occasionally are manipulated by external powers.[17]

Neoliberal Institutionalists make what is commonly viewed as the most comprehensive theoretical challenge to Neorealist orthodoxy. Unlike Neorealists they think of regionalism as one of the central puzzles in International Relations Theory. Explaining regionalism becomes one of their central tasks and one way to challenge the assumptions and inferences of the Neorealist school. It is fair to say that most scholars working on regionalism embrace to a different extent this theoretical construct. Neoliberal Institutionalism has its roots in Liberal thinking about international relations mostly forged in a Western, Northern geopolitical context. Liberals, who believe that common values or interests can induce states to work together, take an optimistic view of the possibility that states may band together in regionalist efforts. Neoliberal Institutionalism is but the latest phase in a long tradition of Liberal thinking on the possibilities of cooperation among states. At least three phases can be discerned before Neoliberal Institutionalism emerged at the beginning of the 1980s: Idealism, Functionalism and Neofunctionalism.[18]

Among the intellectual founders of Idealism are Émeric Crucé, Hugo Grotius and Immanuel Kant. They all called for a voluntary association of states that would be represented within a central body. How a voluntary body was supposed to coerce individual states that did not play by the rules was never spelled out.

A second phase of the evolution of Liberal thinking was characterized by the realization that Idealists' goals had been too ambitious. This gave rise to British Functionalism, a school of thought whose origins can be found in the works of Jeremy Bentham and John Stuart Mill. These thinkers argued that the institutions most likely to succeed would be those that served specific practical functions. States would cooperate to solve common specific problems. The institutions created to accomplish this would be task specific and harmony between states would emerge only with the passage of time through a painstaking bottom-up process.

Neofunctionalism emerged in the 1960s. One of its main exponents, Ernst Haas, criticized Functionalist scholars for failing to emphasize that the process and consequences of international cooperation are *inherently* political. For lessons learned in one functional area to be applied to others political actors would have to make that choice for self-interested reasons.[19] Therefore, Neofunctionalists were more pessimistic about the prospects of building successful international institutions and were not surprised by the mixed record of a lot of them throughout the twentieth century.

Without going into an unnecessary detailed explanation of each of these phases, it is enough to point out here that the evolution of Liberal thinking about International Relations has been from 'a position that featured grandiose objectives, but lacked a plausible mechanism to achieve them, toward a more practical approach grounded in the concrete objectives of national policymakers'.[20] So much so that since the beginning of the 1980s one can discern the maturation of a neo–neo synthesis.[21] Neoliberal Insitutionalism and Neorealism are not as distant as Idealism and Classical Realism. They share a 'rationalist' research programme and a belief in the ontologically given existence of 'anarchy' among nation-states that are seen as by far the most important actors on the international scene. From this common premise the agenda of both research programmes includes, in the words of Ole Waever, 'regime theory cooperation under anarchy, hegemonic stability, alliance theory, trade negotiations, and Buzanian security analysis'.[22]

It would be easy to conclude that a research programme whose main purpose has been the study of regionalism or, in a broader sense, of cooperation among states would be of great help in understanding the working of a sub-regional organization like the GCC. The final communiqués of GCC summits are permeated with references to the need of tackling issues of common concern in a 'functionalist', pragmatic manner.

However, as Mohammed Ayoob points out, Neorealism and Neoliberalism share an epistemological bias in favour of the study of relations between major industrialized democracies, whether manifested in terms of balance or concert, of competition or cooperation.[23] This epistemological bias, which bedevils the whole field of International Relations Theory, is particularly acute in the case of Neoliberal Institutionalism. Discussions of 'long shadow', transparency and sophisticated game theory models bear little resemblance to the interaction between the shaikdoms of the Gulf.[24] In particular, the conditions under which major industrialized democracies are supposed to cooperate in the economic field do not appear in the Gulf or indeed in most of the rest of the world. GCC member states are all more or less trading in one line of production. In this context, free trade agreements are less important than when entered into by countries with diversified, sustainable economies. GCC states import virtually all their industrial and consumer goods and a great part of their labour from outside the region.[25] The challenge becomes more one of coordinating development strategies so as to avoid wasteful duplication, of connecting electric grids, etc. From this point of view GCC cooperation in the economic field has functionalist overtones but is hardly comparable with the one that takes place between the states of the European Union.

Constructivists form the youngest of the three theoretical schools I am discussing and the one that has witnessed a meteoric increase in popularity in the first decade of the twenty-first century. This school is intrinsically more heterogeneous than the two just mentioned. The Constructivists I am referring to are those who view states as social actors. They analyse political identities in specific historical contexts and trace the effects that changing identities have on political interests and thus on national security policies. For them regionalism is based on *regional awareness*, a shared sense of belonging to a particular regional community. Focus is not on material incentives but on ideational forces. Therefore, sub-regional integration is dependent on the compatibility of major values relevant to political decision-making.

The inspirer of many constructivists working on regionalism is Karl Deutsch;[26] more recently Michael Barnett and Emanuel Adler dealt with regionalism in their works.[27] It must be noted, though, how many of the concepts propounded by these constructivist scholars, particularly in the field of alliance formation, are already found in the work of Classical Realist, as opposed to Neorealist, scholars. For Classical Realists material power remains the key independent variable in international relations, but its impact on countries' external behaviour is indirect, complex and problematic.[28] This has led a number of scholars to update and systematize certain insights drawn from Classical Realist thought, broaching a new movement that they chose to label 'Neoclassical Realism'.[29] For them, as for Neorealists, regionalism has much in common with alliance formation, but their treatment of the impact of material power on the foreign policies of states is much more nuanced. In fact, even Neorealists such as Stephen Walt, who is credited with introducing the concept of 'balance of threat' to supplement the traditional 'balance of power' considerations, open the door, at least implicitly, to constructivist interpretations.[30] Threat is not seen as inherent to power but it is also derived from factors such as 'aggressive intentions'. Therefore, the notion that identity can play a crucial role in alliance formation is not confined to the new wave of Constructivist scholars but is very much present in the work of Classical Realists. However, the latter never lose sight of the central analytical concept of power. They do not attach excessive importance to concept such as 'role playing' widely utilized by Barnett to explain the alignment decisions of Arab states.[31] The difference, though, ultimately boils down to one of how much importance to assign to each variable. It is not a fundamental one even if it must be recognized that Constructivist-inspired scholarship did an excellent job of clarifying and systematize Classical Realist insights.[32]

In the case of the GCC states, to paraphrase Alexander Wendt, doctrinal Neorealists would have a hard time explaining why rulers consider an American military presence less threatening than an Egyptian or Syrian one, envisaged by the abandoned Damascus Declaration, let alone the Iranian contingent stationed on the other side of the Gulf.[33] Indeed, many of the insights that the current wave of constructive scholarship in International Relations builds upon are at least implied in the work of Classical Realists such as Hans Morgenthau, Reinhold Niebuhr and George Kennan.[34]

Crucially, for a scholar who aims to examine the international relations of the Gulf in the contemporary era, the Neoclassical Realist framework fully recognizes the divide between 'status quo' and 'revisionist' states.[35]

In the case of the GCC we have seen how the determination of the six rulers to exclude Iraq from the new organization led to its establishment at a very specific time in history: after the outbreak of the Iran–Iraq War. This is explained by their willingness to constitute a status quo organization. In theoretical terms a status quo alliance is comprised of satisfied states that fear the threat posed by a revisionist state or coalition.[36] GCC rulers have always deemed the two regional powers as harbouring revisionist ambitions even if during most of the Iran–Iraq War the Ba'athist regime had been seen as the lesser threat, a shield behind which the GCC states could shelter.[37] In his otherwise excellent paper on threat perception and alliance choice in the Gulf, Gregory Gause tends to conflate Neorealism and Classical Realism. He writes, 'the practical equivalence of power and threat is at the core of both classical realist and neorealist balance of power theories'.[38] However, it appears that the main concern of Neoclassical Realists is not to rescue a paradigm that is often seen as too parsimonious for its own good. It is rather to remind us of the importance of material power as the background, if not the immediate determinant, by which alignment decisions are made. In the words of Joseph Nye, 'military security is a little bit like air, if there is plenty of it nobody talks about it, if it becomes scarce decision makers start thinking of nothing else'.[39]

Another important consideration, when looking at the way GCC states relate to their security needs, lies in the unfeasibility of achieving self-reliance in the external security dimension. The need for support on the part of the United States has become increasingly relevant throughout the first 20 years of life of the organization. This is due to many factors, which will be analysed further in Chapter 5, the most important being the need to 'coup-proof' their military forces.[40] All GCC states felt that military efficiency had to be sacrificed for the sake of regime security. This led to favouring individuals and groups with special loyalties to the regime when making military appointments as well as creating parallel units, such as the Saudi National Guard, that balance the power of the regular military. Furthermore, in the case of Kuwait, the sheer physical size in terms of population and territory makes it impossible for it to mount an autonomous military defense *vis-à-vis* the two regional powers. This despite the improved efficiency achieved by its armed forces following a reorganization programme initiated after the Second Gulf War.[41]

In the case of GCC states, external security has depended on the support of an external power such as the United States since the inception of the organization in 1981. This support used to be 'over the horizon', but in the aftermath of the Second Gulf War it has become far more visible. The United States can be considered almost a local actor given the accords and prepositioning agreements concluded with all GCC states and the degree by which the American presence has become a subject of political debate in GCC states. This lack of autonomy in the military domain makes us wonder whether even Neoclassical Realist interpretations can fully do justice to a hybrid organization such as the GCC. It is apparent that the aspiration to present a united diplomatic front to the external world and the desire to foster economic integration played a part in the decision to set up the GCC. This means that the genesis of the GCC cannot be treated simply as a case of an alliance formed to balance the threat posed by the two regional powers, Iran and Iraq.

Traditional explanations for the genesis of the GCC, laid out in the previous chapter, need to be supplemented by a discussion of the changing identity of the six states of the Gulf as well as the emergence of the new centrist conception of Arab nationalism that developed in the late 1970s and 1980s. Before broaching the Constructivist angle, it is important to stress yet again how culturalist explanations cannot be put forward in isolation from material realities. A Neoclassical Realist framework allows us to incorporate notions of identity while keeping our focus on the importance of material incentives.

The momentous change in Arab political discourse that followed the demise of Pan-Arabism, first as a viable political project, and subsequently as the dominant ideology in the Arab world, has not traditionally been associated with the establishment of the GCC. Barnett, though, convincingly argued that identity politics has defined inter-Arab dynamics and developments over the years and that no understanding of Arab politics is complete without it.[42] His emphasis on a common Arab political 'narrative' sometimes seems to overlook material factors. However, it is true that an understanding of the normative constraints of Arab politics in the last 30 years is essential to make sense of many alignment decisions. Barnett focuses his analysis on the Levant, but this is true even when we look at the Gulf. As Gause argues, words – if it is feared that they will find resonance among a state's citizens – have often been seen as more immediately threatening than guns in the calculations of Arab leaders.[43] In other words, ideological and political threats emanating from abroad to the domestic stability of ruling regimes played an important part in the international relations of the Middle East. In particular, domestic stability is a paramount concern of all GCC states. Whereas for external defense these states have to rely ultimately on the protection of the United States, internal security is something for which they have complete responsibility. The need to ensure domestic stability has undoubtedly affected their foreign policies.

Furthermore, in the case of the GCC, I contend that identity played a role in shaping two crucial features of the alliance: the boundaries of the association, in other words who qualified as a desirable alliance partner; and the definition of the threat.[44] It is my contention that the declining significance of Pan-Arab national identity and the emergence of statist identities in the Gulf, as elsewhere in the Arab Middle East, must be fully accounted for if we are to understand the genesis of the GCC. During the 1970s Arab nationalism, as a political project leading to unification of the Arab world, was no longer realistic. However, all Arab leaders felt compelled to identify themselves with Arabism and to advocate Arab unity as the ultimate goal of intra-Arab political activity. The emergence of a distinct sub-regional grouping of Arab states such as the GCC would have been seen as a betrayal of the ideal of Arab unity. Only the demise of Pan-Arabism,[45] or better, the emergence of a new 'centrist' conception of Arab nationalism,[46] which is fully compatible with the notion of sovereignty, made it feasible for the Gulf Arab states to conduct an experiment in sub-regional integration deliberately centred around the notion of a distinct *khaliji* (Gulf) identity.

The Iraqi invasion of Kuwait further encouraged this process. The invasion could have been interpreted as a 'progressive' act from an Arabist perspective and Iraqi propaganda encouraged this reading. However, one of its consequences was that Arab leaders are now completely unapologetic about arguing openly for their states' interests. They even stopped arguing at the public level that the policies of an individual state will indirectly benefit the cause of Arab unity. This change in attitude is particularly significant in the case of the Gulf Arab monarchies. These states, conscious of their vulnerability, had always utilized foreign aid as a tool of foreign policy, dispensing it generously in the regional arena, and they had tried to cast themselves as the ever-accommodating mediators in intra-Arab disputes. Gulf officials had carefully portrayed the establishment of the GCC itself as a step in the direction of Arab unity.[47] Since the Second Gulf War, though, Gulf leaders have been far more energetic in their assertion of a separate Gulf identity and in stating their need to find solutions to specific sub-regional problems by looking for support from non-Arab actors. For example, all six member states have reached bilateral defense agreements with the United States to guarantee prepositioning of military material and other measures that would facilitate American intervention. However, as former Assistant Secretary of State Robert Pelletreau said, America itself would have preferred a more comprehensive multilateral pact.

The GCC, though, is not as evolved yet as a defense entity to be able to act as a single interlocutor on behalf of its members. Individual states adopted what we could call an 'insurance premium' approach underpinned by the acquisition of foreign weaponry and the investment abroad of petrodollars. This choice, which admittedly is pretty effective, undermines efforts, usually championed by Oman within the organization, to set up an effective deterrence force under unified command. Additionally, relying so massively on the United States and its Western allies for external defense hinders the attempts to set up a comprehensive Gulf security system that would include Iran and eventually Iraq.

From a theoretical point of view, neither Neoliberalism nor Neorealism, with their epistemological agenda biased in favour of major industrialized democracies, can fully account for the genesis of the GCC. Nor can they adequately predict what course the organization will take in the future. The profound change in the notion of Arab identity that followed the demise of Pan-Arabism allowed Gulf leaders to spurn previously accepted norms of intra-Arab political behaviour by setting up an organization that was explicitly sub-regional in character. Likewise, the eventual attainment of a *khaliji* identity by the GCC, particularly in the sphere of external defense, will mark an important step forward in the life of this organization. By charting the emergence and the evolution of a separate 'Arabian', as opposed to Arab, identity, I purport to demonstrate that the politics of identity matter even in fields, such as security studies, that so far have usually been the preserve of scholars adopting Neorealist tools of analysis.

The fields of alliance theory and security studies so far have been the most difficult to penetrate for the new wave of culturalist and constructivist theories of International Relations. They have long been the preserve of Neorealist strategic scholars who have been accustomed to think in terms of balance of power and zero-sum games. I firmly believe that a constructivist approach that focuses on identity can help us to supplement traditional alliance theories such as 'balance of threat' put forward by Stephen Walt,[48] and the 'omnibalancing' framework developed by Steven David to account for alliance formation in the Third World.[49]

While I am convinced that explanations rooted in cultural variables are indispensable to supplement existing theories I do not think they can entirely supplant them. In the case of the GCC cultural variables help explain the lag between structural change and alterations in state behaviour.[50] Namely, why the six Arab states of the Gulf did not create the GCC before. Additionally, matters of identity, as explained before, help us to understand who qualified as a suitable alliance partner and why GCC members spurned overt alignment with either superpower in the first decade of the life of the regional organization. To be sure, though, there were strategic rationales too for these choices.

If we take a positivist epistemological approach to the study of international relations we must recognize that explanations based on identity, while most useful in supplementing and integrating more traditional theories, cannot relegate the latter to the dustbin of social science theory. If we want to give a full account of the formation process of the GCC we must employ tools drawn from both constructivist and more traditional research programmes. This comes at the expense of parsimony, but it is warranted not least because of the hybrid organizational nature of the GCC.

In this regard it is useful to take a step back and examine the GCC in light of the five analytical categories devised by Andrew Hurrell to break up the overtly broad notion of 'regionalism'. The first category Hurrell identifies is what he dubs 'regionalization' which refers to 'the growth of societal integration within a region and to the often undirected processes of social and economic interaction'.[51] He further emphasizes that 'regionalization is not based on the conscious policy of states or groups of states' and that it usually involves 'autonomous economic processes which lead to higher levels of economic interdependence within a given geographical area than between that area and the rest of the world'.[52] This kind of soft regionalism is supposed to be very weak in the Arab world whose states are often seen as being in a relationship of dependency with regards to the major powers in the system.[53] More specifically, the GCC comes under a lot of criticism for its inability to form a complete customs union and for other glaring deficiencies in the realm of economic integration.[54]

However, once we take into consideration another aspect in Hurrell's analysis, 'the increasing flows of people, the development of multiple channels and complex social networks by which ideas, political attitudes, and ways of thinking spread from one area to another', the states of the GCC can be said to constitute a fairly coherent unit. The Independent Forum is an organization founded in 1979, two years before the formation of the GCC. It comprises professionals, bureaucrats and academics as well as other technocrats who felt that the major issues of development and management of resources needed to be tackled at a Gulf-wide level.[55] This is one of the most prominent of a number of professional organizations structured on a sub-regional basis. In particular, Chambers of Commerce and professional organizations now meet routinely on a GCC basis. This has led to the formation of a number of cross-state 'networks'. These are particularly effective in the Gulf because of the personal nature of decision-making in the area. From this point of view it is certain that a transnational civic society operates in the GCC states and is quite relevant to the running of those states. In this Gulf form these fora and organizations are infinitely more efficient and functional than their Pan-Arab counterparts. They were often founded before the GCC and are now the default level of coordination for the national professional syndicates of the six member states.

The second analytical category Hurrell identifies is the inherently fuzzy one of regional 'awareness and identity'. As we have seen this has been the subject of much debate and discussion in International Relations Theory. For present purposes it would be enough to focus on the fact that regions can be seen as imagined communities. They rest on mental maps whose lines highlight some features while ignoring others.[56] These maps are defined by internal factors: a common history, religion, language, etc., as well as by an external 'other' often represented by a security threat. In both cases, as with nationalism, the definition of a particular regional identity involves myth-making and invented traditions fomented by the state. In terms of this second category of regional awareness the GCC fares very well from the points of view of both external recognition and self-representation.

If we look at how the international press refers to the news emanating from GCC states we notice that during the 1980s a new category was progressively created. Throughout that decade actors and events from the Gulf stopped being associated with the wider Arab world. Talk of 'Arab' financial interests was substituted by references to 'Gulf' financial interests. At the diplomatic level the position of GCC states was singled out from the one of other Arab actors and reported separately. In other words, a new discourse emerged in which GCC states assumed an identity of their own and were no longer subsumed within the wider Arab fold.[57] The GCC can claim some credit for this new phenomenon. Annual meetings of the Supreme Council, numerous ministerial meetings and missions by the Secretary General of the GCC were often reported in the world press and started giving the impression of a working sub-regional entity. As we will see this unity was in many cases more apparent than real, but nevertheless it worked well for presentational purposes.

In terms of self-representation the development of a separate distinct *khaliji* (Gulf) identity is underway in all six countries of the GCC. This is well represented by the number of students who describe their 'Gulf' identity as ranking alongside their national or Arab one.[58] Furthermore, the press of all six states now tends to frame international developments according to what their impact on the Gulf at large is going to be. Numerous cultural initiatives such as the opening of museums and the establishment of folk villages are also meant to reinforce the existence of a separate sub-regional identity.

The third dimension of regionalism to which Hurrell alludes is the construction of interstate and intergovernmental agreements. The GCC can be seen as standing out from this vantage point; there are scores of agreements and the regulations jointly developed by the bureaucracies of the six member states. However, Hurrell is quick to point out how a 'high level of institutionalizatio [is] no guarantee of either effectiveness or political importance'.[59] This observation sounds particularly apt when we think of the GCC. We will see how GCC states have not actually implemented the majority of economic agreements. Defense cooperation is also little more than symbolic. A higher level of regional cooperation is often achieved by informal regimes established in other parts of the world that are not accompanied by any sort of institutionalization. A good example is security cooperation in East Asia that, while marred by the historical legacy of colonialism, allows South Korea and Japan to work closely with the United States to face multiple security threats. In spite of its high level of institutionalization the GCC certainly does not operate as a single unit in the defense field.

The fourth category that Hurrell points to is regional economic integration. He correctly emphasizes how this is simply a sub-category that acquired particular salience because of the European 'model' of regional integration driven as it was by economic cooperation. The GCC has certainly looked at Europe as a model, mimicking many of the integrative aspects pioneered by the European Community from separate queues at airports for GCC passport holders to an administrative structure that is clearly modelled on that of the European Community. The local media, which are keen to emphasize this 'benign' regionalist discourse, have often played up these similarities. However, it is clear how decision-making modes within the GCC clearly set this organization apart from the European regionalist efforts. On the one hand, as we will see clearly, intra-GCC trade is negligible by European standards. On the other hand, GCC heads of state enjoy privileged and direct communication channels that cut through the red tape of bureaucracy and make the attainment of a consensus a much more personal affair.

The final category highlighted by Hurrell is what he dubs 'regional cohesion'. This refers to the possibility that eventually the five processes we reviewed might lead to the emergence of a cohesive and consolidated regional unit. Hurrell defines regional cohesion in two ways: when the region plays a defining role in the relations between the states of that region and the rest of the world; and when the region forms the organizing basis for policy within the region across a range of issues.[60] The GCC is of course lacking on both counts. However, it can be said that the organization obtained some success in presenting a unified front to the world on certain issues. This can be ascertained by the frequency by which GCC states are grouped together when their foreign policies are discussed in the press or in government and academic circles. The expression 'GCC states' is by now a mainstay of reports and analysis of Middle East politics.

This consideration leads to the wider discussion of whether the GCC as an institution has made a difference since its inception. If we leave aside for a while the ambitious objectives set down in the Charter of the organization and we adopt a broader definition of what an international institution can achieve, we can conclude that the GCC has indeed made a difference. Joseph Lepgold and Miroslav Nincic define an international institution as 'routinized patterns of multilateral and bilateral practice that define acceptable behavior'.[61] This is of course an extremely broad definition that includes both formal and informal regimes as well as intergovernmental bureaucratic organizations. Even defining the GCC as a mere intergovernmental organization, serviced by a secretariat would be unacceptable to the 'founding fathers' of the GCC who set ambitious goals for their creature. However, I think this is the best benchmark to assess the efficacy of the GCC in the various fields covered by its Charter. Furthermore, the GCC Secretariat was indeed able to operate in a cumulative way over the years, further institutionalizing routinized patterns of behaviour in various fields.

It is important to determine whether the existence of the organization actually made a positive difference, however small, to the six constituent states. This pragmatic approach has the advantage of gainsaying both the ardent critics who argue that the GCC has been a complete failure and the enthusiasts who too often claim illusory successes for this organization. We can answer such a question by drawing on a vast body of theoretical literature in the field of International Relations, economic cooperation and security studies. We should anticipate that the GCC is definitely an intergovernmental organization and that the Secretariat does not hold supranational powers. Governments remain powerfully engaged in the workings of the Secretariat. This does not mean, though, that throughout its history the organization has not made a difference.

From this point of view it is a useful exercise to examine economic, defense and diplomatic achievements separately so as to be able to gauge better the strengths and weaknesses of the organization. In the words of Joseph Nye, 'rather than allowing us to talk about integration in general and confusing terms, this disaggregation will tend to force us to make more qualified, and more readily falsified, generalizations'.[62] In the next chapter we start by focusing on economic integration, which is heralded in the Charter of the organization as one of its most central elements.

4

GCC ECONOMIC INTEGRATION: DISAPPOINTING REGIONALISM AND ENCOURAGING REGIONALISATION

Member states shall establish a uniform minimum customs tariff applicable to the products of the third countries.
(Article 4 GCC Uniform Economic Agreement, 8 June 1981)

The ministers agreed that member states would continue to charge customs duty on goods bought from other states for a limited period.
(Mohammed Al-Mazroui, GCC Assistant Undersecretary for Economic Affairs, 20 December 2002)

Introduction

As in other fields, in the realm of economic cooperation and integration the objectives of the GCC differ sharply from its actual achievements. Senior officials admit that the series of unfulfilled promises and declaratory announcements, in this as in other areas, damaged the credibility of the organization.[1] In this chapter I will first make a distinction between economic and professional regionalization and economic regionalism. In the case of the GCC, while many professional syndicates and organizations now meet on a Gulf basis, the achievements on the part of the member states in coordinating, let alone integrating, their economic policies have been meagre. This vibrancy in the field of transnational civil society is not matched by the governments of the member states. I will illustrate a theoretical model of economic integration focusing on five incremental steps. The progress of the

GCC along this path will be assessed in light of the numerous economic instruments entered into by the six member states. I will devote particular attention to the 'saga' of the establishment of a customs union. This is a veritable test case of the tendency on the part of GCC member states to issue declarations in the economic realm that they then find difficult to implement for historical and political reasons.

I will then illustrate how even in the realm of joint development projects, which are often hailed as the true test of GCC economic integration, the results are not encouraging.[2] I will examine instances of coordination of the oil policies of the six member states. This is one field in which GCC states can claim a preeminent position on the world stage. Finally, I will try to explain some of the reasons that hampered the process of GCC economic integration. In particular, I will contend that in the economic realm the GCC states alternate between periods of bounty, when oil prices are high, and periods of 'crisis in slow motion'.[3] The leaderships of the six constituent states are conscious that something must be done to reform what are extremely cyclical economic systems but are fearful of the political repercussions of serious, lasting economic reform. When times are good it seems easier to GCC governments not to rock the boat, but when the situation is not so prosperous leaders lack the political capital necessary to enact structural economic reform. Even the Emirate of Dubai has proven unable to escape these boom and bust cycles. Furthermore, as a successful trade and business centre it remains even more hostage to downturns in the world economy and to regional instability. The same can be said for those firms, Saudi Basic Industries Corporation (SABIC), that Steffen Hertog aptly dubbed 'islands of efficiency'.[4] They certainly managed to compete in the global market place, but they did so by delocalizing production and behaving as well-managed multinational companies. Their success does little to change the underlying dynamics in most GCC states. In fact, it highlights even more the indolent performance of government bureaucracies.

Economic regionalism versus professional and civic regionalization

It is appropriate to start by affirming an important distinction between economic regionalism as a *conscious policy* of GCC states to coordinate and integrate their economic policies and economic, professional and civic regionalization as the *outcome* of such policies or of 'natural' economic forces.[5] In particular, I contend that while GCC steps to further economic integration fall well short of projected aims, a bright spot is represented by the civic organizations that decided to organize themselves on a Gulf-wide basis. Even more significantly professional organizations, while still constituted on a national basis, meet regularly at the GCC level. The opportunities to do business at the Gulf level have indeed improved since the creation of the GCC. The aim of creating an 'economic citizenship', in accordance with Article 4 of the GCC Charter, is one of the few that have come close to being fully realized. The visa requirements for GCC citizens were scrapped with effect from 1 March 1983. Around the same time the ownership rules for companies were relaxed for GCC citizens well in advance of World Trade Organization (WTO) requirements, even in Saudi Arabia, the most shielded of the six economies.

It can be said therefore that the fact that professional organizations closely coordinate and meet on a Gulf basis is partially the result of GCC policies. It is a lot easier today for professionals and businessmen, who are citizens of member states, to move around/within the GCC and do business. However, even this positive assessment would not take into consideration the genuine enthusiasm of professionals and technocrats throughout the Gulf to see the GCC as a tool to nudge their respective national governments in the direction of economic and political liberalization.[6] The GCC is often seen by restive American-educated technocrats as a possible vehicle of innovation in terms of business practices and transparency. This expectation is unrealistic given that GCC bodies do not have supranational powers and, as we have seen, their decision-making procedures reflect those of the six national governments in their opaque and informal nature. Positive decisions like those regarding visas and company laws have to be implemented by the national bureaucracies of the single states. However, this enthusiasm is a further testament to how sub-regional bodies are seen as something 'good' in today's world in spite of the actual achievements of these organizations.

A further, more daring, instance of the regionalization of civic society in the Gulf is a number of non-governmental organizations (NGOs) that were organized on a sub-regional basis even before the establishment of the GCC. A prominent example is the 'Development Forum', an organization of professionals, bureaucrats and academics. These often American-educated technocrats came together in 1979, two years before establishment of the GCC. Initially, members hailed from five of the six GCC countries, with the exclusion of Oman. Later a few Omani members joined and now the organization has members from all six GCC countries. The membership of around 100 influential professionals meets once a year for a conference whose proceedings are published in book form. During the first decade of the organization they focused on two major issues that affected their countries of origin: the issues of economic development and of the management of resources. They considered development in the Gulf as very lopsided and distorted. Therefore, the forum started by considering how best to deal with the management of large public projects and how to promote a more balanced exploitation of resources.[7] Gradually, members started addressing in their annual symposia more delicate themes such as economic and political liberalization.

Abdulaziz Sultan, an architect who holds a doctorate from Harvard University, is representative of a new breed of Gulf technocrats who resent the lack of transparency and the cliquey nature of Gulf business practices. They see economic liberalization as a necessary precursor of political liberalization. It is not a coincidence that, in addition to his role as coordinator of the Development Forum, Abdulaziz Sultan serves as leader of the Kuwait National Democratic movement. He is aware that many economic problems can be tackled only at the sub-regional level. Interestingly, he adds to the usual reasons that are quoted in the literature as hampering GCC economic coordination and integration the fact that GCC member countries enjoy different levels of democratization. He sees democratic change and the harmonization of political systems as key issues not only as political issues, but also as key elements for economic integration.

In effect the issues of economic and political integration cannot be categorically distinguished. On many occasions further steps on the road of economic integration have been held hostage by political disputes. The fact that professional organizations, economic officials and NGOs now meet on a GCC basis is a good sign. Thus, best practice is spread around the Gulf and there is increased room for business deals to take place across the borders of member states. It is fair to make this point before focusing on the lack of progress in the field of economic integration by GCC member states.

Measures of economic integration

In order to gauge the state of GCC economic cooperation and integration it is useful to refer to the classic work on the subject by Bela Balassa, which GCC officials themselves use as a reference.[8] Balassa distinguishes five sequential degrees of economic integration:

1) *Free trade area*: suppression of discrimination in the field of commodity movements among member countries. However, as long as tariffs among

non-members are not equalized, customs authorities have to distinguish between partner and foreign products according to the shares of value added in the product

2) *Customs union*: complete free trade of commodities within the union and a common tariff wall against non-member countries
3) *Common market*: customs union and abolition of restrictions on factor movements and services. However, non-nationals such as foreign workers are excluded from free movement. This is a crucial proviso for the six GCC countries where at least 35% of the population and 65% of the workforce is made up of expatriates[9]
4) *Economic union*: a common market in which national economic policies are harmonized in order to remove discrimination that was due to disparities in the nations' policies. This implies a joint industrial policy
5) *Complete economic integration*: a common market in which economic policies such as monetary, fiscal, social and countercyclical policies are unified and in which a supranational authority is set up whose decisions are binding for the member states

Balassa's classification is meant to apply to all market economies and it follows closely the blueprint for economic integration adopted by GCC countries. However, it should be noted that joint development efforts, both in the fields of infrastructure and manpower as well as joint policies *vis-à-vis* expatriate workers, are difficult to locate in Balassa's classification. This point is often underscored by GCC officials. They stress how GCC member states are all more or less trading in one line of production. In this context, free trade agreements are less important than when entered into by countries with diversified, sustainable economies. GCC states import virtually all their industrial and consumer goods and a great part of their labour from outside the region.[10] However, this argument is contested by many economic analysts.

Hans Christoph Rieger, looking at the Association of Southeast Asian Nations (ASEAN), stresses how complementarity grows in line with international specialization engendered by trade. Therefore, it should be the objective rather than the precondition of trade liberalization.[11] Once protectionism is reduced there is certainly scope for broader international exchange. Given the pre-existing strengths and weaknesses of the six GCC countries, we can actually design a hypothetical scenario of the different economic activities in which GCC member states could further specialize by following current trends. Bahrain is already the preeminent financial centre in the Gulf. New transparency requirements imposed by the American 'War on

Terror' are bound to decrease its competitive advantage *vis-à-vis* financial centres in Europe and America. This will happen because, as it is recently the case with Switzerland, the traditional discretion that accompanies financial transactions in Bahrain is bound to come under close scrutiny. However, further GCC economic integration will contribute to maintain its edge over rival banking centres. Bahrain could also benefit from more business for its aluminium production plants and shipyards. Dubai, which has so far been the most successful GCC state in diversifying its economy, could further strengthen its commercial vocation as well as its trade and transhipping business and hopefully it could spread its proactive business agenda to the other Emirates. Kuwait may be a centre for the refining industry as well as a financial centre, particularly during periods when trade with its neighbour Iraq is not hampered by political difficulties. Saudi Arabia has an important role to play not only in downstream manufacturing of petroleum products, but also in some basic industries such as cement and chemicals. This after the inefficient and protectionist subsidies to the agricultural sector have been removed and some results from the much heralded but very slow process of the 'Saudization' of the workforce start being achieved.[12] Product and process specialization could lead to intra-industry trade.[13] In general, we can conclude that regional economic integration, when accompanied by other measures to deregulate their economies, would certainly benefit GCC states.

Before reviewing the achievements of the GCC in the realm of economic integration, it is worth noting that within the GCC Secretariat the Economic Affairs sector is placed directly below the office of the Secretary General and is of equal standing with the Political Affairs sector.[14] This is meant to underscore the importance of economic integration within the life of the GCC. The central importance of this field within the life of the organization is invariably mentioned in the final communiqués of the meetings of the Supreme Council of the GCC. The Economic sector is divided into several departments:

1) Economic and social planning
2) Industry, electricity, desalinization and technology
3) Research
4) Commerce
5) Public works, municipalities and housing
6) Petrol and gas department

It is important to emphasize that, much to the chagrin of the first Associate Secretary General for Economic Affairs, Abdullah Ibrahim Al-Kuwaiz, like other GCC departments, these do not have supranational powers.[15] Therefore, unlike, for example, the European Union Commissioners, all the departments can do is to harangue member governments in order to accelerate the implementation of the various economic agreements. The fact that there is no mechanism for the Secretariat General to enforce the implementation of the various treaties is one of the many reasons why the results in the field of economic integration have been so uneven.

Both the Charter of the GCC and its first Secretary General stress that unity is the 'final objective' in the economic field, a lofty goal indeed.[16] In pursuit of such a goal a number of instruments have been ratified and various decisions have been taken. By far the most significant agreement and indeed the cornerstone of all subsequent cooperation in the economic sphere is the Unified Economic Agreement (UEA), which was approved in principle on 8 June 1981, less than three weeks after the adoption of the GCC Charter, and which was then formally ratified by the GCC heads of states at their summit in November 1981.[17] Economic cooperation among Gulf states precedes by many years the adoption of the UEA and this instrument was meant also to broaden and rationalize the previous efforts at economic cooperation.

The UEA consists of a preamble and seven chapters divided into a total of 28 articles:[18]

1) Trade exchange (Articles 1–7)
2) Movement of capital and citizens and the exercise of economic activities (Articles 8 and 9)
3) Coordination of development (Articles 10–13)
4) Technical cooperation (Articles 14–17)
5) Transport and communication (Articles 18–20)
6) Financial and monetary cooperation (Articles 21–23)
7) Closing provisions (Articles 24–28)

The UEA is a very ambitious document that sets out clear objectives for the GCC in the economic field. It is worth reviewing here some of its main provisions while simultaneously assessing what is the status of their implementation a few decades after the signing of the agreement.

Free trade area

The first three articles prescribe the creation of a free trade area and describe the criteria by which a particular product should be considered of national origin. Article 3 states that for products of national origin to qualify as such the value added ensuing from their production in member states should not be less than 40% of their final value. In addition, the share of the member states' citizens in the ownership of the producing plant should not be less than 51% of the final value. This requirement has created quite a lot of controversy in the past as the demand for a certificate of local origin has been criticized by some business people.[19] In practice, even if a standardized GCC form exists, a GCC committee has to confirm the decision that specific products of a specific firm are duty free within the GCC. Having to obtain a certificate of national origin became one of the countless non-tariff barriers that plague business life in the Gulf.[20] Furthermore, some exemptions, allowed under Article 24 of the UEA on a temporary basis, still persist today and there are some ambiguities with regards to the status of handicrafts and art.[21] More importantly, products of national origin are still favoured *vis-à-vis* products from other GCC states in government purchases and public contracts, even if this is expressly ruled out in the UEA. Given the size of government spending in GCC states this is a significant issue. In spite of all these reservations, the creation of a Free Trade Area beginning in March 1983 is the main achievement of the GCC in the field of economic integration.

Customs union

As a further step, Article 4 mandates the creation of a uniform tariff range within five years as a step towards establishing a customs union. A tariff range of between 4% and 20% was established as of 1 September 1983, more than four years earlier than stipulated in the UEA.[22] After this auspicious start, though, finalizing a customs union by agreeing on a single external tariff proved devilishly difficult. Furthermore, the repeated announcements that the establishment of the customs union was imminent did much to tarnish the credibility of the GCC in the economic field. Diplomats and European Union officials came to mistrust the efficacy of the organization in spite of its achievements in other fields.[23] More than 20 years after the signature of the agreement a customs union was still not completed. The saga confirms the importance of the lack of enforcements mechanisms on the part of the General Secretariat. This is in stark contrast with the European Commission that has direct jurisdiction over issues of free trade and competition within the European Union. The European Union as far back as 1989 announced that the achievement of a GCC customs union would be a precondition for a free trade agreement with the European Union. Such an agreement would open European markets to the products of the GCC petrochemical industries, by far the biggest industrial sector in the GCC states. The slow pace in forming a customs union was costly for the six member states.

Finally, after years of hollow timetables, in December 2001, at the annual GCC summit, the GCC countries decided to advance the introduction of their internal GCC Customs Union by two years. A formula for a Common External Tariff was also agreed: there were to be a limited number of duty-free items and the majority of products would be subject to a 5% duty. The Common External Tariff was introduced and was to be fully in effect by January 2003. In a final twist, though, the full implementation was blocked yet again two weeks before the deadline.

Historically, the hypothesis of a customs union is particularly troublesome for these states. The relationship with merchants was the mainstay of the shaikhly regimes before the discovery of oil. Customs were the main source of revenue for them and an important source of patronage. The abolition of the right to set external tariffs is felt not only as a mayor abdication of sovereignty, but also as the weakening of the link to an extremely important constituency. One of the main factors behind the delay in establishing a customs union was the disagreement between the United Arab Emirates, particularly Dubai, and Saudi Arabia on what the tariff level should be on most industrial goods. Saudi Arabia aimed at protecting its highly subsidized infant industries, while Dubai did not want to jeopardize its role as an important commercial and transhipment hub. Furthermore, another major stumbling block was the difficulty in devising a mechanism to apportion tariff revenues among GCC member states.[24]

The difficulty in reaching a customs union has been a thorn in the side of the GCC for a long time and it has overshadowed the achievements of the organization in other fields. If we refer to Balassa's categorizations, it can be seen that this is considered only the second step in a five-step sequence leading to full economic integration. A first deadline to form a monetary union by 2005 was duly missed as was a second one in 2010. Indeed, the prospect of a single currency seems as remote as ever. A monetary union would involve abdicating monetary sovereignty to a GCC central bank. It is true that such a move would involve fewer difficulties than in the case of the euro. The currencies of the member states are stable. Five of the GCC states are linked to the US dollar, whereas the Kuwaiti dinar is tied to a basket of world currencies. Capital flows are completely liberalized. However, the creation of a GCC central bank still appears premature in an organization whose Secretariat is still not entrusted with supranational powers and where no pooling of sovereignty has taken place.

In a final flourish to the customs union saga smaller GCC states have negotiated bilateral free trade agreements (FTA) with the United States starting in 2004. In September 2004, the United States set up a bilateral FTA with Bahrain. In November 2004, United States Trade Representative (USTR) Robert Zoellick announced the intention to create FTAs with Oman and the United Arab Emirates as well. The FTA agreement with Oman was signed in January 2006; the FTA between Bahrain and the United States came into force six months later.

In stark contrast with the drawn-out negotiations underlining the customs union and the prospective deal with the European Union, negotiations for these agreements have been conducted at breakneck speed. In the case of Bahrain the FTA has been signed and ratified in fewer than two years from the start of negotiations. As Jean-François Seznec has remarked, these FTAs have a strategic dimension that goes well beyond throwing in complete disarray the prospect of a functioning FTA with the European Union.[25] Such an agreement may well be signed one day, but these FTAs create almost insoluble problems for the GCC bureaucrats in charge of economic integration, adding the need to implement complicated rules of origin procedures in case the long sought-out accord with the European Union is ever reached. This is because, unlike customs unions, FTAs raise the possibility that imports might enter through whichever member has the lowest tariffs and then get distributed among other member states on a duty-free basis.

It is telling that negotiation with the European Union has carried on in the wake of the signing of the FTAs as if nothing of significance had happened. The fact that the implementation of overlapping FTAs would be devilishly difficult to implement is well understood by technocrats within the General Secretariat. Yet, political leaders are oblivious to this development in their public pronouncements. This hiatus is further proof of the scarce institutional independence that the GCC managed to develop even in the economic field and of its mostly symbolic role in the mind of decision-makers in the six member states.

At a broader, political level these agreements put a wedge between Saudi Arabia and the other GCC members in one of the areas hailed as the mainstay of GCC activities.[26] This is further reflection of a progressive loss of Saudi leadership that will be discussed in the last part of this work.

Joint industrial projects and other economic initiatives

GCC officials stress the importance of joint development projects for the strategy of economic integration of the organization. Activity in this field is categorized as 'positive' integration and it is often emphasized in order to put a gloss on the difficulties encountered in the process of 'negative' integration, namely the creation of a customs union and a common market. Joint development projects did indeed start in earnest after the founding of the organization. After 20 years from its founding, though, we can discern a clear pattern by which activity in this field soars when oil prices are high and then abates when oil revenues start to dwindle. This is the general trend of economic activity in the Gulf and it is not surprising to discern it even in this field. However, it certainly creates many problems in sustaining joint GCC efforts in the economic field.

The Gulf Investment Corporation (GIC) is the pre-eminent institution set up in the field of joint development. It was established by the Supreme Council of the GCC Heads of State at its meeting in Doha on 10 November 1982. The Supreme Council decided on an initial generous capitalization of US$2.8 billion and that it would be based in Kuwait in line with the practice of spreading GCC institutions among the six member states. In later years when oil revenues fell GCC governments began to renege on their commitment and the fully paid up capital was US$2.1 billion. However, at the end of 2008, admittedly right before financial markets were thrown in disarray, the GIC can boast total assets in excess of US$9.148 billion and a very respectable return on paid-up capital of 36.4%.[27] GIC shares are owned in equal proportion by GCC states and the corporation is controlled by a Board of Directors consisting of two representatives from each member state.[28] The aims of the organization are the following:

1) Lending for industrial, agricultural and fishery activities in the GCC where its comparative advantages lies in the ability to provide long-term finance
2) Undertaking technical and economical feasibility studies and providing project selection or rejection, which is a positive externality to other investors
3) Involvement in selected new investment projects either by long-term investment of 20% capital or more and exerting significant influence (associated companies), or by otherwise simply participating (participations)
4) Investing in existing companies, assisting them in expanding, and providing them with management and financial expertise
5) Cooperation with the GCC Secretariat General in organizing conferences or undertaking research and consulting for the GCC[29]

The GIC used to own the Gulf International Bank (GIB) fully, which was acquired in 1991. As a result of a merger between GIB and Saudi

International Bank (SIB), the GIC retained a 72.5% ownership of the GIB. Subsequently in April 2001 that remaining ownership was sold directly to the six governments that comprise the GCC: Bahrain, Kuwait, Oman, Qatar, Saudi Arabia and the United Arab Emirates.[30] The divestment followed a decision by the Board of Directors and the six GCC governments to refocus the GIC on its core missions. However, the GIB was well managed by the GIC in the ten years of its ownership.

Even if its missions appear somewhat outdated in an era of privatization and deregulation, the GIC proved to be an efficient organization. Overall, when choosing its investments, it managed to discriminate between projects and to resist surprisingly well to political pressure. For example, of the 199 projects that the GIC chose for appraisal and evaluation in the first eight years of its existence, only half received a full technical and economic feasibility evaluation and fewer than 10% were finally accepted.[31] This is a commendably low percentage given the political pressure that is usually brought to bear on the organization. The organization, while not a giant given the huge size of the Gulf capital markets, performed well and assisted the GCC General Secretariat by performing serious, in-depth evaluations. In sum, the GIC is probably one of the best-managed projects in the field of GCC economic integration.

Another important GCC specialized agency is the Gulf Organization for Industrial Consulting (GOIC) headquartered in Qatar, which was founded in 1976, before the establishment of the GCC, and whose main mission is the identification, evaluation and promotion of joint industrial projects in the member states. In addition to this primary aim, the GOIC conducts a wealth of studies about the state of industries within the GCC, publishes periodicals and bulletins, as well as maintaining a number of useful databases.[32] It also runs a number of training programmes and symposia. The problem for the GOIC is that while the quality of the studies and of the personnel is good, there simply is not much scope for joint industrial projects in the Gulf. The fact that the studies are rigorous and serious just underlines that with the current cost structures the number of viable industrial joint ventures in the Gulf, which would not require huge subsidies, is quite limited.

The same problem has beset another GCC institution, the Industrial Cooperation Committee of the ministers of industry of the six member states that first met in October 1981 and whose task is to promote joint industrial projects.[33] In this case the main achievements seem to have been the exchange of information and the furthering of projects that do not necessarily involve all six GCC countries. The activity of the committee must be seen in the context of the numerous joint ministerial meetings held at the GCC level. The importance of this constant process of consultation is often discounted by foreign observers. These meetings, which involve almost all the ministries, encourage the spreading of best practice and informal policy coordination between member states.

Among the successes of GCC economic integration must be counted the efforts in the area of standardization and metrology. On 10 November 1982, in addition to setting up the GIC, the Supreme Council approved the transformation of the existing Saudi Arabia Standards Organization (SASO) into the GCC Specification and Measures Organization (GSMO). On 10 October 1983 the inaugural Board of Directors and the organizational structure were established. As in other GCC inter-ministerial organizations the GSMO is governed by a Board of Directors consisting of the ministers representing the relevant ministries in each of the member states, with a rotating chairmanship. The Secretariat General is represented at GSMO meetings by the Secretary General and the Associate Secretary General for Economic Affairs, but crucially the latter two do not have voting rights and the Board of Directors reports directly to the Ministerial Council.[34] This is another illustration of the lack of supranational powers on the part of GCC officials.

In January 1998 the GSMO reported that since its inception it had approved approximately 1000 unified standards for the GCC countries to date.[35] Furthermore, the GSMO plays a part in the European Union–GCC cooperation agreement. The GSMO and the European Commission concluded a Memorandum of Understanding in 1996 covering a Standards Cooperation programme of three years. Subsequently, a European expert took up duty in Riyadh and has worked with the GSMO since December 1996 as coordinator of the European side of the programme. It is planned to introduce telecommunications standards into standards cooperation.[36]

Oil policies

The six GCC states sit on around 46% of proven oil reserves and more crucially they have a production-to-reserve ratio of around 90 years.[37] According to some scholars, most notably Giacomo Luciani, the impact of the oil phenomenon on the role of the state and on economic behaviour in general has been so profound in the Arab world, and in the Gulf in particular, as to give rise to a particular social structure. According to Luciani, a rentier state is a state where the creation of wealth is centred around a small fraction of society; the rest of society is only engaged in the distribution and utilization of this wealth. The government becomes the main recipient of this external rent in the economy. A predominantly rentier state will then play a central role in distributing revenues from oil to the population. Such an economy creates a rentier mentality. Reward in the GCC states, be it income or wealth, is not related to work or risk bearing but rather to chance or situation.[38] Even if we do not share such a radical view, it is certain that GCC energy ministers have a lot to talk about.

Article 11 of the UEA states that member states should endeavour to coordinate their policies with regards to all aspects of the oil industry and to adopt a common position *vis-à-vis* the outside world. The energy committee comprising the oil ministers of the member states has met 25 times in the first decade of the existence of the organization and oil matters are on the agenda of meetings of the Supreme Council. However, from an institutional point of view, four out of six GCC states are members of the Organization of Petroleum Exporting Countries (OPEC) and five out of six, including Bahrain which does not have oil left, are members of the Organization of Arab Petroleum Exporting Countries (OAPEC). Oman follows closely the policies of these two organizations without actually being a member.

In light of the existence of these two organizations, the GCC does not serve as a forum to coordinate oil policies. It must be noted also that oil policies are so vital to the life of the member states that this is an area in which any pooling of sovereignty is unattainable for the foreseeable future. However, there have been some results in the fields of marketing, training of workforces and the need to avoid excessive replication in the refining sector.

Obstacles and perspectives

In order to understand the reasons why the GCC achieved less than was envisaged in the UEA, we have to start from some general considerations about the political economy and the recent history of the six member states. Gary Sick and other analysts remind us of the economic problems that the GCC states face when the price of hydrocarbons falls under a certain level.[39] These include budgetary uncertainties due to the vagaries of the international oil market, the dominance of the public sector, unemployment and underemployment among the local population, inadequate revenues to finance the very generous welfare states, and a lack of transparency in the state budgets. The remedies are similarly well rehearsed and they are quoted in countless reports of The World Bank and the International Monetary Fund

(IMF): reducing government subsidies to the public and private sectors, cutting redundant labour in the civil service, rationalizing non-productive spending, and introducing large-scale consumption taxes as well as taxes on the income of individuals and companies.

Of course all these ills are quickly forgotten when the price of hydrocarbons picks up again. However, as Sick ably concludes, GCC states face a dilemma. If they maintain the paternalistic statism that served them so well for half a century, they risk a domestic struggle over a potentially dwindling body of resources. If, however, they opened the system economically, let alone politically, they risked setting in motion a set of vigorous new institutions that would almost inevitably challenge their ruling style if not their very legitimacy. This formulation encapsulates the essence of the dilemma that was well captured by Tim Niblock even before the founding of the GCC.[40] At the domestic level the cures for the problems are well known and prosaic, but also politically unpopular, so there never seemed to be an appropriate moment to take the kind of bold and painful action required, particularly because the oil price seems to go back to a 'safe' level every time the mechanism of reform is painfully set in motion.[41] This phenomenon is well illustrated in the very slow pace of 'indigenization' of the work forces in GCC states.

If this is the situation at the domestic level in most GCC states, what has economic integration to offer? As long as important reforms are carried out at a glacial pace at the domestic level it is difficult to see how economic integration could proceed much further. This is particularly true when difficult political choices will have to be made such as a significant pooling of sovereignty or the granting of supranational authority to GCC bodies.

These challenges require political solutions and the very able technocrats at the GCC Economic Integration Department cannot be expected to overstep their mandates. They have been able to persuade and cajole member governments into starting down the path of implementation of a customs union. From this point of view the GCC as an organization has been able to build a 'corporate identity' when it comes to economic integration. However, they cannot force implementation on recalcitrant domestic bureaucracies.

A recent development is Yemen's accession to some GCC bodies. While this could be seen as a welcome development from the point of view of regional integration, it actually represents a further potential stumbling block on the path of economic integration. Yemen is much poorer and its socio-economic structure is very different from current GCC members. The prospect of co-opting it in a meaningful process of economic integration is difficult to imagine. Indeed, if Yemen were to become a full member of the GCC this would send a signal that the organization has abandoned the prospect of meaningful economic integration and in future it will satisfy itself with presentational gestures that do not require politically sensitive decisions.

Given their wealth, GCC economic woes are of relatively little consequence when compared with much of the rest of the world. In fact, GCC states can generally choose not to choose when it comes to their political economy in a way that is afforded to very few other countries around the world. There is almost always room for postponement. The next chapter, though, will look at how this prosperity cannot be easily translated into security in either in the domestic or external realm. Their geopolitical and geoeconomic position makes negotiating these multiple tensions difficult, and the leaders of Gulf Arab states often find themselves in a fractious and fragile positions.

5

GCC DEFENSE COOPERATION: BEYOND SYMBOLISM?

We in the Gulf have no liking for foreign troops to defend our own future and to defend our own sovereignty. We believe that we can, by approaching this issue collectively, ensure the survival of our sovereignty and the continuous security of the Gulf.[1]

Many of the Gulf States were very reluctant to have us around before Iraq invaded Kuwait [...] in many ways the war clearly changed attitudes in the Gulf [...] a significantly enhanced willingness to cooperate on security arrangements and joint ventures with the United States and US forces.[2]

GCC Secretary General Abdullah Bishara

Introduction

The conventional wisdom is that, in spite of the absence of any explicit mention in the charter of the organization, the Gulf Cooperation Council (GCC) was founded to guarantee the security of the member states, or more accurately of their dynastic monarchies, *vis-à-vis* internal and external challenges.[3] Therefore, it is a useful exercise to review whether the organization actually served as a forum for external and internal security coordination. In other words, if the establishment of the GCC actually enhanced the security of its member states in the internal and external realms. After a careful review of initiatives in these areas it is my contention that results have been meagre. However, it would be unfair to blame the organization itself because the challenges stem from structural determinants. The support of external allies, chiefly the United States, appears to be a necessary feature in the attempts of the six member states to achieve a modicum of external security.

I will begin this chapter with a brief analysis of the balance of power in the Gulf. This will help to elucidate why self-reliance is inherently difficult to achieve for the six GCC states. I will subsequently review the GCC attempts to institutionalize a common security policy in the external and internal realms. I will then identify what I think are the systemic constraints faced by the six GCC states both individually and collectively. This will help to clarify why the institutional role of the GCC is necessarily limited. I will briefly review the main challenges that the ruling families face both from within and from without in trying to guard against violent change. The GCC will then be assessed using the criteria developed by William Tow to measure the performance of what he dubs Subregional Security Organizations.[4] I will conclude by explaining why the mere existence of the organization does in itself play a positive role in the arena of public diplomacy regardless of the actual achievements in the internal and external security fields.

The realities of power in the Gulf

For most of the past two centuries local actors and even regional powers did not have much of a say in the management of security in the Gulf. The United Kingdom played a hegemonic role and turned this body of water into what Avi Shlaim referred to as a 'British lake'.[5] British influence started in 1793 with the opening of an East India Company agency in Basra even if the first of the treaties with the shaikhdoms that culminated in the exclusive agreements of 1892 was actually signed in 1820. The British negotiated directly with the two regional powers, the Ottoman Empire and Imperial Iran and from the 1910s with the Saudis, but their hegemony until the eve of their departure was uncontested.

Even throughout the turmoil of the 1950s and 1960s with the rise of Arab Nationalism and Nasserite propaganda reaching the shores of the Gulf the British succeeded in providing an illusion of security. They could not possibly have prevented a major Soviet push into the area or a well-organized domestic insurgency, but their mere presence was a reassuring factor for the local rulers and ultimately with the Saudi royal family with whom they had clashed in the past. Their departure left a power vacuum, that while more apparent than real led to all the experiments in regional cooperation and collective security that were analysed in the preceding chapters. This culminated in the creation of the GCC.

But what are the realities of power in the Gulf? The situation is best conceptualized as a scalene triangle in which the two regional powers, Iran and Iraq, are the longer sides.[6] The GCC states, in spite of their geoeconomic importance, are the shortest side and they have to appeal to external powers, chiefly the United States, to preserve their military security.[7]

Iran has always been the foremost sub-regional power. Its population of 72 million makes it one of the three largest states in the Middle East and North Africa.[8] It controls the entire Eastern coast of the Gulf and this puts it in a position to control the northern side of the Straits of Hormuz. It has a long military tradition that derives from its history as an independent state. It is one of the few states in the region not to have been the subject of direct colonial control. Furthermore, in case of military hostilities Iran can benefit from considerable strategic depth as most cities are situated in the interior of the country. Iran has harbour facilities both on the Gulf coast and on numerous islands. These ports, though, are vulnerable as the frequent closures of the oil terminal of Bandar al-Abbas during the Iran–Iraq War demonstrated.[9]

The second sub-regional power is Iraq. It has a population of around 28 million. In geographical terms its access to the Gulf, the Shatt al-Arab, is very narrow. This is an extremely vulnerable waterway that was reopened by the British in the aftermath of the Iraq War of 2003. Previously it had been closed for more than 20 years as it needs to be constantly dragged to be kept operational.[10] The major urban centres, communication lines and industrial complexes are very exposed. In sum, there is a lack of strategic depth.

The GCC states represent the third, shortest, side of this triangle. Their small native population and the extreme vulnerability of major oil installations, particularly refineries, put them perpetually at a disadvantage from a military point of view. All the capitals of the five smaller states are coastal cities and the water desalinization plants are also located on the Gulf coast. It is not surprising then that the six member states of the GCC are compelled to call on an external power, the United States, to redress this imbalance. The myth of self-reliance has been abandoned, even at the rhetorical level after the Iraqi invasion of Kuwait and its subsequent liberation. It is now clear not only that GCC rulers consider self-reliance a chimera, but also that any possibility of building a collective security system that excludes the United States is out of the question. This is the major stumbling block in the discussions between GCC members and Iran aimed at establishing a collective security system and confidence-building measures in the Gulf.[11] It is important to focus on these geostrategic realities before we discuss GCC attempts to institutionalize a common security policy in the internal and external fields.

For example, from a military point of view it is not realistic for Kuwait to implement a 'blocking action' of more than 48 hours in case of military confrontation with either Iran or Iraq. Rhetorical statements abound but analysts, and to a greater extent military men, all agree on this cold assessment of reality.[12] While there is a steady improvement in the training and readiness of the armed forces of all six member states, these will never be in a position to withstand hostile actions on the part of their bigger neighbours. Therefore, the choice of GCC states to rely on indefinite American support is a logical one and sometimes in the realm of the standardization of weapons procurement and interoperability greater integration stands in the way of the desire to rely on many suppliers so as to maximize diplomatic cover when a crisis erupts. Overall, arms procurement complements and integrates a strategy of carefully balanced foreign investments aimed at forging interdependence with external powers.[13]

External defense

For some of the reasons outlined above it is not surprising that after more than 20 years of rhetorical yearning for more integrated defense policies the situation is not different from that prevailing in the 1980s. The six GCC states are equipped with weapon systems acquired from America, Brazil, France, Italy, the UK, Russia and France. While military analysts despair at the resulting operational incongruence, it is difficult to blame the six GCC governments for wanting to take out an 'insurance policy' underwritten by as many insurers as possible. The wisdom of such an approach has been demonstrated by the ability of the six GCC states to muster extensive diplomatic support following the Iraqi invasion of Kuwait in 1991 and the prominent role that defense contractors play in shoring up relations between the United States, Europe and the GCC.[14]

In concrete military terms after more than 20 years the GCC can offer the first phase of a joint air defense command and control system aptly named Hizam Al-Taawun (Belt of Cooperation) that became operational in 2001. This system provides secure communications between the national air defense command and control centres of the six states. It is *not* a truly integrated air defense system.[15] I would argue that this is not the case because what many military analysts omit to highlight is that there is an essential problem of trust within the GCC that prevents a serious integrated defense policy from emerging. At any given point in the life of the organization one or more of the smaller states is fearful of the Saudi hegemony that would result from implementing an effectively integrated defense policy.[16] Throughout the 1980s the more hesitant small state was Kuwait; now this role seems to belong to Qatar.

The point is that there are political considerations preventing further GCC defense integration. The policy of relying on a host of disparate arms suppliers and carefully cultivating diplomatic contacts is seen as a much better way to achieve external security than the idea of establishing a vertically integrated, centralized command similar to the North Atlantic Treaty Organization (NATO) or the US–Korean one. There is a recognition that self-sufficiency in external defense matters is simply beyond the grasp of the six member states and that Saudi hegemony would be too high a price to pay for a truly integrated defense policy.

In spite of these structural constraints and the political choices by smaller member states, symbolic attempts at defense cooperation have persisted for more than 20 years. I would argue that the reason behind these is the willingness to show a united front to the international community. The fact that GCC armed forces could be seen as presenting a united front *vis-à-vis* the two regional powers was seen by ruling elites as carrying positive value in international policy circles. The effectiveness of this choice can be seen in the coverage received by the odd joint military manoeuvre conducted by the armed forces of the GCC states. These mainly 'cosmetic' exercises, as Anthony Cordesman puts it, conducted at the battalion level, are hyped up beyond all proportion in the local, regime-controlled press. Their conduct is meant to transmit notions of 'unity', 'steadfastness' and 'independence' while the only serious military manoeuvres conducted by the armed forces of member states are those carried out under American leadership. At the naval level, progress is being achieved by individual GCC members in their capacity to carry out what are important missions in the Gulf such as mine warfare and patrolling.[17] However, the joint manoeuvres either involve individual navies working alongside the British, the Americans, and the French, or they are conducted at a bilateral level.

The symbolism of GCC defense cooperation is best exemplified by the Peninsula Shield joint defense force. Following a series of joint military exercises during the previous three years, the force was established in 1986 after a meeting in Riyadh of the GCC chiefs of staff. It had been based at King Khaled Military City in Hafr Al-Batin in a strategic location in northeast Saudi Arabia about 65 km from the border with Kuwait. Its nominal strength was about 5,000 men but the real war-fighting capabilities consist of a Saudi Army brigade that was deployed in the area long before the force existed. The second brigade with manpower and equipment from other GCC states is reputedly limited and has no real war-fighting capabilities.[18] The only time the Peninsula Shield Force has been deployed so far has been during the successful Iranian Al-Faw peninsula offensive on 3 March 1986 when it was dispatched to Kuwait as a gesture of solidarity.

In the case of the Peninsula Shield Force its symbolic nature had been recognized publicly even by Abdullah Bishara, first Secretary General of the GCC.[19] Even its alleged function as a 'trip-wire' contingent, though, is called into question by its immobility during the Iraqi invasion of Kuwait at a time when Saudi television did not even give news of the event for the first two days. In light of its modest proportion it is noteworthy that its establishment was quite controversial and that it was finally disbanded in 2006 when the national contingents were sent back to their respective states while maintaining an ill-defined central coordinating element. The initial Saudi proposal of splitting it into two nuclei, and deploying it into the south-western as well as the north-eastern borders, was rejected by Oman on the grounds that this would constitute a 'provocation' *vis-à-vis* Iran. This underlines how different GCC members perceive different threats as more or less important. There is no strategic consensus on who the GCC should guard against. Kuwait, Oman and the United Arab Emirates (UAE) insisted on a proviso that when the force enters a member's territory the command structure reverts from Saudi Arabia to that of the host country.[20] This insistence underlines the preoccupation of smaller member states with Saudi meddling in their internal affairs and underlines the symbolic nature of joint military enterprises. The most that can be said about the Peninsula Shield Force is that it existed but that, I would argue, it was constituted simply to fulfil a symbolic role, proved too onerous in the long run and the force was eventually disbanded.

First Secretary General Abdullah Bishara reinforces this point when he argues that Peninsula Shield was created to prove that 'the Gulf was to all intents and purposes one and that the people of the Gulf would consider any threat to one of them to be a threat to all'.[21] This statement is wildly inaccurate but it is not made naively. It is rather meant like countless other declarations and communiqués to convey the idea that the GCC stands united and it should not be associated with its neighbours.[22] The GCC does not constitute a 'pluralistic security community' defined in Deutsch terms but it strives to project that image with a certain success.[23]

In sum, collaboration in the realm of external defense has not moved beyond symbolism but the symbolic impact has been considerable and, given the structural constraints, it has been what the organization has rightly strived for. From this point of view the showpiece joint military manoeuvres, the token Peninsula Shield Force and the countless communiqués have achieved their purpose. In the mainstream media the GCC states are often lumped together when defense matters are being discussed.[24] This despite the fact that military analysts are unanimous in recognizing that what underpins Gulf security is a solid American military presence.

Internal security

GCC countries have collaborated closely in the realm of internal security. This is an area in which the six member states can act largely independently of external actors and they have done so since the inception of the organization. Actually, collaboration predates its founding and it is conducted mostly at the bilateral level in an informal manner. The GCC Secretariat is largely excluded from dealing with internal security matters even if the Security Department of the Political Affairs section, usually chaired by an Omani official, can from time to time play a liaison role.

The main reasons why the GCC Secretariat plays only a minor role in internal security matters are twofold. Firstly, no one in the security apparatuses of the member states wants to expose the technocrats of the Secretariat to the fairly brutal business of intelligence. Secondly, and crucially, the plotter in one country could well be the relative of the ruler of another country.[25] In other words, the six GCC states have failed to create common expectations concerning non-interference in each other's domestic politics. Fellow GCC rulers in Abu Dhabi and Saudi Arabia gave hospitality to Shaikh Khalifa Al-Thani who had been deposed by his son Shaikh Hamad in the summer of 1995. From the UAE Shaikh Khalifa organized a coup to regain the throne at the beginning of 1996. As a reaction Qatar refused to participate in joint military exercises planned for March 1996.[26] These and other disputes are eventually patched up but in general it can be said that when it comes to internal security familiarity breeds suspicion as well as facilitating cooperation. While GCC states can collaborate swiftly when faced with manipulative mobilization by an external actor there is always an underlying sense that old rivalries could re-emerge quickly when an external threat is not looming. This clearly has an impact on what decisions are delegated to the GCC Secretariat. Security and intelligence officials from each individual country certainly do not coordinate their policies through that body.[27]

In fact, some GCC-wide agreements have been formalized throughout the life of the organization and in the last few years rulers seem to be more concerned with Islamist opponents than with palace plotters. Furthermore, even if the GCC as an organization does not have much of a role in combating internal dissent GCC forums and meetings have undeniably helped principal decision-makers informally to coordinate the security policies of the six member states. This is because the threats faced by the ruling families of the six member states are of a similar nature.

An attempted coup in Bahrain in December 1981, a few months after the establishment of the organization, provided the spark for the start of various attempts to formalize GCC internal security cooperation. As mentioned earlier the inaugural meeting had purposefully underscored economic cooperation as the main focus of the incipient organization. However, on 13 December the Bahraini government announced the arrest of 73 alleged saboteurs. The Prime Minister Shaikh Khalifa bin Salman Al-Khalifa placed responsibility squarely on the new Iranian revolutionary regime. He charged Iranian rulers with wanting to exploit the Shi'ah populations in the GCC states to try and foment instability and chaos even if none of the arrested men was in fact of Iranian nationality.[28] This episode, and the fact that the Dubai authorities had provided crucial intelligence leading to the apprehension of the suspects, considerably increased the appetite for multilateral cooperation in internal security.

It was Saudi Arabia that took the lead in attempting to institutionalize hitherto informal cooperation. The Saudis had pushed for such an agreement from 1980, before the formation of the GCC. The five smaller GCC states that had reason to fear Saudi hegemony were confronted with the prospect of successful external manipulative mobilization on the part of Iran and despite earlier misgivings they all agreed, with the exception of Kuwait, to proceed along this path.[29] Within one year Saudi Arabia had signed bilateral security agreements first with Bahrain and then with the UAE, Qatar and Oman. A draft multilateral agreement was ready to be signed at the fourth Supreme Council Conference in Doha in November 1983. The bilateral agreements and the draft multilateral agreement provided for joint intelligence and training, the extradition of suspected activists and, crucially, border cooperation and a right of hot pursuit in the territory of the member states.

Kuwait, however, refused to sign even a bilateral agreement with Saudi Arabia, let alone accede to the multilateral regime envisaged by Prince Nayef, the Saudi Interior Minister. The Kuwaiti parliament did not like the extradition clauses and the right of hot pursuit, feeling that the gap between the relatively liberal national legislation of Kuwait and the stern Saudi one was too wide. The Kuwaiti government went along with this interpretation and it also feared that signing a bilateral or a multilateral internal security agreement would put it in a collision course with the new Iranian regime. It must be noted that at the time the Kuwaiti government was still striving to establish a good relationship with the Iranian revolutionary regime. This in spite of a number of terrorist attacks that had taken place in the city state and for which the Iranian regime had been blamed by the local press and by international commentators alike.[30] It was only the dissolution of the Kuwaiti parliament in 1986 and the modification of the draft agreement submitted by Saudi Arabia to excise the right of hot pursuit that allowed the eventual ratification of a multilateral agreement by the Supreme Council in December 1987. The fact that only the dissolution of the sole democratic body in the six GCC states at the time allowed the signing of a multilateral security agreement illuminates how the attitude towards sub-regional cooperation and the GCC in particular is ambivalent in the five smaller states.

The enthusiasm for 'cooperation' and 'regionalization' at the societal level is matched by a healthy distrust of possible Saudi hegemony. First Secretary General Abdullah Bishara, a Kuwaiti, elucidated this concept clearly and succinctly when he stated,

> I can understand both points of view. On the one hand you want closer cooperation to face internal security threats. On the other hand, heads roll often in Saudi Arabia whereas the carrying out of a death sentence in Kuwait is a very rare event.[31]

This attitude encapsulates well the ambivalence felt by many Kuwaiti citizens. This attachment to a more liberal political discourse is remarkable given that Kuwait has been throughout the years on the target list of several militant organizations.[32] However, the spate of attacks in GCC countries that followed the American intervention in Iraq has induced GCC states, particularly Saudi Arabia and Kuwait, to close ranks again.

The draft internal security agreement which was ratified by the Supreme Council in December 1987 with the exclusion of the right of hot pursuit consists of 39 articles divided into four chapters. In addition to some general principles relating to collaboration among security services the agreement tackles the issues of information exchange, extradition and propaganda aimed against regimes in any of the six member countries. The agreement is riddled with convenient loopholes. For example, it is up to each individual government to decide whether a particular crime is political and therefore excluded from the provisions of the agreement. This said, GCC countries have a good track record in dealing with internal dissent. In particular, information regarding the large number of expatriates, a constant preoccupation of GCC decision-makers, is centrally stored in a Saudi data bank. Most collaboration, though, happens through informal channels and the formal agreement is rarely invoked.

In sum, collaboration in internal security matters is far from being symbolic but, unlike external defense initiatives, member states have not had until recently any interest in publicizing it. Internal security services that collaborated closely were associated with the authoritarian nature of the regimes and did not convey the same benign image in the international sphere that was associated with coordination in external defense matters. This has changed after 11 September 2001 and the spate of related incidents that culminated in the spectacular attacks on Saudi targets in May 2003. It is not a coincidence that in February 2005 Saudi Arabia sponsored a major international conference that focused on combatting terrorism around the world and that massive publicity campaigns have been launched throughout GCC states highlighting the plight of those harmed in terrorist attacks. Increasingly, the efficiency of internal security apparatuses acquired a positive value in the international arena and, like in the area of external defense, GCC member states have started boasting about their increased cooperation and coordination. Like in the case of external security, 'cooperation' and 'integration' now are seen as a positive value in the realm of internal security and intelligence sharing. The difference is that whereas the six GCC states will not be able to attain independence in the military field in the foreseeable future, internal security cooperation against external manipulative mobilization has been a mainstay of the six member states since their inception. The fact that it is not channelled through the GCC is consistent with informal patterns of decision-making and the rules of shaikhly exchange.

Internal and external security policies: an assessment

William Tow in his study of sub-regional security cooperation identifies four criteria against which he deems Subregional Security Organizations, to borrow his term, should be judged. These are a useful starting point in trying to assess how the GCC has fared in the first quarter century of its existence and, crucially, whether it could have done more given the structural constraints outlined above. The tasks that Tow identifies for an organization such as the GCC are as follows:

- Broadening sub-regional economic and development cooperation and policy cooperation on sensitive political and security issues.
- Converting shared ideological and political outlooks into a tangible mutual security approach to neutralize threats from both internal and external sources and to advance their common security interests.
- Balancing national security with region-wide and international security ties.
- Compelling major world powers to accept their collective and security agenda.[33]

It can be broadly said that in relation to security matters the GCC has fared well in around one-and-a-half of these fields. The frequent meetings of interior ministers, foreign ministers and security officials have certainly broadened cooperation on sensitive security issues. The fact that this agenda has not been pushed through the organization itself should not detract from the importance that frequent meetings and mid-level coordination have had in tackling collectively internal security challenges.

This brings us to the second point that Tow outlines. In this respect we can posit that while progress has been made in the internal security realm the results in the field of external security have been lacking. However, I would argue that the much-quoted disagreements between 'lower' and 'upper' Gulf states in identifying the most pressing threats are only part of the picture.[34] A more structural constraint is given by the fact that GCC states know that they cannot achieve self-sufficiency in external defense matters for the foreseeable future. This leads them to utilize arms procurement as a diplomatic tool. This is a choice that is often mischaracterized as being wasteful and counterproductive but which in fact constitutes a sort of 'insurance policy' aimed at securing continued American military support and, more broadly, a diplomatic reward among great and middle powers.

As for the last two points outlined by Tow, GCC states have little chance of making major powers accept their collective security agenda. However, they are fortunate because their national interests broadly coincide with the regional interest of the great power of the day. The United States has concretely showed how it is committed to defend the territorial integrity of the Gulf shaikhdoms by coming to the rescue of Kuwait after it was invaded in 1991. In March 2003 the American intervention in Iraq lessened considerably the menace posed by one of the two sub-regional powers.[35] The chequered history of GCC external defense cooperation must be assessed in light of these structural constraints.

A tentative way forward for the GCC in the field of external security may be constituted by a more unified approach when dealing with the United States. For example, in the wake of the Second Gulf War all six member states have reached bilateral defense agreements with the United States to guarantee prepositioning of military materiel and other measures that would facilitate American intervention. However, the United States itself would have preferred a more comprehensive multilateral pact.[36] An ability to speak with one voice on defense procurement matters would enhance the leverage of the six GCC members without foregoing their traditional utilization of arms procurement as a foreign policy tool.

Conclusion

GCC security collaboration has evolved beyond symbolism in the field of internal security; it has not done so in military matters. At a basic level the risk that GCC regimes would incur in setting up effective standing armies clearly outweighs the benefits that could be gained in military efficiency. The traditional separation between regular army and 'national guard' and other separate units, whose most conspicuous example can be found in Saudi Arabia, is bound to endure. Under these circumstances little could be gained by closer military cooperation.

In the field of internal security there has been effective cooperation predating the founding of the organization. GCC regimes face similar threats. The fact that collaboration in this field has not been channelled through the GCC Secretariat is in line with local bureaucratic culture and should not been seen as impinging on the effectiveness of the organization. Many meetings of security officials have been organized under the auspices of the organization and they clearly yielded results.

More in general, collaboration in the external security sphere and increasingly in the realm of intelligence sharing has played an important role in enhancing the image of the GCC on the world stage. It is at this discursive level that efforts in the realm of security cooperation should be judged. The fact that the GCC will increasingly be seen as speaking with one voice on security matters, whatever the reality on the ground, is in itself positive. Geostrategic constraints allow for very little room for manoeuvre for the six member states. The possibility of establishing a collective security system in the Persian Gulf involving the two sub-regional powers is remote. For now the security of the Persian Gulf depends on the willingness of the United States to intervene militarily and to maintain a large military force in theatre despite local ambivalence to it. The situation is made more dangerous by the possibility of nuclear proliferation. While almost everyone theoretically exposes the desirability of a collective security system the obstacles seem difficult to surmount. The triangular balance of power that has characterized the Gulf in the last decades is structurally determined. The only evolution is constituted by an ever-growing involvement on the part of the United States.

This situation is very clear when we look at the way GCC states reacted to the development of the Iranian nuclear programme, which we will examine in Chapter 7. In the meantime, though, the next chapter looks at how the GCC as an organization fared in the field of diplomatic coordination. Given the security realities outlined above, the stance taken *vis-à-vis* Iran in relation to its nuclear programme is better conceptualized as a diplomatic rather than as a security issue when it comes to the Gulf Arab states. Therefore, a thorough understanding of GCC diplomatic performance in the first 20 years of its history provides a good basis on which to assess the GCC approach to Iran in the twenty-first century.

6

GCC DIPLOMATIC COORDINATION: THE LIMITED ROLE OF INSTITUTIONS

Be polite; write diplomatically; even in a declaration of war one observes the rules of politeness.[1]

Otto von Bismarck

Introduction

In this chapter I propose to analyse GCC diplomatic coordination and performance in the internal and external realms in the first 20 years of its history. After an examination of several episodes in the life of the organization I conclude that institutionalization played a very small role in the life of the GCC.

I will focus on how the Gulf Cooperation Council (GCC) reacted to the cases of the Iran–Iraq War, the Bahrain–Qatar disputes, and the Abu Musa and Tunbs territorial dispute between the United Arab Emirates (UAE) and Iran. I will also dwell upon its dealings with the European Union in their fruitless attempt to reach a free trade agreement (FTA). It will be apparent how the organization did not behave very differently from other international organizations such as the Arab League. In other words, it has proved its worth as a forum for policy coordination but individual states have rarely sacrificed their foreign policy priorities on the altar of reaching a common stance. Sovereignty is still paramount in GCC states even if the close personal ties between the rulers certainly constitute an asset when it comes to policy coordination.

In this chapter I purport to explain these overarching principles by using the method known as 'narrative explanatory protocol'.[2] The aim is to construct an account that is verisimilar and believable to others looking over the same events, not to offer 'if–then' predictions or law-like statements. I will supplement the deductive arguments with inductively derived insights. It is possible that in future the GCC will change its nature and become an organization possessing supranational powers. It is my contention, though, that so far the organization has served as a useful loose forum when it comes to diplomacy. In the words of Erik Peterson, 'the GCC has not by any means replaced the individual foreign policies of the member states but rather has served as the vehicle for the implementation of consensus policies among them'.[3] Even if these words were written almost 20 years ago they remain true to this day. I will try to explain this point by looking at some crucial events in Gulf history since the founding of the organization to understand what role the GCC played. The events have been selected because they represent crucial moments or issues on which a sub-regional organization such as the GCC could have been expected to take a stand.

The Iran–Iraq War was a protracted international conflict involving the two foremost regional powers in the Gulf. It was also instrumental to the creation of the GCC itself since it allowed member states to refuse membership in the organization to Iraq. The dispute over the Abu Musa and Tunbs islands seems like the perfect case in which the GCC could have displayed its joint diplomatic clout since the UAE could have legitimately asked the organization to give the issue prominence through its strength in unity. The case of the disputes between Bahrain and Qatar seem a textbook case for the Commission for the Settlement of Disputes, whose establishment is explicitly called for in the sixth article of the GCC charter. Its rules of procedure are further spelled out in a 13-point document approved by the Supreme Council.[4] Finally, negotiations with the European Union have been so far the only case in which both organizations have engaged on a *multilateral* basis to achieve an FTA. Taken together these case studies give a fair picture of the diplomatic *modus operandi* of the organization.

Diplomacy in the GCC

The approach to disputes and disagreements between member states has always been based on the notion of trying to reach consensus (*ijma*) through informal means. GCC institutions have played only a limited role in facilitating the mending of fences between member states and the adoption of common diplomatic stances. However, I will argue that this is not necessarily a limitation on the part of the organization. It is more an indication of the fact that the GCC is rooted in Gulf political culture and in more general diplomatic principles. Often failure to reach an agreement or forge a common position is a signal of the unwillingness to make a difference in opinion emerge. In the same vein a lack of follow up and limited enforcement are present even within the national administrations of the GCC member states.[5]

In Gulf politics resorting to institutions to come to a binding decision is frowned upon as is recourse to judicial settlement in business circles. Abdullah Bishara referred to the GCC as a 'gentlemen's club' in which clear, if unstated, rules of conduct were to be followed and deference accorded to more powerful players.

For all of its shortcomings, the organization played an important diplomatic role, as we shall see, particularly during the Iran–Iraq War, allowing some of the smaller member states the cover of a common GCC position vis-à-vis one or the other belligerents.[6] This is a similar process to that exemplified by the possibility of Germany taking cover under a common European Union position when it comes to Middle East matters, especially concerning the Israeli-Palestinian conflict.

Furthermore, even in the heat of intense disagreements when meetings were boycotted by one or the other of the heads of state, GCC technical cooperation at the ministerial and administrative level continued unabated. This is an aspect of the GCC that is too often overlooked by critics who focus on the lack of binding agreements between member states. It actually provides a welcome pattern that gives rise to knowledge networks between officials in the six member states and facilitates the solution of day-to-day administrative problems.

Even in the UAE, which as we have seen is not comparable with the GCC given the amount of sovereignty vested in the federal government, individual Emirates take significantly different stances on major international political issues. This has been the case throughout the Iran–Iraq War and certainly with regards to issues of economic integration. Yet these intense and sometime bitter disagreements do not preclude this much more cohesive political unit to operate effectively.

The Iran–Iraq War (1980–88)

Traditional accounts of GCC behaviour throughout the Iran–Iraq War stress the progressive tilting of its diplomatic position towards Iraq as the Iranian military situation improved, particularly in the aftermath of March 1982.[7] Before looking at the behaviour of the GCC as an actor it is essential to sketch out the overall dynamic of the conflict particularly in relations to Iran, Iraq and the superpowers.[8]

The war can be schematically divided into three parts if we take as a guiding principle the balance of power between Iraq and Iran. In a first phase, which we can date from September 1980 to March 1982, Iraq seemed to have the upper hand on the battlefront as judged by territorial control. The new Ronald Reagan administration that had taken over in January 1981 and the GCC states seemed uncertain about how to react. The United States perceived Iraq as a Soviet client and Iran as a radical regime bent on spreading its Islamist ideology throughout the rest of the Middle East. Even the Soviet Union reacted negatively to the Iraqi invasion of Iran recognizing Saddam Hussein's regime as the aggressor and temporarily suspending weapons shipments. This reflected their irritation at not being informed.

The second phase of the war started with the Iranian counteroffensive of March 1982. This was the first of a series of successful Iranian counterattacks that brought the war onto Iraqi territory while Iranian war aims came to include explicitly the overthrowing of the Ba'athist regime in Iraq. The Iranian war changed from a defensive undertaking to an offensive operation aimed at punishing the aggressor. The conflict assumed increasingly ideological overtones. On one side Iran fashioned itself as the leader of revolutionary Islam, on the other side Iraq came to be perceived as a secular bulwark and as the defender of the status quo.

In Washington, DC, the danger of an Iranian victory became more palpable and overcame the reluctance to support in any way an ally of the Soviet Union. Therefore, a cautious rapprochement began between the United States and Iraq. The United States started utilizing loan guarantees to provide Iraq with grain and other raw materials. The Soviet Union, alarmed at the prospect of an Iranian victory, resumed selling military supplies to Iraq.

De facto from the start of the conflict the United States had two overarching aims. It wanted to prevent the decisive victory of one of the sides and it aimed at preventing a spillover of the conflict that would endanger freedom of navigation and the free flow of oil from the Gulf. As we shall see most GCC states shared these goals even if there were significant differences within the organization.

A third phase of the conflict opened in 1986 with the progressive deterioration of the Iraqi military situation. From this point of view the Iranian conquest of the Al-Faw Peninsula in February of that year marks a turning point. Its location at the opening of the Gulf overlooking Kuwait made it an extremely important strategic asset. As discussed in the previous chapter this was the only time the GCC Peninsula Shield force was mobilized. The fall of Basra and the dismemberment of the Iraqi state came to be seen as concrete possibilities. This episode was a catalyst as it nudged the United States closer to Iraq and heralded a renewed commitment on the part of the Soviet Union in support of Iraq.

Since 1984 the United States and Iraq had restored diplomatic relations that had been suspended 14 years earlier. It was during that period that the United States started selling dual-use equipment, such as Bell helicopters, to Iraq as well as acquiescing to French sales of missiles and fighter jets that allowed Iraq to hit Teheran and other important Iranian centres in the so-called 'war of the cities'. The United States always encountered problems in exporting weapons to Iraq because of opposition from Congress to direct arms sales to a country that was seen as a traditional enemy of Israel.

Starting in 1986 the United States assumed a more direct role in an escalating conflict. From the fall of the Al-Faw Peninsula the United States started to share tactical intelligence with the Iraqi armed forces. The value of this intelligence has been hotly argued since that time.[9] It must be remembered, though, that even low-grade battlefield information can prove very valuable to a country that does not have access to satellite reconnaissance.

The Iranians, frustrated by the Soviet and Western support to Iraq, started to attack neutral shipping in the Gulf, in particular the oil tankers that were departing from Kuwait. After a series of Kuwaiti diplomatic moves and counter-moves in December 1986 the United States offered to protect Kuwaiti ships by reflagging them with an American flag. This decision was taken as a reaction to a Soviet offer to do the same thing.[10] The prevention of a Soviet role in the Gulf had been a long-standing foreign policy aim of the United States. This spurred the Americans to take upon themselves, with the help of some Western allies, the burden of ensuring free navigation in the Gulf. It was, however, a risky undertaking and on 17 May 1987 two Iraqi Exocet missiles hit by mistake the frigate USS *Stark*.

From that moment on the pressure on Iran to accept an armistice became very intense. Since 1982 Iran had always insisted on the overthrowing of the Iraqi regime. This was insisted upon as a precondition for the return to the borders pre-existing the Iraqi invasion that was called upon by numerous United Nations instruments. This was of course a precondition that was not contemplated by the plan that the United States was trying to force on the two parties. Therefore, the United States Navy started to attack Iranian oil platforms, such as the Sirri platform, and organized an international embargo on the sale of any kind of weapon system to Iran.

The downing of Iran Air Flight 655 on 3 July 1988, which killed 290 innocent passengers and crew, and a new series of Iraqi offensives finally gave Ayatollah Khomeini the opportunity to accept United Nations Resolution 598 and to sue for peace on 18 July 1988, a decision that, a few days later, he described as 'more deadly than drinking poison'.[11] The Iranian military effort had started to falter from within putting the regime in danger. The attack by the USS *Vincennes*, which has been proved to have happened as a consequence of overtly aggressive behaviour on the part of the cruiser, gave Ayatollah Khomeini a good way out from what was becoming an unsustainable situation militarily, economically and politically.[12]

The war cost between US$150 billion and US$300 billion to the two regional powers according to different estimates. The number of casualties varies considerably according to the sources as it is subject to some political manipulation. It can be stated with some certainty that there were at least 350,000 Iranian casualties and around 150,000 Iraqis died in the war.[13]

The GCC and the Iran–Iraq War

The attitude of the GCC states oscillated throughout the war according to the events happening in the battlefield and mirrored to some extent that of the United States. The GCC served as a useful forum from its inception to give cover to the smaller Gulf monarchies and to allow a certain extent of parallel diplomacy in order to let member states embark on individual diplomatic demarches under the cover of a certain common position. In particular, throughout the course of the war the support for Iraq on the part of Kuwait and Saudi Arabia was at certain times overt whereas Dubai and Oman can be said to have been leaning more towards Iran in trying to find a negotiated settlement. The GCC as an organization, as we will see, served as a useful cover for these different bilateral positions. As Gerd Nonneman points out, the same technique to send different messages to different audiences can be noticed in the domestic realm by scrutinizing the differences between governmental policy and the permitted expression of alternative views in the media throughout the war.[14] These were two sophisticated methods of sending messages to both belligerents without breaking diplomatic cover.

Overall it can be said that their diplomatic attitude reflected that of the United States as the Six became increasingly worried about the possibility of an Iranian victory. As we shall see, though, it is impossible to talk of a single diplomatic stand as each GCC state pursued an independent foreign policy *vis-à-vis* the conflict.

The first phase of the conflict

In the first phase of the war, when it was hoped that the Iraqi blitz would succeed, GCC states were on the whole cautiously supportive of Iraq. However, there was no consensus on the degree of support to lend to Saddam Hussein as everyone waited to gauge what would be the results on the battlefield. As a stalemate set in after the first month of the conflict the position became more articulated on the part of the future six members of the GCC. The main diplomatic aims became to end the war soon and to prevent an Iranian victory at all costs.

Two broad fronts came into being, the Emirates of Dubai, Sharjah and Umm Al-Qaiwan, and even more significantly the Sultanate of Oman maintained a neutral diplomatic stance between the belligerents, not wanting to damage relations with Iran. The motives were mixed: in the case of Dubai the significant trade relations with Iran highlighted in a previous chapter played an important part alongside the presence of a sizable population of Iranian origin. For the two other Arab emirates the determining factor was the joint management of the Mubarak oil field of Abu Musa island, of which more later. Finally, with regards to Oman, Nonneman highlights the fact that Sultan Qaboos always had more leeway than other Arab leaders to pursue a pragmatic foreign policy because of the relative insulation of Oman from Arab nationalist currents. Furthermore, the geopolitical significance of the Strait of Hormuz imposed extra caution when dealing with Iran, both under the Shah and with the new regime of the Islamic republic.[15]

On the contrary, Kuwait and Saudi Arabia sided more decisively with Iraq at the beginning of the war. The hope was for a successful *blitzkrieg* that would reverse what were seen as the more pernicious provisions of the 1975 Algiers treaty. Nonneman goes as far as to argue that at least Saudi Arabia was informed in advance of Iraq's plan to invade Iran.[16] Be that as it may, Kuwait and Saudi Arabia certainly displayed full-blown support for Iraq in the first few months of the war spurred undoubtedly by the increasingly radical rhetoric of the new leaders of the Islamic Republic.

This lack of unanimity, even within the UAE, let alone the newly formed GCC, is reflected in the first declaration of the first regular session of the Supreme Council that met in Abu Dhabi on 26 May 1981. The Iran–Iraq War is mentioned only in the second-to-last paragraph and the drafters studiously avoid taking sides limiting themselves to expressing a vague desire for the cessation of hostilities and including no call for withdrawal to international borders, a definitely pro-Iraqi stance by international standards.

> Their majesties and highnesses backed the efforts spent on putting an end to the Iran–Iraq war, as it is considered a problem which threatens the security of the area and increases the likelihood of foreign intervention in it, and they affirmed the necessity of doubling efforts to find a final solution to the conflict.[17]

This follows a discussion of organizational matters, the appointment of the first Secretary General of the organization, and a mention of the need for further economic integration. Even more tellingly, it is preceded by a denunciation of Israeli actions against the Palestinians and a declaration of support for Syria. The haziness of this stance vis-à-vis a major regional conflict breaking out on their doorstep sets the tone for the diplomatic activity of the GCC throughout its history. The traditional caution of most Gulf Arab monarchies is compounded by the difficulty in reaching a consensus on most diplomatic issues.

The second phase of the conflict

During the second phase of the conflict the six generally displayed heightened support for Iraq, but the differences in their diplomatic stances did not disappear and this made it difficult to achieve a common GCC position. Nonneman puts a positive interpretation on this lack of coherence by underlining how the GCC served as a forum that allowed the six to follow consciously diverging policies reconciling conflicting interests and aimed at different constituencies, both domestic and international. Indeed, we will see how the lack of the GCC to serve as a forum to mediate disputes amongst its member states was more worrying from the point of view of the institution. In particular, Nonneman underlines how the collective vehicle of the GCC allowed the two more pro-Iraqi actors, Kuwait and Saudi Arabia, to retain a possible line of communication with Iran.[18] This assessment is certainly borne out by an analysis of the diplomatic demarches of the different GCC members throughout this phase of the conflict.

In May 1982 the Ministerial Council drew together the foreign ministers of the six gathered in Riyadh. Their communiqué called on Iran to be more forthcoming to peace initiatives and mentioned the Islamic Conference Organization (ICO) as a possible organization under whose aegis the two parties could meet to resolve their differences. The choice of the ICO as the recommended venue to reach a ceasefire was a curious one. The ICO has never served as a venue for peacemaking throughout its history, even if it hosted several important diplomatic encounters on the sidelines of its meetings. However, it is interesting that it was felt that an *Islamic* venue would be preferable to the United Nations as it would cut out the two superpowers from exerting an overbearing influence. To this very day the ICO still plays a significant role in world politics, but it would be interesting to see its emergence as a significant diplomatic actor in the twenty-first century.

The GCC foreign ministers were correct in feeling that this was a crucial moment. Iran had gone on the offensive and Saddam Hussein had agreed to withdraw to the international border. If the occasion were lost the war was bound to continue for a very long time. Saudi Arabia and Kuwait started buttressing Iraq financially to the tune of US$26 billion each. As Iraq tried to internationalize the conflict by attacking Iranian oil installations, Saudi Arabia and Kuwait finally succeeded in producing a GCC initiative explicitly criticizing Iran: the organization sponsored a United Nations resolution condemning Iranian attacks on international shipping.[19] Kuwait and Saudi Arabia had finally succeeded in convincing the more reluctant member states to adopt bolder language. In May 1984, amidst fiery Iranian rhetoric directed at the six and the first attacks on neutral, mostly Saudi and Kuwaiti, ships, the organization sponsored a United Nations resolution condemning Iranian attacks on international shipping.[20] These attacks proved to be the tipping point even for traditionally Iranian-leaning member states such as Oman.

The downing of an Iranian F-4 Phantom fighter jet over Saudi territorial waters by the Saudi Air Force escalated the tension with all the Gulf states. There was the concrete possibility that the war could not be contained and the conflict would spread. Saudi Arabia appealed directly to both the ICO and the non-aligned movement at the United Nations to help bring an end to the war. These diplomatic demarches culminated in a May 1985 visit to Teheran by Prince Saud al-Faisal which was reciprocated by Foreign Minister Ali-Akbar Velayati at the end of the year. These initiatives did not signal the end of Saudi support for Iraq but underscored the fear of escalation felt by the six. Furthermore, a number of sources point to Iran–Saudi negotiations throughout this period and the facilitation of American weapon sales to Iran as well as the start of the supply of refined oil products.[21] Nonneman calculates that by the beginning of 1986 Gulf aid to Iraq amounted to about US$40 billion. Of this sum all but US$3–5 billion came from Saudi Arabia and Kuwait.[22]

On the contrary, GCC communiqués throughout this period are studiously even-handed even if they constantly refer to the need by all parties to accept the two relevant United Nations resolutions, which Iran always refused to do. This symbolizes a certain support for Iraq as Security Council resolutions were certainly biased against Iran throughout this period. They never recognized clearly that the onus for the start of the conflict should be placed on Iraq and they never called for a return to the international border until the Iraqi war effort had been blunted.[23]

The four southern members of the GCC had by now recognized that neutrality was their best option but they allowed themselves to adopt a shared pro-Iraqi tilt when acting under GCC cover. This enabled them to be good, collegiate GCC members while not antagonizing Iran bilaterally. Looking at the communiqués it is also worth noting how denunciation of the Zionist regime and appeals to Muslim solidarity through the Islamic Conference are more prominent and more starkly conveyed when compared with references to the Iran–Iraq War.[24] The impression is that the matter is too sensitive and too close to home to actually take a definitive stance. In contrast, declarations denouncing the occupation of Palestine and proclaiming the need for Islamic unity *vis-à-vis* the Zionist threat could be dispensed more liberally as they did not risk exposing the fault lines running through the foreign policies of the six. In fact, they acted as solidarity promoters.[25]

The third phase of the conflict

A third phase of the conflict in relation to the GCC states can be said to have started in February 1986 with the capture of the Al-Faw Peninsula by Iranian forces. This event sent shivers down the spine of GCC rulers, as well as American decision-makers, and increased the direct and indirect support of Saudi Arabia and Kuwait for Iraq while making the position of the 'neutral' GCC states more difficult.

From a military point of view the fall of the peninsula did in fact represent a prominent setback for Iraqi forces and posed a direct threat to Kuwait bay. Iraq decided to escalate the tanker war by attacking Iran's oil terminals in the southern Gulf so as to make international intervention to end the war more likely. The dissolution of the National Assembly in Kuwait in 1986 made the start of the reflagging operation easier to achieve for the government of Kuwait as this had previously been blocked by the resistance of nationalist deputies. The operation duly began in on 21 July 1987, the day after the passage of United Nations Security Council Resolution 598, which eventually formed the basis to end the war. Only ten days later hundreds of pilgrims died in Mecca following violent demonstrations by Iranian pilgrims.[26]

The tone of the Supreme Council communiqués as well as the foreign ministers' meeting changed remarkably. The Iran–Iraq War still did not feature prominently, but the tone became increasingly stern *vis-à-vis* Iran. In March 1986 GCC foreign ministers condemned Iran collectively, something that had never taken place before.[27] Even more strikingly, the Supreme Council in its 29 December 1987 declaration noted

> with great regret Iran's procrastination regarding accepting the resolution [United Nations Security Council Resolution 598] and urged the international community led by the Security Council, to shoulder its responsibility to adopt the necessary steps to implement Resolution 598 as soon as possible.

It further expressed its hope that

> Iran will take an attitude responding to the will of the international community and to answer the appeal of the Islamic nation by ending the war, establishing peace, halting the bloodshed of Muslims, and conserving its energies in order to confront the enemies of the Islamic nation.[28]

These were harsh words when compared with previous statements by the Supreme Council and they point squarely to Iran being the party responsible for dragging on the war.

The events at Mecca did indeed play a significant role in stiffening Saudi attitudes and resulted in a collective denunciation couched in very harsh terms. This was coupled with grievances over other hostile acts. At the same meeting the Council discussed the events in Holy Mecca and the sedition which the Iranians aroused at the House of God; what the State of Kuwait has encountered – shelling by missiles and Iranian aggressions against Kuwait's security and stability; the Iranian aggressions against the embassies of the State of Kuwait and the Kingdom of Saudi Arabia in Teheran; the striking at oil tankers and commercial ships sailing to and from the ports of the GCC member states in Gulf waters; and what such aggressions represent in terms of violating international law and the UN Charter.[29]

Finally, the Council called on Iran to 'adhere to the principles of mutual respect in a manner that guarantees the reestablishment of security and stability in the region'.

It must be reiterated that these stern calls come in the context of a six-page-long communiqué that tackles many issues in the region as well as the internal workings of the Council. However, these are expressions of unprecedented harshness *vis-à-vis* Iran.

The atmosphere had indeed changed, though, and while Iran tried to divide the six by singling out Saudi Arabia and Kuwait as propaganda targets, the GCC functioned as an umbrella to express a more severe condemnation of Iranian actions. From this point of view the GCC served a useful purpose during this last phase of the war.

The last year of the war, marked by further escalation of the conflict, still saw the GCC as a useful forum through which to convey collective messages, while single member states pursued individual initiatives. In June 1988 a communiqué of a foreign ministers' meeting reiterated a call for Iran to accept United Nations Security Council Resolution 598 while actually *congratulating* Iraq for its military victories, chiefly the recapture of the Al-Faw Peninsula that had been completed on 18 April. During the same period Saudi Arabia broke off diplomatic relations with Iran over Teheran's refusal to accept a quota of 45,000 pilgrims for the Hajj. Other member states, though, still maintained relations with Iran. For example, Qatar, Oman and the UAE received envoys during the same month who were presenting evidence of Iraq's use of chemical weapons.[30]

Finally, after Iranian acceptance of United Nations Security Council Resolution 598 on 18 July 1988 the GCC, in a sudden role reversal, played a useful role in convincing Iraq to accept a ceasefire on 6 August. The consensus among the six was that there was no reason for Baghdad to refuse prompt acceptance of a ceasefire. Led by Saudi Arabia, the GCC put pressure on Iraq finally to bring the war to an end.

It is also important to remember that throughout the war the GCC was conducting diplomatic *démarches* towards the warring parties and throughout the Arab world mostly through the person of its Secretary General, Abdullah Bishara. These, of course, had to respect a consensus between the six and therefore they were not always incisive; however, they proved rather useful in presenting a common front at events such as Arab League summits. They increased in number and deepened in substance during the last phases of the conflict.

In sum, we can say that the GCC proved a useful forum for the six member states throughout the Iran–Iraq War. In addition to providing collective cover for some irksome diplomatic stances it proved to be a useful organization to advance common diplomatic positions in multilateral fora such as the United

Nations, the League of Arab States or ICO. However, the institution never developed a supranational role in foreign policy matters. The Secretary General acted as an emissary, but there was not even an attempt to forge a common foreign let alone a security policy.

Abu Musa and the Greater and Lesser Tunb

In relation to this dispute the GCC as a body did not behave differently from the League of Arab States. In other words, it was a forum in which to air grievances and express common positions, but it did not have an independent role as an institution.

In his exhaustive study of the issue, Thomas Mattair, who embraces and exposes the Emirati position, concludes that 'the consistent message has been that Iran can only improve its relations with the Arabs if it resolves this dispute'.[31] This, as we shall see, is probably an overstatement. However, it is worth analysing the evolution of the dispute to ascertain whether GCC support for the UAE ever translated into a reorientation of the foreign and security policies of single member states.

Actually, since its inception, the GCC communiqués and actions with regards to Abu Musa and the two Tunbs closely reflect the conduct of the Arab League throughout the 1970s with regards to the same dispute. In other words, statement succeeded statement and expression of brotherly solidarity followed expression of brotherly solidarity, but the dispute did not affect the dynamics of relations with Iran for any single state. Geopolitical and geoeconomic factors as well as events in the global political context were still driving the foreign policies of individual GCC states *vis-à-vis* Iran. For example, we have seen how during the Iran–Iraq War the dispute did not prevent individual GCC states from acting as mediators between the belligerents when they deemed it in their interest to do so. Likewise, after the Lebanon War of July 2006 the dispute over the islands had no discernible effect on the propensity of Saudi Arabia and Iran to deal with each other regarding their common interests in the regional arena. Friction has always been determined by diverging interests on issues considered much more relevant, such as the situation in Iraq after the regime change in 2003 or the balance of power within Lebanon.

The impression is that the intermittent surfacing of the dispute over Abu Musa and the two Tunbs is much more the symptom of troubled relations on other issue areas than an actual cause of friction. It could be said that it is something that GCC states, with the notable exception of Ra's al Khaimah, bring up when they want to raise the temperature of relations with Iran. For example, it is worth noting at the outset how the Emirate of Sharjah, which claims territorial sovereignty over Abu Musa, continued to share revenue from the jointly owned Mubarak oil field with Iran throughout the Iran–Iraq War and beyond.[32] The symbolic importance of the issue is usually outweighed by more pragmatic factors.

In fact, the reactions of Arab League members, such as Iraq and South Yemen, throughout the 1970s to the Iranian occupation of the islands can be said to be more bellicose in tone than anything that has been ever uttered by the GCC. The organization, in this as in other matters, with the notable exception of Palestine, has always tried to maintain a moderate tone.

In May 1983, after the first wave of Iranian military successes, the UAE and Kuwait were given a mandate by other GCC members to try and mediate on behalf of all six states. The attempt came to naught, but it is worth noting how the dispute over the islands did not prevent the UAE from trying to act as an intermediary. Furthermore, this episode shows how from early on the GCC would delegate the handling of difficult disputes to the diplomatic offices of single member states or individuals. The organization has never taken upon itself the task of tackling a really difficult dispute involving either member states or regional powers. It just provided collective diplomatic cover for the more meaningful bilateral diplomatic initiatives of its member states. The war actually led to the further militarization of the three islands, particularly the Greater Tunb. They served as bases for regular Iranian armed forces and for the naval branch of the Iranian Revolutionary Guard Corps.[33] Particularly during the last two years of the war an increasing number of attacks were launched from there against shipping in the Gulf. This underscored their importance from a military point of view and not only as symbols of sovereignty. In spite of these strategic considerations the GCC states, let alone the organization itself, did not make their relations with Iran dependent on the issue of the islands.

As Mattair concludes, 'while maintaining sovereignty over the islands throughout the war, the UAE and its GCC partners were mostly preoccupied with the larger issues of the war'.[34] The issue of the islands kept being muzzled around the time of Operation Desert Storm and in the aftermath of the liberation of Kuwait in the early 1990s. Likewise the issue did not surface in Arab League deliberations. As President Rafsanjani signalled his intentions to establish a new more pragmatic relationship with GCC states the issue did not feature explicitly in the final communiqués of the Supreme Council. Saudi Arabia and Iran re-established diplomatic relations in March 1991 and the issue certainly did not constitute an obstacle to this climate of renewed collaboration. The closing statement of the Twelfth Supreme Council meeting in December 1991 in Kuwait did not mention the issue while expressing 'its satisfaction about the positive and concrete development of relations' with Iran and expressing 'its desire to push forward bilateral relations'.[35]

The issue started to surface in GCC collective statements only after Iran violated the Memorandum of Understanding with Sharjah in 1992. On that occasion it started to require visas for the Egyptian teachers sent there to teach at the local school in the southern part of the island. There has been speculation in diplomatic circles that this move was decreed by the Supreme Leader and enacted by the Iranian Revolutionary Guard Corps to sabotage the new conciliatory line of President Rafsanjani.

Irrespective of the motives behind the decision it sparked a long series of GCC diplomatic protests that lasted throughout the 1990s and into the twenty-first century. It is worth noting that these protests did not affect the bilateral relations of single GCC states with Iran and after the initial reaction to the Iranian breach of the Memorandum of Understanding on Abu Musa they became almost ritualized, appearing as footnotes in various GCC communiqués.

However, with the benefit of hindsight we can conclude that the breaching of the Memorandum of Understanding on the part of Iran proved to be a strategic mistake. What was a sleeping territorial dispute was revived and it became a convenient political issue to be raised by any GCC state when it felt it needed a good pretext to raise the temperature in its relations with Iran. Furthermore, it hindered what should be an almost physiological dialogue with its Arab neighbours, particularly the UAE, so much so that the first visit ever by an Iranian Head of State to the Emirates took place only in May 2007 after a tacit agreement was reached to the effect that the issue of the three islands would not be discussed.

In the aftermath of the restoration of diplomatic relations between Saudi Arabia and Iran in March 1991 the communiqué following the Twelfth Summit of the Supreme Council does not even mention the issue of the islands and expresses 'its satisfaction about the positive and concrete developments of relations' with Iran.[36] This followed a series of conciliatory diplomatic steps *vis-à-vis* Iran before and after Operation Desert Storm aimed at freeing Kuwait from Iraqi occupation. From the Iranian point of view the pragmatic line of President Rafsanjani seemed to be bearing fruit and ushering in a new era in the regional relations of the Islamic Republic. However, in August 1992 Iran denied access to some Egyptian and Palestinian teachers who were returning to Abu Musa to start teaching in the new academic year. This was followed by a request that all Arab citizens be issued Iranian visas in order to travel to the island. This request was unprecedented and constituted a clear breach of the 1971 Memorandum of Understanding between the leaders of Sharjah and Iran.[37] This was followed by an intensification of building activity in the northern part of the island, which was administered by Iran.

The breach of the Memorandum of Understanding immediately drew protests from many quarters, including from GCC Assistant Secretary General Saif Al-Maskari, who was among the first to protest on 1 September 1992, declaring his surprise at the Iranian actions and warning that they would have 'extremely negative' repercussions on GCC–Iran relations.[38] It is true that since 1992, with two exceptions that will be discussed below, the final communiqués of the Supreme Council always drew attention to the islands dispute. Furthermore, the UAE has become bolder in the last decade reminding the outside world that the 1971 Memorandum of Understanding did not imply a recognition of Iranian sovereignty even on the northern half of Abu Musa and that the UAE still claims sovereignty over all three islands and that it is ready to bring the case to the International Court of Justice (ICJ) at The Hague. However, what is interesting from a GCC point of view is how the three serious attempts to resolve the dispute since 1992 have not been led by the GCC as an institution or even by its Secretary General. The UAE and Iran conducted negotiations twice on a bilateral basis and, more significantly, the single mediation attempt was conducted by a tripartite commission of GCC member states with the endorsement of the organization, but without resorting to its offices. This model is very similar to that utilized by the European Union in its dealings with Iran at the beginning of the twenty-first century. It certainly provides an added flexibility that is precious in fast-changing negotiations.

The first bilateral attempt was conducted in 1992 immediately after the breaching of the Memorandum of Understanding by Iran when it was thought that the dispute could perhaps be solved expeditiously. This first attempt failed as Iran made it clear that it did not intend to revert to the *status quo ante*. Significantly even this bilateral attempt was broached by Syria, a third party, which enjoyed close relations with Iran, endorsed UAE rights, and had an interest in Gulf stability.[39] This reinforces the long-standing pattern of resorting to third parties to mediate disputes in the Gulf, rather than multilateral organizations such as the Arab League and the GCC that are instead utilized as diplomatic fora. There seems to be a need to resort to leaders with their own power base when broaching serious and delicate matters.

In the intervening three years the GCC resumed its usual role of a collective forum that allowed smaller states such as Bahrain and Qatar to support the UAE position without endangering their crucial relations with Iran. Then in September 1995 a second set of bilateral negotiations was jumpstarted to try and reach an understanding between Iran and the UAE. Even in this case the talks were broached by a third party, in this case a GCC leader acting individually. The Foreign Minister of Qatar, Shaikh Hamad bin Jassim bin Jabir Al-Thani, hosted a round of talks in Doha in the November. Even in this case third-party mediation was resorted to following time-honoured Gulf diplomatic practice.[40]

The talks failed when Iran refused to accept the UAE agenda for the talks. This by then had considerably broadened to include the possibility of a referral to the ICJ on the issue of the sovereignty of all three islands. This demarche, which made the dispute escalate beyond the level of a return to the *status quo ante*, made a possible resolution more difficult to achieve and was perhaps spurred by the solidarity that the UAE had encountered both within the GCC and at the League of Arab States. The idea of a referral to the ICJ was first broached by the new Secretary General of the GCC, Shaikh Fahim bin Sultan Al-Qasimi, a UAE national from the ruling family of Ra's al Khaimah, in December 1993 and was then incorporated in the final communiqué of the GCC Supreme Council Fifteenth Summit at Manama in Bahrain in December 1994. However, collective support in a GCC setting should not be confused with the willingness of other GCC states, particularly Saudi Arabia, to spend valuable political capital when its national interest is at stake. A decade later we can conclude that the idea of broadening the subject-matter of the talks to include sovereignty did not serve well the UAE national interest. Saudi Arabia and the other GCC members have usually put their bilateral interests before GCC solidarity when dealing with the islands issue.

A further proof of the preference accorded in the Gulf to mediation by third parties is the attempt made to settle the dispute in 2000. Saudi Arabia had been chafing at the need to include ritual statements condemning Iran in final GCC communiqués. President Khatami of Iran had visited Saudi Arabia in mid-May 1999 and Saudi Arabia clearly saw this as an opportunity to get relations with Iran back to an even kneel. Therefore, at a Ministerial Council meeting in June 1999 in Riyadh Saudi Arabia insisted that the ritual condemnations in GCC statements be toned down. The reaction of UAE officials was furious and they let it be known that the UAE was actually ready to forego membership of the GCC over the matter.[41] This reaction in itself is telling of the actual conception that some individual member states have of the GCC as an organization. The GCC is conceived of as a forum that can be abandoned or at least boycotted in case of diplomatic strife. It is very different from an organization such as the North Atlantic Treaty Organization (NATO) or the European Union whose membership is never in doubt and where boycotts of meetings are reserved for the most dramatic circumstances.

In any case, the GCC Secretary General, by then Shaikh Jamil Ibrahim Al-Hujailan, started touring the capitals of GCC members to end the public row.

The solution found was the creation of a tripartite committee composed of Saudi Arabia, Qatar and Oman that was supposed to report by May 2000 on a mechanism to resolve the dispute. The communiqué issued by the Supreme Council meeting in late November 1999 in Riyadh was unusually conciliatory *vis-à-vis* Iran as the deliberations of the tripartite committee were awaited. The committee failed in its task and nowadays the UAE seems to be insistent in its determination to make the issue of the islands a central one in GCC–Iran relations. In the years since 2000, though, it has emerged clearly that the other GCC governments are not willing to make their bilateral relations with Iran hostage to this issue. In particular, the symbolic importance of the three islands seem to take a back seat *vis-à-vis* the tensions emanating from the escalation regarding the Iranian nuclear programme.

From the point of view of the workings of the GCC, one theme emerged clearly: GCC rulers, in the case of a dispute with a preeminent regional power such as Iran, preferred mediation, conducted through the usual rules of 'shaikhly exchange', to reliance on the GCC as a multilateral organization in order to try and solve the dispute.[42] For a number of reasons, including the nature of the domestic regimes of member countries, the GCC is not seen by its members as an institution that can be entrusted to act autonomously on the regional stage. GCC functionaries are always seen as subordinates to be entrusted with specific tasks and not as counterparts. From this point of view the GCC Secretariat is not perceived to be an independent actor by the leaders of the member states and indeed does not act as one.

The Bahrain–Qatar disputes

It is useful now to review an intra-GCC dispute to see how the organization fared in mediating disputes among its member states. As we have seen previously, the GCC charter provides for a 'Commission for the Settlement of Disputes' that is supposed to adjudicate in precisely this type of situation.

However, the commission was never activated and intra-GCC disputes have been settled outside the GCC institutional framework.

It should be noted, first, that traditionally in the Arabian peninsula sovereignty was exercised over peoples and not over territory. This led to a host of disputes when territorial borders became suddenly very important in the granting of oil concessions. Furthermore, GCC states are particularly jealous of their sovereignty and sometimes even disputes that are not endowed with a financial component spiral out of control. The process of settling border disputes continues apace but some are still left unresolved.[43]

The dispute between Qatar and Bahrain is a longstanding one and involves a number of islands lying between them and, crucially, for the purposes of oil exploitation, the exact line of the maritime boundary.[44] Actually, it was the need to proceed with oil exploration that prompted the British to intervene in the 1930s. The dispute became the object of mediation efforts and finally of a British adjudication in 1939 that satisfied neither party and left tensions simmering.

In a nutshell, while involving a large number of smaller islands and shoals, the dispute was twofold: the Bahraini ruling family claimed a piece of land on the northern coast of the peninsula of Qatar basing its claim on the fact that the area had been the ancestral home of the Khalifa family before its conquest of Bahrain in 1783. Qatar countered that the Bahraini Hawar islands were extremely close to its peninsula.[45]

While the British were therefore enforcing their adjudication while continuously carrying out mediation efforts the dispute remained dormant, but soon after independence in 1971 it started causing enough dissension that the Saudi government took up the mediating role that the British had relinquished. In particular, King Khalid bin Abdul Aziz Al-Saud started undertaking the role of mediator between the two states in 1976.[46]

Five principles were established on which negotiations to reach a comprehensive settlement were to be based; these were later amended in 1983.[47] The preference for a mediated agreement was clearly expressed but importantly one of the principles stated that if this failed the entire gamut of disputes would be submitted to arbitration. The mediation efforts continued after the establishment of the GCC but they were conducted under 'the continuing patronage of Saudi Arabia'.[48] The pivotal role of Saudi Arabia was never in doubt. The GCC did not constitute much more than a venue for the tripartite meetings of Bahrain, Qatar and Saudi Arabia.

The subsequent mediation efforts on the part of the GCC have to be seen as a continuation of this Saudi attempt. They did not emanate from GCC institutions themselves and did not imply an autonomous initiative by the

GCC Secretary General. In other words, the GCC put a 'cover' over what was essentially a Saudi effort. And even this would be a generous interpretation since the other GCC leaders were not consulted on the subsequent mediation efforts undertaken by Saudi Arabia.

The dispute flared up again in March and April 1986 during a particularly delicate period of the Iran–Iraq War. In April 1986 after Bahrain named a navy vessel 'Hawar' and announced military exercises, Qatar on 26 April attacked construction crews sent to build a coastguard station on the reclaimed coral reef of Fasht Al-Dibal located between Bahrain and the Qatari mainland and arrested 29 workers. It then proceeded to declare an 'exclusion zone' around the disputed area.

Despite this escalation the situation returned to the *status quo ante* within a month. Both parties agreed to freeze the situation to avoid an escalation at a delicate time of the Iran–Iraq conflict. Saudi Arabia took the lead as King Fahd dispatched his defense minister to the two capitals and tasked GCC Secretary General Abdullah Bishara to mediate the dispute. It is perhaps noteworthy that the GCC Secretary General was chosen to mediate the dispute, but it must be clearly stated that he did so on behalf of King Fahd of Saudi Arabia. He was not acting in an independent role as GCC Secretary General when he negotiated a settlement. In his own words, 'My power emanated from King Fahd, because I went on his behalf and I had to report to him. I only implemented his instructions'.[49] Saudi Arabia took the lead in imposing an interim solution on its two restive neighbours.

In fact, it was at a meeting of the Tripartite Committee during the 1987 Supreme Council GCC meeting in Riyadh that the dispute was put on course to be eventually resolved. On that occasion both Qatar and Bahrain agreed to submit the dispute to the ICJ at The Hague for a final ruling binding upon both parties in case mediation efforts failed. This followed the dispatch of letters by King Fahd of Saudi Arabia to the Emirs of Bahrain and Qatar setting up a specific roadmap for a solution of the dispute. A Tripartite Committee was formed that met six times between January and December 1988 to prepare for a joint submission to the ICJ.[50]

As the two parties could not agree on the scope of the dispute, in spite of Saudi prodding, the issue was taken up again at the following GCC Summit Meeting in December 1988 where the two parties renewed the mandate of the Tripartite Commission and the role of Saudi Arabia as the sole mediator.

At the GCC Supreme Council meeting of December 1990 in Doha the issue was taken up again on a tripartite basis, without the involvement of the other GCC members who were understandably subsumed by Iraq's invasion of Kuwait, which had wiped out the territorial sovereignty of a member state. It was here that the basis was laid for Qatar's unilateral submission of the Case to the ICJ in 1991.

The dispute was ultimately resolved by the ICJ with a final judgment issued in March 2001 that was slightly more favourable to Bahrain, particularly in terms of the maritime boundary, than the British adjudication of 1939. The case in the ICJ was interesting as it involved the alleged forgery of several documents and the intervention of Dr John Wilkinson, Tutorial Fellow at St Hugh's College, Oxford, who was called upon to judge the veracity of the suspected documents.

Apart from the legal case the settlement of the dispute was certainly helped by the coming to power in both states of a new generation of rulers. The political willingness to settle the dispute undoubtedly abetted a fast resolution of the legal process, proving once again the primacy of political considerations when dealing with border disputes in the region.

It is also interesting to note that Bahrain and Qatar, after their disputes had been satisfactorily settled, tried to build a causeway linking their states. Saudi Arabia, the erstwhile mediator, tried to prevent them from doing so because of concerns over the fact that the bridge would pass over its territorial waters.

The event, a major border skirmish between two member states, was not even mentioned in the communiqués of the Supreme Council as business went on as usual even if it was discussed by the Tripartite Commission on the sidelines of these very meetings. The crucial decision to submit the dispute to the mandatory judgment of the ICJ was taken after all on the sidelines of the GCC Summit in Doha in 1990. The fact that the dispute could not be solved through the mechanisms specified in the GCC charter may be read as a failure for the organization. A more benign interpretation would posit that the dispute and the way it was solved demonstrates that the low degree of institutionalization of the GCC is in fact a positive characteristic. It allows the organization to weather major crises between its constituent states shielding it from having to take decisions that would potentially lead to its breakup.

European Union–GCC negotiations: dialogue of the deaf?

Another interesting case study to gauge the nature of the GCC diplomatic persona is to retrace, albeit briefly, its conduct during the negotiations it entertained into with the European Union for more than 20 years. We alluded to them in the chapter analysing GCC economic integration and the customs union 'saga'. However, it is useful to review the subject from the point of view of GCC diplomatic cohesiveness and the difficulty for the General Secretariat to muster a united front of the 'six' *vis-à-vis* the European negotiators. From the beginning, these negotiations have aimed to establish an FTA. This outcome might be definitely out of reach after Bahrain, Oman, Qatar and Kuwait concluded bilateral FTAs with the United States in fewer than three years from 2004 to 2007. However, the long history of negotiations is indicative of the diplomatic behaviour of the GCC, as well of course of the European Union.

Gulf states had been part of the Euro-Arab dialogue, launched in 1974, that achieved little and came to an end in 1989.[51] The European Union–GCC Cooperation Agreement, signed in 1988, was supposed to herald a new era in the relations between the then European Community and the Gulf. European officials were hoping to achieve the first FTA negotiated by Europe on a multilateral basis and therefore attached particular symbolic importance to this relationship. The 1988 Agreement came into force on 1 January 1990 and provided a framework for interregional cooperation whose chief aim was the establishment of a free trade area.[52] Furthermore, a political dialogue was started to complement the trade and cultural aspects. The agreement provided for a fairly institutionalized setting whose premier expression are the annual Joint Ministerial Council meetings. In fact, after almost 20 years the free trade area has not been established yet and it may have been compromised by the United States bilateral FTAs, whereas the political dialogue yielded a long series of rather vacuous communiqués expressing common positions on the political issues of the day, with the exception of course of really contentious issues. From this point of view the two organizations found common ground but crucially the trade aspect that required painful domestic compromises remained unresolved.

It is particularly interesting how the European Union feels it has a lot to share in terms of its experience as a peace-maker and purveyor of confidence-building measures 'in the framework of cooperative and collective regimes on regional security' without being willing to provide any military guarantees.[53] This leaves the field chiefly to the Americans but even to the UK and France operating on a bilateral basis.

This ambivalence on the part of the European states, wanting to preserve their lucrative bilateral links while pushing the multilateral framework for declaratory purposes, has been one of the main obstacles to a functioning, multilateral European Union–GCC relationship. However, the difficulty on the part of the GCC in presenting a united front in trade negotiations has been throughout the years even greater. The limited institutionalization and the lack of supranational powers on the part of the GCC Secretariat have proved a formidable obstacle.

In order to give an impression of the pace at which the General Secretariat was able to muster a mandate for negotiations it would be enough to record a few milestone dates. After the Cooperation agreement came into force in 1990, it took another seven years for the GCC to agree on the FTA's mandate. As we have seen in a previous chapter the customs union, a precondition for a multilateral FTA with the European Union, was finalized only in 2003 and was soon thrown into disarray by a wave of rapidly concluded bilateral FTAs between the United States and some GCC states. This was in addition to European misgivings about free access of GCC petrochemical products to its market, what Abdulla Baabood and Geoffrey Edwards quite aptly label an 'institutional mismatch' has plagued European Union–GCC relations.[54]

Ultimately, it was not until 2004 that the European Union opened a delegation in Riyadh, with an ambassador accredited to the six GCC states.[55] In other words, it took 16 years from the signing of the Cooperation agreement. It is a fact that certainly has to do with the reluctance of the Europeans to deal with the Gulf on a multilateral basis, but it also highlights the low priority that GCC institutions command in the international arena.

The opening of the delegation and the renewed emphasis by the European Union in bringing about the conclusion of an FTA was probably due to the successful completion of the European Union–Saudi agreement of August 2003 regarding the Kingdom's accession to the World Trade Organization (WTO).[56] However, these hopes were soon to be dashed by the conclusion of the already mentioned bilateral FTAs with the United States. It must be noted, with the experience of the GCC customs union in mind, that the signing of an eventual agreement would only be the first step. As we have seen in a previous chapter with regards to the customs union, practical implementation would be very arduous given the lack of supranational powers on the part of the General Secretariat.

In 2006, even if one were to exclude the rather fundamental notion of how to conciliate an eventual European multilateral FTA with the bilateral American FTAs already signed by some GCC states, the European Union included clauses that will quite possibly rule out the possibility of an FTA with the GCC. Up to this point outstanding disputes had been concentrated in four areas: market access, rules of origin, government procurement (a particularly crucial one in a place like Saudi Arabia), and investment protection and guarantees criteria.[57] These are fairly usual, if in this case quite thorny, areas of negotiation when aiming at a trade deal. However, probably influenced by contemporary American initiatives, the European Union decided to introduce human rights and good governance clauses into its negotiating stance drawing the ire of the GCC delegation. The joint European Union–GCC communiqués had so far touched upon political notions, but always at the regional and international without touching on domestic concerns. The actual incorporation of these clauses in the trade deal has proven unacceptable for the GCC delegation and has highlighted the fact that these issues did not arise in its parallel negotiations with China.

Another issue that highlighted the institutional, and in this case even societal, mismatch has been European Union insistence on a parallel process of 'decentralized cooperation' to involve civil society actors in the Gulf in business, academia and the arts. This process of track-two diplomacy was interpreted by the GCC, and Saudi Arabia in particular, as interference in the domestic affairs of its member states and eventually dropped. NATO is experiencing similar problems with its efforts in the Gulf even if it wisely chose to carry out its Istanbul Cooperation Initiative on a purely bilateral basis.[58] These episodes highlight the limited role that GCC institutions can play in carrying out multilateral negotiations even when they are headed by very capable functionaries. The lack of supranational authority is an obstacle that is very difficult to surmount.

Conclusion

By analysing the way the GCC has dealt with key internal and external disputes, as well as its drawn-out dealings with the European Union, we can conclude that the GCC acts as a loose forum on the diplomatic scene. However, this looseness is the key to its strength as closer, concerted diplomatic action would make the differences between the national interests of the constituent states come to the fore.

In internal GCC disputes the organization has not been effective to date. Some border disputes are still an issue, whereas others such as the Bahraini-Qatar dispute discussed here have been solved outside the realm of the organization. As recently as 2005, Saudi Arabia warned Bahrain and Qatar not to build a causeway linking the two states as this would encroach on Saudi territorial waters. It is difficult to imagine such disputes arising within other multilateral organizations that are nominally committed ultimately to achieving unity among its members.

GCC members are brought together by common threats in either the internal or the external realms. Regime security is the foremost priority in the foreign policy of all the six member states. If there is no perception of a common threat, GCC states revert to competing among themselves, and GCC institutionalism is certainly not enough to keep them from doing so. In other words, we can say that in the first 20 years of its existence the GCC has not developed independent agency and likewise it cannot be said to shape the interests of its member states. Furthermore, GCC member states definitely do not constitute a security community.

Perhaps the only exception was in the economic area where Secretariat personnel for many years pushed the rulers in order to herald the customs union. However, as we have seen the fate of the customs unions hangs in the balance as a result of the bilateral FTAs concluded with the United States by single-member states. This only reinforces our previous conclusion.

In general, smaller GCC states display a greater tendency to defy the traditional 'rule of shaikhly exchange' that has characterized intra-GCC relations for the first 20 years of its existence. There is, for example, a greater tendency to defy notions of Saudi leadership, the bilateral FTA issue being just the most egregious example. This new tendency can be attributed partially to a perceived waning of American soft power in the region, following regime change in Iraq in 2003 and a more general 'hollowing out' of the regional level as the Iran–United States confrontation is increasingly played out at the global level. Under these circumstances smaller GCC states feel that the imperative of regime security can probably be attained by keeping a rather low profile. This stance is well exemplified by the behaviour of the GCC states during the confrontation between Iran and the international community about the Iranian nuclear programme. This and, more broadly, their attitude *vis-à-vis* nuclear energy are discussed in the next chapter.

7

THE GCC, IRAN AND NUCLEAR PROLIFERATION IN THE GULF

> IAEA [International Atomic Energy Agency] supervised programs start off as peaceful but you are never 100% sure of what is going to happen 15 years from now.[1]
>
> Egyptian diplomat

Introduction

In this chapter I propose to reflect on the likelihood of one of the members of the Gulf Cooperation Council (GCC) deciding to acquire a latent nuclear capability or even a nuclear device in response to regional or global threats. I will focus in particular on the GCC response to the challenge posed by Iranian nuclear activities. My analysis will be informed by an examination of past defense and foreign policy choices by individual member states and it will include an evaluation of the possibility that the GCC, as an organization, may provide an umbrella for a civilian or a military nuclear project.

The GCC Supreme Council at its 27th meeting on 9–10 December 2006 in Riyadh called for the establishment of a peaceful civilian nuclear programme on a *multilateral* basis under International Atomic Energy Agency (IAEA) supervision. In the words of the final communiqué, the Supreme Council of the GCC has commissioned a joint study to be conducted by the GCC member countries to explore the possibility of forging a joint program in the field of nuclear technology for peaceful purposes according to international criteria and systems.[2]

The announcement created quite a stir in Western policy-making circles.[3] A nuclear arms race in the Gulf as a response to proliferation efforts by one of the two foremost regional powers would certainly constitute a deterioration of the Gulf 'security sub-complex'.[4] The strong, negative security interdependence between the GCC, Iran and Iraq would certainly worsen. The imbalance of power between the three sides of the scalene triangle we described in a previous chapter would grow.

The decision of the GCC Supreme Council certainly resonated in policy circles. However, the fact that as part of the same announcement it was made clear that this programme would be set up on a *multilateral* basis under GCC supervision makes the likelihood of its actually coming to fruition fairly low. The possibility that single states such as the United Arab Emirates (UAE) could proceed on an individual basis cannot be discounted, but the possibility that the GCC could set up a collective programme is extremely remote.

I will argue that the announcement is better interpreted as a diplomatic gesture aimed at Iran and not as an actual action plan. This in light of the chequered results obtained by the GCC in other fields of cooperation and the fact that single GCC members would be extremely unlikely to embark in such a crucial project on a collective basis under the umbrella of the GCC.

Iranian actions and its intent to develop a full nuclear cycle that will bring it a 'switch away' from building a nuclear device is of course a crucial variable in the decision-making process of GCC states. However, I will argue that the classic balance-of-power conundrum in the Gulf would not change if one of the two foremost regional powers, Iran or indeed a resurgent Iraq, were to acquire nuclear weapons. GCC states would still have no choice but to rely on an external balancer for their defense.

In order to lay out my argument the bulk of the chapter will be a detailed examination of what has been the diplomatic reaction of GCC states to the incipient Iranian nuclear programme. This will help put Iran's December 2006 announcement in its proper context. I will then provide a fair assessment of what are the prospects of a civilian nuclear programme in GCC states, particularly given the lack of an economic rationale when fully costed. I will then proceed to assess the even more remote possibility of a GCC member state setting up a military nuclear programme.

I will then discuss the political dynamics that lie at the basis of weapons of mass destruction (WMD) proliferation in the broader Middle East. I will argue that the solution of political problems, not any technical of legal issues, is the key to non-proliferation efforts in the region. In particular, as long as diplomatic recognition amongst regional states and between these and external powers is not universal, it is very difficult to envisage current nuclear powers renouncing their strategic deterrence. Likewise, as long as security guarantees that are perceived to be satisfactory are not extended by the United States to every state in the region, WMD proliferation efforts will continue.

I will conclude by discussing some additional factors that make in my opinion GCC members, and even more the GCC as an organization, unlikely to jumpstart a nuclear programme, be it civilian or military.

The GCC states and the Iranian nuclear challenge

Proponents of the 2003 Iraq War anticipated that the removal of Saddam Hussein's regime would dramatically improve security in the Gulf. Under Saddam Hussein's leadership, Iraq had adopted a threatening posture that precipitated three wars and generated great uncertainty and instability in the region. Yet, contrary to these expectations prospects for Gulf security prospects seem to have significantly deteriorated in the aftermath of the war.

While the removal of the Ba'athist regime has eliminated the risk in the medium-term of Iraq being a state threat to the region, internal unrest in Iraq and the perception of rising Shi'ah Islam, however vague this notion may be, have profound implications for GCC states.[5] The security situation in Iraq, combined with a fragile and divisive political process, has the potential to heighten regional tensions and pit Iraq's neighbours against each other.

Indeed, in the eyes of GCC states Iran is emerging as the real beneficiary of Saddam Hussein's fall, and as such it has become a much bigger threat to stability in their neighbourhood. As we have seen well before the establishment of the Islamic republic, the Shah was seen as an arrogant and overbearing leader who considered himself the natural leader of the area, a 'toff' to use the expression of a British-educated leading GCC diplomat. However, Gulf Arabs had no reason to expect domestic tampering on his part. This fear has become palpable in the aftermath of the Islamic Revolution. These days the creation of a stable security system in the Gulf appears even more distant with the coming to power of a second generation of Iranian revolutionaries. These leaders are committed to acquiring the complete nuclear fuel cycle. This programme draws support from all actors across Iran's political spectrum, and it has gained significant symbolic meaning for Iran's population.

On this and other issues Iranian leaders are willing to challenge the United States and much of the international community. Nevertheless, while Iran's involvement in Iraq dominates headlines in the GCC states, only recently did its nuclear programme attract significant attention.

One would expect GCC states to play a role in the negotiations aimed at convincing Iran to renounce access to the complete nuclear fuel cycle. Yet they have remained on the sidelines. At first glance this passive posture seems to make little sense. Yet a more thorough examination reveals intricate layers of logic and reasoning that explain the persistent and uneasy silence of the GCC states.

Defining priorities: a nuclear Iran versus Iraq

Iranian officials regularly tour the Gulf Arab states to assure them of their peaceful intentions, especially regarding the nuclear issue. But in the dissolution of the scalene triangle of power currently unfolding in the Persian Gulf, the main actors, are distant powers, and Iran's closest neighbours have reason to act as mere spectators. The restraint and inaction of the Gulf Arab states reflect both their distrust of Iran and their reliance on the United States as their ultimate security guarantor. Simply put, GCC states play a limited role, if any, in the current negotiations to ensure that Iran's nuclear programme remains aimed at civilian purposes.

In May 2005, on the eve of then-Secretary of the Iranian Supreme National Security Council Hassan Rowhani's visit to Persian Gulf countries, Richard LeBaron, US Ambassador to Kuwait, criticized Iran for its 'appalling human rights record, its pursuit of nuclear weapons and weapons of mass destruction, its interference in the internal affairs of Iraq, its opposition to the Middle East peace process and its sponsorship of terror'.[6] LeBaron called on the GCC to 'take a firm stand against Iran's nuclear ambitions' and be more diplomatically active on this front. The Kuwaiti Speaker of Parliament, Jassem Al-Kharafi, who enjoys relative independence compared with his Arab counterparts and clashes periodically with Kuwait's ruling family, quickly rebuked him for interfering in Kuwait's relations with Iran and jeopardizing their bilateral relations.[7] Top Kuwaiti officials preferred to keep silent.

Gulf Arab officials certainly worry about Iran's nuclear aspiration. From August 2002 to late 2005, however, they remained mostly silent and hesitant, perplexed by Iran's actions and distracted by events in Iraq. In January 2005, the GCC Secretary-General Abdel Rahman Attiya was quoted as saying: 'Saudi Arabia and the other GCC countries can't find any justification for such nuclear activity which poses great dangers for all the peoples in the Gulf region.'[8] Only later did heavyweights such as Saudi Foreign Minister Saud al-Faisal and

Saudi Ambassador to the United States Turki al-Faisal join the chorus. The former spoke of a potential 'disaster' should Iran stay the course, and the latter criticized Iran's inflexibility on the nuclear issue.[9]

But it is telling that the most vocal in his angst at the prospect of a nuclear Iran is former GCC Secretary-General Abdullah Bishara. He is now freed from the shackles of having to play an official role and he can be more outspoken in his comments, a situation that reminds us of recently retired British and American foreign officials. Iran's nuclear programme 'totally turns over the balance of power, and makes Iran the master of the region and the influential instrument in its decisions – the GCC position should be united, strong and clear', he said in April 2006, complaining that 'the Gulf states' position does not satisfy me, nor do I feel at ease about it'.[10]

Indeed, the Gulf Arab concern has not translated into an integrated campaign to obtain Iranian cooperation with European negotiators. On the contrary, the LeBaron incident typifies the way Gulf Arab states have chosen to cope with the Iranian nuclear challenge. Essentially, their strategy seeks to keep the discussion away from the public arena, to placate Iran to avoid antagonizing a powerful neighbour, and to rely on European Union diplomacy and American military forces to constrain and deter Iran. This two-level strategy, criticized by many, characterizes relations between Iran and its Arab Gulf neighbours and makes perfect sense in light of the enduring realities of power in the Gulf. It is a cost-effective way of conducting their relations with the foremost regional power, a more pragmatic approach than both the many idealistic collective security schemes put forward by solicitous academics and the policy of confrontation suggested by more hawkish American and British analysts.[11]

There are additional reasons why Iran's nuclear question does not receive that much coverage in the GCC states. First, the nuclear issue is overshadowed by a more imminent and more visible development: Iran's involvement in Iraq. GCC regimes see with great anxiety the internal shift in Iraqi politics that is bringing to power an emboldened Shi'ah majority whose rise generates internal and regional concerns. Iran's intentions in Iraq remain unclear, creating immense potential for misinterpretation and miscalculation.[12] What is Iran's vision of Iraq's future? Is Iran actively undermining US efforts in Iraq to control the country, or is its involvement in Iraq part of contingency planning? Is Iran shrewdly positioning its clients in Iraq, or is it hedging its bets and hoping to shape Iraq's future regional posture? Regardless of Iranian preferences, though, what seems evident is that Iraq cannot currently project power in the Gulf and it has lost its role as balancer in the triangular power structure outlined in previous chapters.

That the situation in Iraq dominates the media coverage and public debate in the Middle East makes the perils emanating from Iran – especially Iran's ability to stir Shi'ah passions in other countries – even more palpable. Iraq's slow descent into civil war is broadcasted and commented on daily on Arab satellite television. Iraq has become an emotional and omnipresent issue in the Arab world. Support for the Iraqi 'resistance' and fear of rising Shi'ah Islam are powerful rallying cries, especially when paired together.

Often, statements from the GCC states' own senior officials only strengthen the perception that Iran is the main patron and beneficiary of Iraq's troubles.[13]

Iran has always had hegemonic ambitions in the Gulf.[14] Its historic regional ambitions, its support of Shi'ah groups in the 1980s and early 1990s, and Ayatollah Khomeini's eagerness to export the Islamic Revolution still resonate in the minds of Gulf decision-makers. An attempted coup in Bahrain in the early 1980s and the suspected irredentism of Shi'ah communities there and in other GCC states are, rightly or wrongly, linked to agitation on the part of the Iranian government. Iran's historic role in the Gulf makes it a much more worrying neighbour than other actors, including the United States: Iran is there to stay, and its ambitions, real or perceived, shape GCC states' behaviour. This translates into justified circumspection in making public statements that may antagonize the Iranian leadership, a circumspection that goes hand in hand with the private manifestation of alertness when weighing Iranian influence in the Gulf.

The narrative of the Iran–Iraq War, with Iran portrayed as the aggressor, despite evidence to the contrary, is indicative of this mindset. The Saudi-Iranian rapprochement of the 1990s and the pragmatic and conciliating policies of former presidents Rafsanjani and Khatami towards their Arab neighbours have partly alleviated GCC fears, but the hardening of Iran's position *vis-à-vis* the West may have implications that would reverse the *détente* of the last decade.[15] Despite this *détente*, long-held suspicions and prejudices that Arabs maintain toward their neighbour still linger and are likely to inform Gulf reactions to Iran's blatant involvement in Iraq.

Conversely, because of its sensitivity, complexity and apparent remoteness, Iran's nuclear challenge rarely made the headlines in the Gulf. It is often kept in royal *diwan*s and for discussion with senior US and European officials. In the public sphere it is tackled with unease and perplexity.

In responding to Iran's nuclear challenge, GCC regimes are constrained by two powerful and convergent forces: their own public opinions and resilient pan-Arab norms. Paradoxically, there is a significant measure of sympathy in the Arab world for Iran's nuclear ambitions.[16] An unscientific poll on the

Al-Jazeera website showed that 73% of the respondents (arguably mostly Arabs) did not believe that Iran's nuclear programme constituted a threat to neighbouring countries.[17] In October 2005, a poll showed that 63% of respondents in six Arab countries (including Saudi Arabia and the UAE) considered that international efforts to get Iran to stop its nuclear programme should cease.[18] Indeed, a significant achievement of President Ahmadinejad is that he succeeded in shaping the debate about the nuclear crisis in the Arab world. By courting an already sympathetic public, he amplified the rift between pro-American Gulf Arab rulers and their deeply anti-American populations. Indeed, Ahmadinejad's rabid anti-US and anti-Israel rhetoric, his eagerness to defy what is perceived as Western obstruction, and his claims to represent an oppressed but rising Islamic nation resonate well among populations convinced that the colonialist West is again up to no good.

The complexity of the issue and poorly conducted public diplomacy have convinced many that American and European attempts to restrict Iran's access to a complete fuel cycle reflect an inherent Western tendency to check any rising power instead of an attempt to forestall a crisis of a global dimension. More specifically, at the popular level many Arabs feel some pride at seeing an Islamic nation, even a non-Arab one, develop nuclear technology and challenge the United States on the world scene. With the George W. Bush Administration's hawkish foreign policy in the background, the widely shared sentiment is that the counter-proliferation doctrine is only another instrument of Western and US imperialism. The nuclear apartheid argument resonates more than the necessity to abide by international agreements such as the Nuclear Non-Proliferation Treaty (NPT) and related obligations. Iran itself has sought to portray the issue as one of sovereignty and prestige, while systematically obscuring its own breaches of the NPT. Additionally, in the eyes of many Arabs the possession of military nuclear capabilities by other regional powers provides Iran with arguments to defend its strategic needs in a region where the myth of self-sufficiency in defense reigns. It would be wrong to dismiss outright the influence of public opinion in GCC states when it comes to this issue. For rulers engaged in a delicate balancing game, appearing too close to the US position is a liability, and the example of Islamic dissent in Saudi Arabia is certainly a reminder of this.

GCC leaders are also limited by surviving pan-Arab norms that shape public and official expectations in the Arab world beyond the Gulf. The ever-present issue of Israel's nuclear capabilities constrains them because it gives other Arab states a say in how they define the Iran problem.[19] Pan-Arab and pan-Islamic norms and expectations require GCC regimes to appear more anti-Israeli than anti-Iranian, despite the immediacy and potency of the Iranian threat, and to criticize US policy towards Iran despite the United States' role as their main security guarantor. The Egypt-inspired Arab League's insistence on a region-wide focus reflects an eagerness on its part to remain engaged as a key actor, keep the foreign policies of the GCC anchored in the Arab state system and prevent them from articulating a completely autonomous agenda.

In reality, these pan-Arab norms have become less salient to GCC threat perceptions. These are significantly different from the Israel-centred concerns of the Levantine Arab states. For them, the centre of gravity of the Middle East has shifted from the Levant to the Gulf, and the nature and scope of Gulf volatility has little to do with the Arab–Israeli conflict. Indeed, some Gulf states (Bahrain, Qatar, UAE and Oman) have initiated contacts with Israel, but the low-key and commercially driven nature of this interaction has ensured that it remained largely off the public discussion.

Nevertheless, overcoming this taboo has been more difficult than expected because of the convergence of official Arab pressures (mainly through efforts by Arab League Secretary General Amr Moussa) and the considerable support for Iran manifest in public opinion throughout the region. In a telling example, the GCC leaders failed to mention Iran's nuclear ambitions as a main concern in the final statement of their December 2005 Supreme Council. Instead, and as urged by Amr Moussa, Secretary General of the Arab League, they agreed to condemn Israel's nuclear arsenal. But the recent Saudi suggestion that a nuclear-free Gulf should precede a regional pact on WMD signals willingness to put this obstacle aside.[20] Only in May 2006 did GCC leaders issue a relatively tough statement after an extraordinary summit on the situation in Iraq and Iran.

The costs of negotiating with Iran

For those who worry about Iran's nuclear aspirations, there is something deeply disconcerting about the absence of any GCC involvement in the negotiations aimed at stopping, or at least slowing, Iran's nuclear progress.

GCC states undoubtedly prefer a non-nuclear Iran but they are unwilling to assume the costs of negotiations with Iran. The existing asymmetry of power between GCC states and Iran, combined with the Gulf Arabs' lack of political options, complicate the situation.

Discussions between Arab states and Iran in formal and informal settings over security arrangements and stability in the Gulf have been ongoing since the *détente* of the 1990s. But real progress depends on a key issue unlikely to be resolved in the near future: the presence and role of the United States in the region. Iran considers the United States to be the key factor of instability and an aggressive outsider in the Gulf, while GCC states see the United States as the foremost element of their defense posture. Iran's overarching strategic objective in the Gulf is to obtain a major shift in the US posture, preferably the departure of US military forces.[21] For their part, GCC states seek to maintain good relations with Iran while continuing to rely on the US security umbrella. Consequently, demands for an immediate withdrawal of US troops are simply a non-starter. These contradicting perspectives make it difficult for the GCC states and Iran to actually implement those confidence-building measures that are often heralded as a panacea.[22] The obstacles that lay in the path of a comprehensive Gulf security regime are of a deeply political, not technical, nature, and therefore they are much harder to overcome.

In a diplomatic effort to persuade Iran to suspend its uranium enrichment activities permanently, GCC states have economic and political levers that can influence how beneficial or damaging the United States or the EU's "carrot-and sticks" approach ultimately is, but ultimately, this influence is marginal. For GCC states far more important is the question of whether the benefit of joining these efforts outweighs the potential fallout if Iran goes ahead with its programme.

Indeed, for Gulf states to antagonize Iran by siding fully and overtly with the United States would not be beneficial. It will bring no substantial benefits and will instead likely yield more tensions in the future. It is significant in this regard that recent warnings about the Iranian nuclear programme have been delivered mainly by the GCC Secretary General, who, as we have seen, cannot wield any sort of supranational power, only later by foreign ministers and never by heads of state. Furthermore, these officials explicitly recognize Iran's right to a complete nuclear fuel cycle for peaceful purposes under the auspices of the IAEA. The latter is seen by the United States as a prologue to weaponization or at the very least an unacceptable element of nuclear ambiguity. In contrast, warnings about Iranian influence in southern Iraq and the rise of Shi'iah influence were delivered personally and through major outlets by Egyptian President Hosni Mubarak, Jordanian King Abdullah and Saudi Foreign Minister Saud al-Faisal and resonated throughout the Arab world.

The GCC states are inclined to question the utility of pressurizing Iran on the nuclear issue, as they rightly assume that only the European Union and United States have the economic and military heft to give their words power.

This assumption is perfectly acceptable and drives GCC members to question the need for involvement. Furthermore, there is a perception that not even these incentives would convince Iran to renounce its nuclear aspirations. Most Gulf decision-makers are convinced that Teheran is set on its course and nothing except a grand bargain with the United States, improbable as it is, will change its strategic rationales.

Moreover, GCC states judge that Tehran probably does not identify them as a major threat to its security, and certainly not a driving factor behind its nuclear ambitions. Iran's rationales for developing a nuclear capability are based on strategic and prestige grounds in which its Arab neighbours play, as such, a minor part. This probably correct judgment, corroborated by Western analysts, however, comes with an important corollary that should not be overlooked: the risk is that an Iran armed with nuclear weapons will lead to a diplomatic stand-off in the Gulf and reduce considerably the margin of political and diplomatic manoeuvrability of its Arab neighbours. Iran could demand an end to the rapprochement between some Gulf states and Israel, have a bigger say in oil policy, or be in a position of immense strength on GCC–Iran disputes (i.e. Abu Musa and the Two Tunbs). Certainly the acquisition of nuclear weapons, or more simply the acquisition of a full nuclear cycle that leads to a posture of nuclear ambiguity, will bring significant strategic advantages to Iran. It would turn it into the foremost regional power in the Middle East on a par with Israel and, at least in the eyes of the most radical elements in Iran, would provide welcome leverage to defy US pressure.

A recommendation from hawkish analysts is that Middle East states, namely Saudi Arabia and, to a lesser extent, Egypt, signal to Iran that its nuclear ambitions will force them to reconsider their own nuclear posture and precipitate a regional arms race.

Some even argue that Saudi officials have made this clear to Teheran. However, the persuasive value of such an argument is uncertain and probably counterproductive. Iran is already living in a neighbourhood of nuclear powers – including the United States. It is certainly not convinced that it is starting an arms race, but rather that it is entering late in the game, especially in view of the world's passive reaction to Iraqi use of WMD against Iran in the 1980s. It will take more to change the rationale behind Teheran's nuclear venture than raising the prospects of an arms race. Even if that were the case, it would only comfort Teheran in its decision to acquire a nuclear capability.

In addition, the perception that Iran is stubbornly set on its nuclear course makes GCC states wonder why they should pay a political price by subscribing to a lost cause. A grim acknowledgement among Iran experts in the West is that Iran will likely acquire the expertise to produce weapons-grade fissile material. Those who believe that a diplomatic solution is possible envisage a tougher inspections regime to prevent Iran from diverting nuclear fuel for military purposes, but reluctantly acknowledge that this would mean that Iran would possess a complete fuel cycle capability. If this were indeed the case, Iran would nevertheless come close to have its own policy of 'strategic ambiguity'. This would be a major step forward on the path of being recognized as a nuclear power. Under these conditions, it is legitimate to ask what benefits GCC states would obtain from joining a losing battle.

Despite this grim picture, GCC states have not been totally absent from the diplomatic game. In reality they are actively courted by both high-level Iranian and American officials.

Iran has repeatedly approached its Gulf neighbours to reassure them about its intentions and to limit the damages of President Ahmadinejad's rhetoric – his comments casting doubt on the historical veracity of the Holocaust were made from Mecca, on the sidelines of a meeting of the Islamic Conference Organization (ICO), to the embarrassment of his Saudi hosts. Supreme Leader Khamenei has encouraged or dispatched to key Gulf states mediators such as former Foreign Minister Velayati (now Khamenei's diplomatic advisor), Expediency Council Chairman Rafsanjani, who enjoys good relations with several Gulf leaders, and Secretary of the Supreme National Security Council Larijani. Iran has also tried to enrol them in its own public diplomacy effort against the West or as mediators, a role that would suggest that the nuclear challenge is really about Iran–West relations instead of a regional crisis.

Gulf Arab leaders have also visited Teheran, but there is little evidence that such visits have delivered any tangible result except short-term *détente*. On the occasion of the visit of Qatar's Emir Hamad in May 2006, Qatar and Iran agreed in principle to sign a security agreement, but more revealing was the public argument over the naming of the Gulf – an emotionally charged fixture in the region.[23] Even a later announcement that the GCC would send to Teheran a delegation headed by the Omani foreign minister to restate its concern about its nuclear programme sounded more like an improvised and futile initiative than a smart move which was part of a bigger diplomatic campaign.

While Oman enjoys good relations with Iran, its foreign minister certainly cannot claim to speak for the GCC as a whole. A more politically significant event would have been a visit by the Saudi foreign minister. Moreover, the Omani foreign minister himself denied that he was formally asked to represent the GCC, claiming that 'those are just ideas'.[24] Qatar's foreign minister further confirmed the lack of a common GCC position when he stated that 'There is no initiative in a real sense by the Gulf states, it is more that we support and encourage a diplomatic solution to this issue.'[25]

A more indirect and in many ways creative avenue through which GCC states are tackling the Iranian nuclear challenge is by emphasizing the environmental hazards linked to Iran's nuclear programme. The legitimate concerns GCC states have about nuclear safety are grounded in two widely shared assessments: first, that the nuclear technology acquired and developed by Iran presents a high degree of risk and unreliability; and second, that the populations and basic infrastructure of the Gulf monarchies are, with the exception of Saudi Arabia, concentrated on the coastal region and would be highly vulnerable to a nuclear accident. A Saudi journalist complained that 'the Bushehr nuclear reactor [...] is closer to Manama or Doha than to the Iranian capital'.[26]

Iran has been trying to assuage these fears – 'There is nothing to worry about, we have spent a lot of money on [environmental] safety and the security of the plant', an Iranian spokesman even stated[27] – and has made offers of limited technological and scientific cooperation. These reassurances have however fallen short of GCC hopes. Iran has also refused to allow GCC inspectors from visiting key nuclear facilities, including the Bushehr reactor. This, combined with IAEA reports, creates concern in GCC capitals.

The implications of a showdown

If a confrontation with Iran ensues, the GCC will have to act confrontation with Iran is in sight. If the United States, with or without approval of the international community, decides to impose sanctions or undertake coercive action against Iran, GCC states will be hard pressed to choose a side, but in all likelihood they will opt to side with the United States lending them basing rights.

Yet this will be an extremely unpleasant and decidedly risky decision. It would shatter the illusion of *détente* patiently fashioned throughout the 1990s, create lasting Iranian resentment and bring no guarantee of a more peaceful future. The prospect of a fourth major armed confrontation in the region since 1980 is sobering, and its potential impact on Gulf security and economic development devastating.

Some analysts are convinced that the Gulf Arab states will provide the United States with the logistical and political support it will need to deter, contain or punish Iran.[28] They contend that Gulf leaders are on board for such scenarios, and have prepared throughout the past decades for this eventuality. Because GCC states cannot be seen as leading the charge against Iran, they demand in private that the United States and European Union be more assertive in countering Iran's nuclear ambitions.

While this line of argument has some validity, it lacks contextual nuance. Going beyond the issues of US intentions and capabilities, especially while the United States is deeply and unhappily entangled in Iraq, it is essential to speculate whether GCC states would acquiesce to US-driven escalation with the risk that Iran may then attempt to destabilize them or whether they prefer to accommodate a powerful nuclear Iran. Hawks argue that GCC states will always prefer a weak and angry Iran to a powerful one.

Yet, if this implies internal instability and a major blow to their economic development, combined with additional volatility in Iraq, it is difficult to imagine the GCC states choosing this path without scrupulously assessing the alternatives. To associate themselves so blatantly with the United States in military strikes or a war where Iran will be perceived as a righteous victim by their own populations will consume much, if not all, the domestic and regional political capital they have, and ensure Iranian hostility for decades to come.

Another element critical to upholding the above argument is improving military capabilities of the GCC states. Awash with money from energy revenues, these states are already investing significantly in arms procurement and force modernization.

To be sure, Gulf states need to enhance their defense posture and work harder toward an integrated, Gulf-wide defense system. There are signs that GCC states are moving in this direction, but for now GCC defense cooperation remains largely symbolic, as evidenced by the January 2006 announcement that Peninsula Shield, a joint GCC force long-heralded as the nucleus of a credible integrated GCC defense system, would be dismantled. In fact, it would be counterproductive and somehow delusional to build up offensive capabilities. As we have seen in a previous chapter at a very basic level the risks that GCC regimes would incur in setting up effective standing armies clearly outweigh the benefits that could be gained in military efficiency. Professional standing armies have a tendency eventually to seize power in the Arab Middle East.[29] GCC elites realize that their conventional capabilities are no match for Iran's, and that their own military assets will only complement US forces marginally, if at all.[30] As already discussed, weapons acquisition by GCC states is best conceptualized as an 'insurance policy' underwritten by as many insurers as possible. While military analysts despair at the resulting operational incongruence, the decision to rely on a wide array of suppliers makes much sense given the geostrategic realities of the Gulf.

As many have observed, military solutions to delay or stop Iran's nuclear programme are not easily feasible. In GCC eyes, however, they will likely have disastrous consequences. First and foremost, military force would prompt Iran to activate its networks and assets in Iraq, fuelling an already highly volatile situation and ruining for good any hopes the United States might still entertain of delivering peace to Iraq; in Afghanistan, jeopardizing a fragile success made possible by Iranian goodwill; in the Levant, where Syria and Iranian-backed Hezbollah and Islamic Jihad can easily provoke a military escalation; and, evidently, in the Gulf. Iranian President Ahmadinejad has demonstrated his willingness at least to embarrass his Arab colleagues. When he calls for the vanishing of Israel from the pages of time, not only does he provoke the international community, but also he exposes a gulf between GCC rulers and their own populations.

That Ahmadinejad seems to be reclaiming Iran's self-allotted responsibility as the champion of the Islamic world certainly adds another layer of apprehension. If Iran is willing to embarrass or challenge its neighbours on purely ideological – that is, anti-US – grounds, it will appeal to many Sunnis offended by their countries' alignment with the United States and moderation on the Arab–Israeli conflict, regardless of increasing Sunni–Shi'ah tensions. This is a risk that Gulf Arab leaders, to their credit, fully appreciate.

Moreover, any military option would also lead Iran to withdraw from the NPT and end legal international control of its programme through inspections and safeguards. With the backdrop of the Iraq WMD fiasco, GCC states, as many other countries, believe that, despite its many limitations, United Nations- and IAEA-generated information is probably of better quality than Western intelligence on Iran's nuclear programme. This is why Arab Gulf states prefer a situation in which IAEA inspectors can monitor Iran's nuclear progress. With Iraq fresh in mind, it is only predictable that questions as to the quality of intelligence and the wisdom of a coercive approach will dominate the debate.

Finally, expecting limited strikes effectively to deter Iran from going ahead is probably wishful thinking and ignores the power of Iranian pride and nationalism. If anything, it will guarantee that Iran will push ahead and go for nuclear weapons instead of only the capability to build them. GCC leaders, most of whom have dealt with Iran for much longer than any US government, probably comprehend this predicament and will lobby heavily to prevent such an escalation.

Short of military action, any strategy of containment or punishment would require GCC states participation, or at least their assent. From maritime interdiction to the implementation of sanctions, the toolbox envisaged is wide and possible to utilize. However, one cannot expect Iran to endure that which contained and eventually brought down Saddam Hussein, at least not without retaliation. The GCC states, regardless of their own reservations about the wisdom of sanctions or the war, accepted that the United States and its allies use bases located on their soil for land, naval and air operations. In Saddam Hussein's case, the capacity of Iraq to instigate domestic unrest or even acts of terrorism was negligible. On the contrary, Iran has proven to be very skilled at developing its own regional and international networks and at nurturing groups with loose ideological affinities. In its own way Iran has developed its own deterrence capability that GCC leaders have to take into account in their decision-making process.

Only a strategy of deterrence would bring at a bearable level the political and security costs that Gulf Arab states would incur should there be a showdown. Such a strategy would rely on redlines, escalation levels, and military capabilities defined in accordance with and provided by the United States and its allies. Nevertheless, even such an approach would be hardly satisfactory. If Iran manages to define the terms of the confrontation, or if Islamic fundamentalists seize the opportunity to denounce their leaders as Osama Bin Laden did during the 1990s, then the Arab Gulf states will simply be trapped. One needs to imagine a replay in the Gulf of the 1980s missile crisis in Europe.

A key factor in determining where GCC states stand will be international legitimacy. In February 2006, in the wake of the IAEA decision to refer Iran's file to the United Nations Security Council, the Secretary General of the GCC stated that the GCC 'did not oppose' this move. This suggests that, with the cover of international law, it is likely that the GCC will endorse a United Nations-sanctioned decision to impose targeted sanctions against Iran.

Differing threat perceptions

Beyond the fact that Arab states feel powerless to influence Iranian policy, other structural factors shape GCC policy assumptions and decision-making regarding Iran.

First, it is essential to acknowledge that Western powers and Gulf states perceive the Iranian menace very differently. For Western powers, and especially the United States, whose economic, cultural and political ties with

Iran are weak, Iran is perceived as a hard security threat, a function of the perceived nature of the regime in Teheran. For Western analysts and policy-makers this threat is almost quantifiable and very material and is dominated by terrorism, WMD and missile capabilities. This is the direct result of decades of estrangement and tensions between Iran and the West that have reduced relations to a primitive state. Business interests, cultural exchanges, personal experiences, even Iranian lobbies in the West play a limited role in how assumptions are formed and policy formulated at the highest levels of government.[31]

In particular, US–Iranian relations have remained at their nadir for the past 25 years. For Americans, Iran evokes hostages in Teheran and Beirut, shady arms deals – including Iran-Contras – violent anti-US and anti-Israeli rhetoric and support for various radical groups, and, as of recently, WMD and Iran's role in Iraq's unrest. Other psychological and domestic obstacles reinforce this inability to conceptualize Iran as nothing other than a threat, and certainly not as an opportunity.

While both the United States and Iran made overtures to one another at some point, particularly in the last year of the Bill Clinton administration and in the immediate aftermath of regime change in Iraq in 2003, the fact remains that neither convergent interests in Afghanistan and Iraq nor hopes that a reformist takeover of Iranian politics would translate into genuine diplomacy and *détente* materialized into serious dialogue. Contrary to its predecessors who sought US recognition, the new leadership in Teheran has deemed irrelevant the need for rapprochement with the United States. This confrontational posture makes it harder for the United States to explore ways to talk to Iran.

While Iran's image in Europe has improved during former President Khatami's term – Europeans were intrigued by his 'Dialogue of Civilizations' initiative – the dominant feeling that started prevailing after the election of Ahmadinejad has been one of suspicion and frustration. Perhaps more than anyone Europeans understand the complexity of Iranian decision-making and the difficulty of getting the Iranians to negotiate, commit and act. The diplomats they meet do not wield enough power to balance the role of the Revolutionary Guards and other powerful actors, or to commit the Supreme Leader to any agreements. As a result, Paris, and more recently London and Berlin, have all become strong critics of Iran. Because they felt that their efforts were failing despite advocating a diplomatic solution early on and putting forward what was in their eyes a generous package in August 2005, they started blaming Teheran for its inflexibility, and aligning themselves with Washington. Furthermore, Iran's reputation is still reeling from its support for terrorist actions on European soil in the 1980s and 1990s – bombs that went off in Paris and Berlin, assassinations that eliminated Iranian dissidents, and the decree that targeted the author Salman Rushdie.

The GCC perception of Iran is more nuanced: because of the wider range of Arab–Iranian interactions, Gulf Arabs do not see Iran exclusively as a hard security threat. This does not mean that Gulf Arabs underestimate or are unaware of the Iranian military menace: as argued above, they worry about Iran's rising power in the region and they certainly do not consider it a benign actor.

However, Gulf Arabs and Iranians maintain multidimensional if complex relations that add nuance to and sometimes mitigate their assessment of the other's intentions and capabilities. Underlying the widely reported spats over the naming of the Gulf lies a complex, interdependent relationship often overlooked in the West. It would be enough here to mention the crucial role that Dubai plays as a transhipment hub for goods bound to Iran, the large expatriate community in the UAE as well as in other GCC states, and the many business and cultural ties that bridge the two shores of the Gulf. Visits by Iranian parliamentary, business and cultural delegations are routine and a complex web of ties links communities on the two sides of the Gulf.

Central to this dynamic is a key distinction with the West: while the West and the United States in particular have issues with the nature and behaviour of the regime in Teheran, GCC states worry about Iran itself, regardless of who calls the shots in Teheran. Of course, under Ayatollah Khomeini their relations with Iran were disastrous, but the Gulf Arab historical narrative is filled with occasions of Iran bullying its neighbours prior to 1979 and perceptions of a Persian sense of civilizational supremacy.

After all, as we have seen in the previous chapter, it was the Shah who took control of three disputed islands claimed by the UAE – a move then weakly protested by the United States.

Also, and perhaps wrongly, many in the region believe and fear that a pro-West Iran is a much bigger strategic prize for the United States than for the Gulf states. The United States would certainly welcome strategic changes that would bring it closer to a millennium-old civilization: a huge market, an educated population and a geographically appealing location. As a reminder of US past inclinations, the twin-pillar strategy of the 1970s initially rested on Iran: Saudi Arabia, the second and 'weaker' pillar, was only added at the urging of State Department Arabists and for its financial power.[32]

While the early 1990s witnessed a serious deterioration in their relations, GCC–Iranian contacts improved later in the decade as a result of a Saudi-driven rapprochement with Iran, and a sense that Iran had made regional confidence-building a key element of its national security strategy. Part of the rift after the 1990 Gulf War was due, to a degree, to GCC distrust of its neighbours and an unwillingness to accept anymore the logic of regional balance. In other words, Iran's deep enmity for Saddam Hussein's Iraq was not reason enough to rebuild ties. The United States had proven a reliable and capable ally, and Iran had nothing to offer aside from calling for a regional security pact with the Arab states, an idea they quickly rejected. The US dual containment strategy was providing a welcome shield from potential aggression. Iran, meanwhile, stepped up its support for Shi'ah groups in the Gulf, escalated tensions with the UAE over the disputed islands, allegedly had links to the Bahraini Hezbollah that attempted a coup in Manama in 1996, and organized major military exercises.[33] This strategy was probably aimed at signalling to its Arab neighbours that it would play a major regional role, and that their support and hosting of the US military presence was seen as a direct threat to Iranian security.

It is also important to remember that because of their history and geostrategic location, GCC states have different interests when dealing with Iran. While they all agree on the need for a US security umbrella, each state seems to pursue separate and evolving strategies when dealing with Iran, making it difficult to talk of a 'GCC position' *vis-à-vis* Teheran. Oman and Qatar have a long history of trading and negotiating with Iran. As already mentioned, Dubai plays an important role in Iranian economic life by serving as a major transhipping and financial centre even if the UAE as a whole may have the worst 'formal' relations with Iran. On the other hand, Saudi Arabia and Bahrain are traditionally more wary of potential Iranian manipulative mobilization of their Shi'ah communities. In the wake of the 1991 Gulf War newly liberated Kuwait was very friendly with Iran in the 1990s, but after regime change in Baghdad their relations have cooled significantly.

Overall, though, either to avoid ruining a fruitful economic relationship or antagonizing a powerful and overbearing neighbour, all GCC states concur on the wisdom of letting the United States and Europe deal with the Iranian nuclear challenge.

The GCC nuclear option

It is in this context that the announcement by the GCC Secretary General that a nuclear programme should be established on a *multilateral* basis must be viewed. The programme has no economic rationale when fully costed. The increasing security costs make nuclear energy production a questionable enterprise even in G8 countries, let alone in leading Organization of the Petroleum Exporting Countries (OPEC) producers such as Saudi Arabia and Kuwait.[34]

Furthermore, as it should be clear from previous chapters, the GCC Secretariat does not have either the technical expertise nor the supranational powers to implement a full-blown programme of nuclear development under IAEA supervision. The lack of supranational coordination and trust that has hindered the establishment of a customs union and a free trade area would *a fortiori* prevent the successful completion of such a complex endeavour. The issue of joint management would be even problematic.

Such a programme requires a scientific and industrial wherewithal that is simply not there and whose build up would require at least a decade under the watchful surveillance of the United States, the ultimate guarantor of external security for all the GCC states. Saudi Arabia, acting alone, is a more credible candidate but even in the case of a purely Saudi programme the obstacles are daunting. Let us just consider what would be the reaction of the United States and of Israel, the pre-eminent regional power.

The Saudi and American security apparatuses are deeply intertwined, a link cemented by multibillion dollar deals.[35] This makes it very difficult for Saudi Arabia to set up a clandestine programme similar to the Libyan one as well as making the country vulnerable to the withholding of American spare parts and training if diplomatic relations were to worsen. A good example of what could happen is Iran in the aftermath of the Islamic Revolution. On that occasion much of the sophisticated military equipment that had been previously acquired ceased to operate within a few months for lack of replacement spare parts.

Furthermore, it is highly doubtful that Israel would let a Saudi civilian nuclear programme evolve to the stage when the Saudis could claim even a *latent* nuclear capability under IAEA guidelines. The Israelis have clearly demonstrated in the past that they see the establishment of a nuclear programme by a country that does not entertain diplomatic relations with them as a clear red line that cannot be crossed.[36]

It should be further remembered that civilian nuclear reactors can become a major security threat to the host countries in the case of military hostilities. Even the shell of a reactor of the latest generation, if punctured by a missile or an artillery round, is likely to constitute a grave environmental hazard to the host country. This should be kept in mind when evaluating current UAE civilian nuclear projects. The UAE is one of the most vulnerable countries to an Iranian attack and a civilian reactor would constitute an easy target for Iranian short-range missiles. The short distance between Iranian shores and the territory of the UAE would make anti-missile technology almost useless.

Therefore, when looked at in the context of the balance of power in the Gulf region the possibility that the GCC states would have an interest in developing a latent nuclear capability through a civilian nuclear programme looks remote. The idea that GCC states could set one up collectively is highly unlikely. The UAE is moving towards a civilian nuclear programme individually in an incremental fashion. However, even in this case the security implications of having a civilian nuclear reactor extremely vulnerable to missile attack should not be underestimated and may deter the government unless a sustained *détente* takes hold in the Gulf.

WMD proliferation in the Middle East

Some broader considerations about the state of WMD proliferation in the Middle East are in order. This will help to shed some light on the difficult position in which the GCC member find themselves. The actual incentives and costs of proliferation in the region are frequently clouded by media reports, subsumed by benign normative considerations that characterize WMD as 'evil'. These normative judgments are not shared by regional decision-makers who think of WMD as a useful device to ameliorate their standing in the regional security complex.

More fundamentally, there are profound political differences that underlie the lack of compliance with arms control treaties and prevent the emergence of a new security architecture in the Middle East.

For example, the idea of a regional or sub-regional nuclear weapons-free zones (NWFZs) is widely touted both in media and diplomatic circles. However, the NWFZs that have been established around the world so far have been 'easy' ones where no nuclear powers were present beforehand and all states extended diplomatic recognition to each other. Furthermore, from a Realist perspective, the NWFZ covering Latin American and the Caribbean, enshrined in the Tlatelolco treaty whose protocol has been ratified by all the P5 nuclear weapon states, is located in the Western hemisphere where American hegemony was until recently virtually unchallenged.[37] In a sub-region like the Gulf, where the American security overlay is significant, but as we have seen there is still an element of resistance embodied by Iran, it is more difficult for an external power to bring to bear its hegemonic influence.

Prima facie the status of compliance with non-proliferation agreements in the Arab Middle East is not dismal. Most Arab states have signed the

Chemical Weapons Convention (CWC) and the earlier Biological Weapons Convention (BWC) and have deposited the instruments with the relevant international bodies. Those that have not signed are Sudan, Syria, Somalia, Lebanon, Libya and Egypt with regards to the CWC. With regards to the BWC all member states of the Arab League have signed. However, four of them, Syria, Somalia, Egypt and UAE, have not deposited the instruments of ratification. In the case of Syria and Egypt this last act has been explicitly linked to the behaviour of Israel. Israel has signed the CWC but has not deposited the instruments of ratification and it has not signed either the NPT or the BWC.[38]

The focus of much of the world's diplomatic activity and media attention is of course the behaviour of the two non-Arab regional powers, Iran and Israel. Their behaviour is what stands in the way of the full implementation of existing non-proliferation agreements in the Middle East. Israel has not signed the NPT and it is believed to have an extensive nuclear arsenal that crucially includes second-strike capabilities. Simultaneously, Iran, as we have seen, in terms of both declaratory policy and verified activities, is in compliance with the whole gamut of existing non-proliferation agreements. It has even signed the Additional Protocol of the NPT in 2003 as a gesture of goodwill. However, most of the international community does not trust the final goal of Iranian activities to be a peaceful nuclear programme. This is because Iran embodies a discourse of resistance to American hegemony in the region and its active support of non-state actors at war with Israel.[39]

This demonstrates how the obstacles to a Weapons of Mass Destruction Free Zone (WMDFZ) in the Middle East, far from being legal or technical, are political. Therefore, the political disputes in the region, chiefly the Arab–Israeli conflict, whose resolution has always been seen as a precondition for the establishment of a Middle East WMDFZ, are the core obstacle. Not surprisingly this indicates the primacy of politics in the realm of non-proliferation agreements in the region, which too often is disingenuously tied to issues of international law or technical verification. In other words, a technical infraction by Iran is treated by relevant international bodies in a wholly different manner from a technical infraction from South Korea. The same way as possession of intermediate ballistic missiles by North Korea is treated differently from the same British capability.[40]

This situation puts GCC governments in a difficult position as they are caught between an American military presence that is bound to be unpopular with local populations and the inability of dealing with Iran without an external security overlay.

Most Arab states, not to mention Iran, would consider the establishment of a multilateral arms control regime in the Middle East as a sign of 'normalization' with Israel. This is considered unacceptable before a comprehensive political agreement is reached.[41]

The first proposal for a Middle East NWFZ was formulated by Iran in 1974 and it received the immediate support of Egypt, but it is still viewed in Israel as a diplomatic manoeuvre aimed at compromising the security of the Jewish state. Not surprisingly, many decades later the actual implementation of an NWFZ in the region is still a remote possibility and the attention of the international community is focusing on the chances of additional proliferation.[42]

Meanwhile, the Israeli nuclear posture is regarded domestically as a success. Furthermore, the leaders who advocate territorial concessions and a return to the 1967 lines are those who always leaned towards maintaining the nuclear option indefinitely. This is in stark contrast to the political leaders who frame the issue in terms of 'defensible borders'. Therefore, in Israel it is the people pushing for a peace deal who are highlighting the strategic value of a nuclear deterrent.[43]

The Arms Control and Regional Security (ACRS) Working Group on regional security met between 1992 and 1995 and collapsed even before the end of the Oslo peace process. This demonstrates the sensitivity of the issue of a new regional security architecture in the region. And yet a new regional security compact is a necessary precondition to expand membership and the ratification of existing non-proliferation agreements. The collapse of the multilateral talks in the 1990s, though, is an indicator of the fact that a political resolution of current regional conflicts is a necessary but perhaps not a sufficient condition to achieve a WMDFZ in the Middle East. In fact, the retention of a strategic deterrent by the state of Israel could be an important card in trying to sell a peace deal to the Israeli public.[44]

This is particularly true at a time when the qualitative edge in conventional capability is eroding as other regional states gain access to sophisticated Western weaponry. Therefore, even if we conceive of the creation of a WMDFZ in the region as a process and not as a cathartic event, the resolution of current political disputes must be considered the key to initiate this process.

In conclusion, at a broader regional level there can be no progress in the direction of an NWFZ in the Middle East without a comprehensive political settlement. Many regional states still do not extend diplomatic recognition to each other and in this context agitating for an NWFZ can only be categorized as diplomatic manoeuvring. Even after a comprehensive peace process is reached Israel will probably decide to retain the current strategic deterrent capability as an insurance policy against new, more bellicose regimes coming to power in the neighbouring states. Nuclear weapons are seen as a necessity, and not only an advantage, in a tense region. Until this perception is reversed, it is difficult.

In fact, if we were to venture a prediction regarding nuclear weapons proliferation there is no ground for optimism. In addition to the much scrutinized Iranian nuclear programme, Egypt and UAE have approached the IAEA to jumpstart peaceful nuclear programmes under agency supervision. Other regional states are sure to follow leading to a more volatile situation in which these programmes start off as peaceful but there is no certainty of what is going to happen in the space of two decades. At this later date even the current signatures on the Comprehensive Test Ban Treaty (CTBT) could be called into question.

The picture is a little rosier when it comes to other WMD non-proliferation treaties. Significant work could be done with regards to the CWC and BWC. This provided that states in the region begin to recognize that setting in motion a string of commitments to non-proliferation is a common good. Additionally, normalization and communication ought to be treated as analytically different. These are two principles that are essential to further progress.

Communication should not necessitate agreement; hostilities can be resumed if a deal is not reached. However, to decouple communication analytically from normalization would be very beneficial to non-proliferation efforts. Similarly, diplomatic steps could be taken and incentives offered to have states in the region stop conceiving of adherence to non-proliferation treaties as a tit-for-tat issue. If this approach were to prevail we could have some concrete progress. Israel could sign the BWC and deposit the instruments of the CWC in order to build confidence without much prejudice to its security posture. Likewise, Syria and Egypt could deposit the instruments of these two treaties without waiting for Israel to sign the NPT. The message would simply be that chemical and biological weapons are considered unacceptable instruments of war by all states in the region.

Conversely, given the absence of a political deal, nuclear proliferation is instead too sensitive to be tackled before a comprehensive political deal is reached or at the very least diplomatic recognition is extended to each other by all states in the region.

Conclusion

Given the nature of the sub-regional security complex the possibility that GCC states could set up a nuclear programme on a multilateral basis is remote. However, there are certainly some steps that could be taken to contribute to an alleviation of tension in the Gulf. For example, Gulf Arab states could examine ways to reduce further the American footprint while maintaining the US security umbrella. So far, the United States has provided for their external security, but on a bilateral basis and to the detriment of institutional mechanisms that could alleviate some of Iran's fears. While this flexibility suits the United States and Gulf leaders well, it creates uncertainty in the region and promotes Arab Gulf lethargy in the realm of defense and strategic thinking. Until the GCC states can conceptualize their security interests in a more independent way, they will remain in the backseat. Minimizing the American footprint in the Gulf will give Arab Gulf leaders more room to manoeuvre *vis-à-vis* Iran. One needs to realize and accept that the United States need not a large ground force to deter Iran or guarantee stability in the Gulf. The current expansion of air and navy bases in Qatar, UAE and Bahrain suggests that the United States is thinking strategically about its military posture in the region. The question is how much of this change is driven by GCC preferences.

Moreover, since it is likely that in case of a showdown Iran will adopt a more aggressive rhetoric than a military posture, Arab Gulf states could harness and refine their 'soft power' tools to counter any Iranian attempt to hurt their Islamic legitimacy, and shore up their counter-terrorism capabilities. The GCC has engaged in a well-conceived public diplomacy campaign, a message that emphasizes that Iran's nuclear programme is a regional and global concern, not just a point of tension between Iran, the United States and Israel, an emphasis on Iranian past behaviour, and a careful handling of US requests, pressure and profile.

Ironically, Gulf Arab states only realize in hindsight how good they had it in the 1990s when a balance of weakness, guaranteed by the United States, was in place in the Persian Gulf. This was probably an unstable equilibrium, but in retrospect it did offer the conditions for GCC states to focus on internal matters without worrying too much about their neighbours.

It is also paradoxical that Arab Gulf states are uneasy about a genuine rapprochement between the United States and Iran or regime change in Teheran. Such an improvement may alter US preferences and entail major strategic changes in the region, and they could be on the losing side. This eventuality is remote and it ought not to affect Gulf short-term calculus. GCC states have an interest in a relative *détente* between the two countries that would allow them to focus on their economic development and reduce the dangers of domestic unrest.

While any GCC–Iran security arrangement is contingent upon an improvement in US–Iranian relations, Arab Gulf states can prepare the groundwork by engaging both parties at a more sophisticated level. In light of the discussion above the Western attempts to foster a reformist agenda on the GCC states in the wake of 11 September look disingenuous at best and potentially perilous. The NATO endeavour is the focus of the next chapter and it is a good illustration of the more general difficulty in fostering reform from the outside that has bedevilled Western decision-makers in past decades. It is striking how this simple social fact is still routinely ignored when designing outreach programmes aimed at the Arab Middle East.[45]

8

THE GCC, NATO AND THE GULF SECURITY COMPLEX

> Of course we cannot operate, let alone integrate, with the Kuwaiti or the Emirate navy. However, the Gulf is a hot point and NATO [the North Atlantic Treaty Organization] feels it is important to be there and to demonstrate a new willingness to operate out of area.[1]
>
> NATO Rear Admiral

In a previous chapter we discussed the state of GCC defense integration and we reached the conclusion that it has evolved little beyond symbolism. More importantly, we also noted how a strong bilateral link with the United States remains the fundamental security guarantee for each and every GCC member state. It is therefore pertinent to analyse a more recent trope in the Gulf security discourse, the pious hope that NATO and other multilateral organizations could have a significant role to play.[2] We could dub this as the new wave of 'multilateralitis' in Gulf security to differentiate it from previous multilateral experiments of the 1970s that, as we have seen, have not yielded any result and to infuse it with an appropriately negative connotation.

This new attempt on the part of NATO to establish a presence in the Gulf is two pronged. Firstly, there is the will to establish a multilateral strategic presence in the Gulf. It has been made clear that this will never match the Article 5 'iron clad' commitment to collective defense present in the NATO Charter and that expansion of membership to GCC states is out of the question.[3] However, a NATO presence would give the *impression* that it is not the United States, and to a lesser extent the United Kingdom and France, that is solely responsible for the external defense of the GCC states *vis-à-vis* other regional powers, Iran and possibly one day a resurgent Iraq. From this point of view the initiative is welcomed by a plurality of the GCC states as a declaratory gesture in relation to the rest of the world. The second part of the initiative is more interesting and it is worthy of close scrutiny as it is almost hubristic in its ambition. NATO aims at encouraging Security Sector Reform (SSR) in the Gulf through an initiative patterned after the Partnership for Peace (PfP) that successfully integrated a number of former Warsaw Pact members into NATO throughout the 1990s. For our purposes it is also worth noting that NATO eschewed a multilateral approach in its dealings with the GCC and decided to deal with all those that had signed up on a bilateral basis.

This chapter explores the current and future role of NATO in enacting SSR in the Gulf through the recent Istanbul Cooperation Initiative. It is grounded in recent scholarship on military reform, democratization and collective security. Enough time has elapsed since the inauguration of the initiative that an initial balance sheet can be drawn. The chapter aims at starting to fill the gap between the theoretical literature elaborated by authors who focused on other regions of the world and the reality of SSR experiments in the Gulf and in the Broader Middle East. Furthermore, from a policy point of view it explores the possibility of NATO playing a role in any of these fields of SSR in the Gulf and the Broader Middle East. The main conclusion is that the new initiative is bound to display a significant gap between policy commitment and actual implementation because of a host of political, military and historical reasons.

The NATO Istanbul Cooperation Initiative

On 29 June 2004, NATO announced at its summit in Istanbul, Turkey, a new initiative relating to the Middle East region, with an initial focus on the six countries of the Arabian peninsula, which comprise the Gulf Cooperation Council (GCC). This initiative is one of a number of outreach programmes that have been promoted by the United States and its European allies in the wake of the attacks on 11 September 2001. There are other prominent programmes of this kind. One is the Greater Middle East Initiative, later renamed the Broader Middle East and North Africa (BMENA) Initiative, that the United States government tried to organize at the level of the G8.[4] A second one is the Middle East Partnership Initiative (MEPI), which the United States manages directly through the State Department.[5] Originally the American government wanted the NATO Istanbul Cooperation Initiative (ICI) to be merged with the pre-existing Mediterranean Dialogue (MD) programme. However, its European allies, particularly the French government, expressed resistance to the idea. They considered the MD, with all its limitations that will be discussed below, as a program that was already functional while the new initiative was seen as something still tentative. Following this pressure the decision to keep the two initiatives separate was adopted by the NATO Supreme Council.[6]

The common denominator of all these programs is the intention to spread democracy and rule of law throughout the Arab Middle East, having identified their absence as one of the primary factors behind the geopolitical instability of the region. The size and ambition of these programmes have been considerably scaled back after the first few years and it became clear that they were viewed with extreme scepticism in the region (and beyond) and the problems arising from regime change in Iraq have given some pause to decision-makers in NATO countries. However, these programmes, particularly those promoted at the multilateral level, are bound to survive in modified form because of a mixture of bureaucratic inertia and vested interest on the part of the organizations involved.

In its ICI, NATO focused specifically on the topic of SSR, identifying it as a building block for democracy building in the Gulf. From a functional point of view NATO aims to offer a rich menu of options for training and collaboration on topics ranging from counterterrorism to greater transparency in defense budgeting and decision-making.[7] As we already mentioned the new partnership project is explicitly modelled after the PfP aimed at countries that were former members of the Warsaw Pact that was implemented during the 1990s.[8] The other example held forth is the 13-year-old MD. Four GCC states – Kuwait, Bahrain, Qatar and the United Arab Emirates (UAE) – initially adhered to the initiative. Saudi Arabia, the bigger GCC country, keeps being courted by NATO. 'I do want to stress here today that NATO would very much value the participation of Saudi Arabia', NATO Deputy Secretary General Alessandro Minuto Rizzo said at a meeting with Gulf Arab states in the Saudi capital on 22 January 2007.[9]

NATO is certainly driven by the post-Cold War need to define new missions for the alliance. Building on its work with the former Soviet states, NATO has become more confident about its ability to offer practical security assistance to countries beyond the European landmass. The old confinement of operations 'North of the Tropic of Cancer', always tenuous at best, completely vanished with the Alliance conducting a major operation in Afghanistan and mooting a possible logistical role in Sudan. This in addition to the crucial role being played in the Balkans, an area of operation more congruous with its historical mission.[10]

The PfP that involved former members of the Warsaw Pact did indeed yield some excellent results. Member countries undertook a specific set of political pledges, such as commitment to the rule of law and a democratic framework. In particular, they made specific commitments closer to areas of traditional NATO concern such as transparency in national defense planning and budgeting. The set of practical activities included in the bilateral individual partnership programmes ranging from securing weapon stockpiles to anti-mine activities, touching on fields such as air defense and naval exercises. The ultimate aim is to promote the development of effective defense institutions that are under civilian and democratic control and that are capable of cooperating with NATO forces if the need arises.

However, it is highly doubtful whether NATO experience in Eastern Europe will prove a useful guide in building a partnership with GCC countries. The approach taken so far by NATO officials in charge of the initiative makes a brave assumption, namely that these countries are eager to jettison the legacy of the past and are in favour of modernizing their security apparatuses along Western lines in the near term. However, as we have seen in previous chapters, rulers of GCC states adhere to an extremely gradual model of reform that is dictated endogenously. The idea that this change can be dictated, or even strongly supported, from the outside is perceived as very problematic.[11] The premise of NATO officials is that this is a demand-driven process. However, it should be investigated whether the four GCC countries that accepted the initiative did so under the impression that they were accepting an offer that they could not refuse in the current political climate and in particular as a result of the Global War on Terror, then referred to as the Long War.

Furthermore, the fact that political reform could in fact 'spill over' from SSR is even more remote. In fact, it is likely that the security sector, widely considered in the region and elsewhere as a defining feature of sovereignty, will be the last to be put up for reform. This does not mean that there is not a big role for outsiders to play. The British played a crucial role in setting up the security sectors in Oman and Bahrain; the United States had a vital role in assisting Saudi Arabia in the organization of its defense. At a more tactical level, it may be enough to mention the group of hastily converted French commandos who raided the Great Mosque of Mecca after it was seized on 20 November 1979 by several hundred militants led by Juhayman al-Utaybi.[12]

In the past though, this collaboration had always been conducted as discreetly as possible. The NATO initiative with its strong public diplomacy component marked a strong discontinuity with previous Western security initiatives in the Gulf and is in contradiction with the traditional US Central Command (CENTCOM) policy of having as small a 'footprint' in the area as possible. The consequences of such an approach ought to have been to be thoroughly investigated. Instead, the dominant attitude within NATO seems to have been *omnia munda mundis*, i.e. since our intentions are good there is nothing to worry about and, on the contrary, we should actively propagandize our new found role in the region.[13]

An issue of incentives: do efficient, professional armies make sense for GCC states?

At an even broader level, as we have seen in a previous chapter, it is very doubtful that it would make sense for GCC states to create efficient armies capable of cooperating fully with NATO to face a variety of threats. The risks that GCC regimes would incur in setting up effective standing armies clearly outweigh the benefits that could be gained in military efficiency. The traditional separation between regular army and 'national guard' and other separate units such as tribal levies, whose most conspicuous examples can be found in Saudi Arabia and in the UAE, is bound to endure. GCC officials often pride themselves in working for states that constitute one of the few areas that has been 'revolution-free' in Eurasia in the last 70 years. They are absolutely correct. It is important to note, though, that this important result has been achieved by carefully managing the security sector so that it will not pose a threat to the ruling regimes.

Indeed, an overview of the history of the Arab Middle East in the last 50 years demonstrates that monarchical regimes have many reasons to fear professional armies.[14] An interesting exception is Jordan where the monarchy successfully blended tribal elements in its military establishment while preserving a good degree of operational efficiency. However, a close look at how this was achieved demonstrates that few of the elements of that experience are replicable in GCC states. King Saddam Hussein took outmost care all his life to nurture his ties with the military establishment, chiefly drawn from Trans-Jordanian elements of society.[15] Unlike its GCC counterparts the Jordanian army never had to rely on rank-and-file soldiers drawn from abroad, even if it benefited greatly from British officering in the first 30 years of its life. On the contrary, to this very day most GCC armies include a percentage of Pakistani and other foreign soldiers. This makes the Jordanian army a much more versatile instrument than most of its GCC counterparts.[16] Furthermore, King Saddam Hussein has always styled himself a soldier and has maintained the closest possible relationship with the military. In the Gulf this may be said of Shaikh Mohammad bin Rashed and Sultan Qabus, but not of the other rulers.[17] The two monarchs had a close relationship throughout the 1980s and collaborated on security matters. However, given the specific experience of state formation in Jordan, it would be very difficult to replicate national security establishment along Jordanian lines in the other GCC states.[18]

NATO experience in Eastern Europe: not an apt precedent

The ultimate objective of SSR is often defined as being the creation of armed, uniformed forces and security services that are functionally differentiated, professional forces under objective and subjective civilian control, at the lowest functional level of resources.[19] If we take these criteria as benchmarks it is immediately apparent how far we are from such a situation in all GCC states. In fact, it would be very difficult to retain objective and subjective civilian control while building up professional forces that are capable of integrating seamlessly with NATO assets. Furthermore, the idea that this can be achieved 'at the lowest functional level of resources' betrays a fundamental misunderstanding of what drives the procurement policies of most GCC states. Procurement in GCC states is as much a foreign policy tool as it is an instrument of defense policy.

The rationale behind the setup of the GCC security sector

Judging from the remarks of NATO Secretary General Jaap de Hoop Scheffer and other senior NATO officials it transpires that the ICI is driven by a fundamental misunderstanding of the rationale behind the current organizational structure of GCC armed forces and security services.[20] This is a misunderstanding that GCC government officials have an interest in fostering as they strive to appear keen in participating in these reform initiatives whilst concurrently prolonging indefinitely the dialogue with NATO. In fact, it would be curious if GCC officials were to internalize the strong normative component inherent in the NATO initiative. The case of Ukraine, which was involved in a bilateral partnership programme, is explicitly heralded by NATO officials as a successful precedent for NATO-inspired SSR reform. However, that example clearly elucidates the fundamental misunderstanding at the heart of this latest initiative. In the aftermath of the Cold War Ukrainians were ready to jettison a legacy of totalitarianism. The defense sector in particular had to be reinvented from scratch after the dissolution of the Soviet Union. This process was greatly aided by the eventual prize of NATO membership, something that is explicitly not on offer to GCC states.[21] In fact, it is difficult to fathom why the six GCC states would yearn for radical reform. Gulf rulers ought to be quite satisfied with the way they managed their countries in such a turbulent region since independence. Saudi Arabia in particular has a long, independent history and rightly values its bilateral defense ties with the United States. For example, the Saudi National Guard has been trained by the Vinnell Corporation since 1975.[22] In terms of external security, it is not clear what a multilateral umbrella could add to the package apart from all the chicanery and tortuousness in decision-making that are now on display in the case of the Afghanistan mission. As for SSR, Gulf countries quite simply do not have a domestic incentive to change as current arrangements have proved their worth throughout the last few decades.

It is not a coincidence that NATO's MD, which was initiated in 1994, has dragged on for more than ten years with few tangible results. It is noteworthy that the seven partner countries involved in this dialogue – Algeria, Egypt, Israel, Jordan, Mauritania, Morocco and Tunisia – are generally considered better candidates for SSR than the four GCC countries involved in the ICI. The regimes of these GCC countries take comfort in this lack of genuine results as they speculate that the initiative will be kept at the level of an interesting dialogue without the need for them to enact reforms that would be costly in terms of political capital.

For example, there are very good reasons why defense budgeting, whose transparency is one of the avowed objectives of the ICI initiative, is opaque in GCC states. It provides one of the main sources of patronage for influential members of the royal families. Even more specifically 'commissions' for cabinet members brokering the deals are significant.[23] Another good reason for the acquisition of very sophisticated weapon systems that do not seem to be operable in any given scenario is that it constitutes a sort of 'insurance policy' underwritten by major Western powers. There is therefore an expectation gap between NATO officials and representatives of the four ICI countries with regards to the final goals of the initiative. This aspect ought to have been investigated before considerable resources were devoted to the programme.

Furthermore, the initiative risks to have some moderately negative consequences at the domestic political level. We have seen how in the case of Mauritania, which incidentally is located more than 1000 km from Mediterranean shores, the issue of NATO membership has turned into a domestic political football. The government utilized it to claim that they are acting with the implicit approval of the 'powers that be', chiefly the United States, and the opposition denounced membership in the MD as a sign that governing forces are subservient to the United States. The issue has acquired symbolic significance and it is at the centre of bitter contestation between government and opposition.[24] Of course the similarities should not be overemphasized, but it is easy to see how the Islamist opposition in GCC countries, far more effective than its liberal counterpart, would quickly move to exploit the situation. It is noteworthy that in the case of Jordan there has clearly been no distinction drawn between NATO and the United States at the level of public opinion. NATO is associated with the United States in all its good and bad aspects. It is therefore puzzling that the NATO ICI initiative explicitly incorporates a strong public diplomacy component.[25] If there is something that NATO can contribute, a fairly doubtful proposition in itself, it would be better provided in a very low-key manner.

Another factor that should give pause for thought when considering this NATO ICI is that after it started to become clear that the initiative was not going to yield concrete results in the foreseeable future, various NATO actors re-elaborated its aims according to their particular interest. Therefore, for example, Italian officials would cheerfully admit off the record that they did not expect these countries to change the fundamental nature of their security sectors. However, they pointed out that this would be a good way for Italy to gain a role in the lucrative GCC arms trade while lacking the strong bilateral ties that France and the UK, not to mention the United States, have long enjoyed in the Gulf. The same sentiment is expressed by officials from newer NATO members such as the Czech Republic and Poland.[26] The fact that NATO officials from different countries express dissimilar views on the nature of NATO ICI is the sign of a troubled initiative.

When asked directly NATO military leaders quickly acknowledge the limited military value of the whole enterprise. A leading NATO Rear-Admiral discussing the issue under Chatham House rules (which do not allow his remarks to be directly attributed to him) had this to say about the NATO ICI initiative: 'It is a political initiative, there is no gain in military terms', further adding, 'it was very difficult to integrate even a single Russian ship in Operation Active Endeavor in the Mediterranean but the political significance of a Russian ship showing the flag in Naples is huge'. Finally he concluded,

> Of course we cannot operate, let alone integrate, with the Kuwaiti or the Emirate navy. However, the Gulf is a hot point and NATO feels it is

important to be there and to demonstrate a new willingness to operate out of area. [...] I feel that the North of the Tropic of Cancer limitations are now irrelevant.[27]

This particular set of remarks is just an explicit rendition of a sentiment that is very widespread in the military wing of the alliance. The NATO ICI initiative is seen as something that will be relevant in political terms even if militarily it will not make much of a difference. Therefore, one is led to believe that the whole initiative has much less to do with actual concern for the state of the security sector in the GCC states and a lot more with the need to find a new role for the alliance. However, it appears as if NATO has already has its hands full as it tries to win a decisive victory in Afghanistan. After regime change in Iraq and the continuous upheavals in Lebanon and the Palestinian territories, GCC states are among the few stable allies the United States can count on in the Arab Middle East. The new NATO ICI initiative will certainly not yield any significant advantage to either NATO or the GCC states. More worryingly, it has the potential of upsetting the fairly robust domestic political balances in these countries.

In fact, the initial requests lodged by the four participating Gulf countries demonstrate the hollowness of the initiative even from a technical point of view. The four countries have requested border surveillance equipment and assistance in setting up domestic security operations, which was indeed one of the fields specifically mentioned by the ICI policy document. These requests mirror those made by Jordan in the context of its bilateral relations with NATO. However, these are fields in which NATO has little to offer the new partners.

Conclusion

The NATO ICI initiative is certainly *mostly representational* in nature. Military officers are very sceptical of the eventual synergies emanating from it. So far it has resulted, as predicted, in a conscious gap between half-hearted policy commitments and their poor implementation on the part of GCC states. The results of the MD after many years in terms of military integration and interoperability are there to testify to the *mostly symbolic nature* of these partnerships. The initiative did indeed yield some *symbolic* results. However, these worked in the opposite direction to those intended by the promoters of the initiative. In particular, Gulf governments taking part in the initiative are perceived by the public as even more tied to the United States than they already were. The idea that a multilateral umbrella can in some way smooth the current perception of dependency is misplaced. The case of Jordan is there to demonstrate this fact.

It is not surprising then that the two GCC states that are stronger militarily, Saudi Arabia and Oman, have not joined the initiative. They were the ones that had the diplomatic and military wherewithal to refuse the NATO entreaties.

The NATO ICI initiative has not contributed significantly to the enhancement of Gulf security. In the dreadful hypothesis of a military confrontation with Iran, there will certainly not be a consultation at the NATO level to decide how to move forward and to organize the defense of GCC states. These decisions will be taken by American officials in bilateral consultation with GCC governments, as has been done in the past. NATO and the United States are in any case likely to be conflated in the perception of most people in the Gulf, as it has already happened in Jordan.

Furthermore, NATO's ICI initiative has not spurred a wave of SSR in GCC countries. As we have seen in previous chapters the rulers of these states know what is in their best interest when organizing the security sectors of their countries. The attitude of NATO officials, who are acting in good faith, is naïve and can at times be categorized as patronizing. The comparison with the successful PfP is misleading at best given the completely different, economic, social and political context.

CONCLUSION

There is a growing body of literature highlighting the renewed importance of regionalism in world politics.[1] It is often stated that the erosion of state power *vis-à-vis* multiple globalization processes points to the need to take back the political initiative by bringing states together. The identification of this 'urge to merge', though, cannot be carried out without taking into account the specific nature of the constituent states embarking on a given regionalist enterprise.[2]

States may all perform, or try to perform, the same functions, but they do that in very different ways from a cultural and institutional point of view and this is reflected in the nature of their regionalist undertakings. The case of the Arab states of the Gulf is not an exception from this point of view and throughout my research I realized that it would be very difficult to understand the workings of such an organization without a clear grasp of the way policy is formulated at the domestic level in the six constituent states. Furthermore, the GCC is an example of how an organization can change over time as the interests of the member states vary and, in the case of the GCC, often diverge.

Processes of 'transnationalism' that bring business and civil actors together are also increasingly identified as pivotal in international relations giving rise to a feeling of 'regioness' that is independent of the workings of regional institution or at least partially detached from them.[3] Even in this case, though, comparative area knowledge is essential as civic organizations and business actors vary widely in their practices, not least according to whether they operate in an autocratic or a democratic environment. In the Arab Middle East an integrated labour market was created in the 1970s and this led to an influx of Arab workers to the Gulf. Immigration and labour policies are sensitive issues from both an economic and security point of view for the Gulf Arab monarchies and it is interesting to see how these states have trod very lightly in delegating powers to the regional level when dealing with these matters.

In this work I analysed the Gulf Cooperation Council (GCC) from an historical and an institutional point of view. I also assessed the role it played in the international relations of the Gulf. I came to the conclusion that the analytical tools used to assess other regional organizations, in particular the European Union, limit our understanding of the GCC with the analytical tools developed to determine the progress and scope of all other regional organizations and in particular the European Union. I also discussed what role the organization and its constituent states play in the international relations of the Gulf and specifically how they relate to regional and global powers.

The actual workings of the organization and its policy output disprove both obsequious and disparaging readings. The GCC is a sub-regional forum devoid of any supranational powers. It operates according to rules of the game that very much reflect those that predominate in its member states. It would actually be surprising if things were different. One cannot expect regional structures and institutions to replicate smoothly around the world.

Therefore, avid proponents of regionalism in the Gulf, who somehow expect best practice and transparency in the field of governance to percolate down from the GCC to the domestic level, will be disappointed. In fact it will be difficult to find transparency and efficiency within the General Secretariat itself. Equally, though, cynical observers have to marvel at the resilience and flexibility of this organization. It has to be acknowledged that what did not work at the Pan-Arab level may very well work in a sub-regional setting.

Moreover, as we have seen in the initial chapters, the frequent parallel with the workings of federalism in the United Arab Emirates (UAE) are also misguided. The UAE federation, despite some sycophantic claims to the contrary, would have never come about without the oversight and encouragement of Britain, the departing colonial power. On the contrary, the creation of the GCC was the sovereign decision of independent states. The tension between individual Emirates and the Federal government has come to characterize politics in the UAE.[4] Within the GCC that problem never arose as the General Secretariat was never delegated any supranational powers.

As for the interaction between leaders, GCC decision-making reflects the 'rules of shaikhly exchange' that are proper to the domestic institutions of the constituent states.[5] It would be wrong to dismiss the organization because of the lack of follow-up by the General Secretariat and its other bodies over treaties such as the Unified Economic Agreement or the inconsistency of its common defense pact. GCC countries are aware, even if they are coy about expressing this publicly, that they will never achieve self-sufficiency in external defense matters. They will always require the presence of an out-of-area hegemony to balance the power of Iran and, in the long run, of a reconstituted Iraq. The external balancing power is currently the United States and it is likely that it will play such a role for the foreseeable future.

The 'turning east' policy of the GCC states and the recent infatuation with the possibility of China playing a more substantive role in Gulf security has more to do with frustration at the output of American policy in the region than with a cool-headed analysis of available security options. If seen from this point of view the lack of integration and interoperability achieved by the GCC armies individually in their long history can be seen as the natural extension of an awareness that self-sufficiency in the realm of external defense is a chimera. From the point of view of regime security the risks that GCC regimes would incur in setting up effective standing armies clearly outweigh the benefits that could be gained in military efficiency as professional armies have a long history of mounting military coups in the region.

Slightly more problematic are the meagre results obtained in the field of economic cooperation. This is a field where more could certainly be done without directly jeopardizing the security of the ruling families. It is no coincidence that this is the issue area where the Secretariat has made the utmost effort to make individual GCC governments stick to their commitments. The complete overhaul of the GCC Economic Agreement adopted at the 22nd Session of the Supreme Council in December 2001 is a testament to the considerable efforts of successive GCC functionaries. The emphasis on deadline and benchmarks marked a radical departure from previous GCC efforts in this field. And yet the customs union proved elusive for so many years and after coming into effect it was compromised in fewer than three years by the signing of a number of bilateral free trade agreements on the part of single GCC states.

Even in the economic field, though, it is difficult to expect more from the rulers of GCC states. Their regimes are buttressed by what Tim Niblock aptly labels eudemonic legitimacy, stemming from the ability to deliver policies, welfare and performance which the population seeks.[6] The upsetting of some of their domestic constituencies in the name of a more balanced economic system is a risky undertaking. In any case, when compared with the massive effect of Dutch disease on all the GCC economies, the lack of integration is probably a minor impediment.

Likewise, the feebleness of GCC institutions has to be seen in light of the limited scope of institutionalization at the domestic level. We can consider for example the recurrent practice of settling business disputes through extrajudicial settlements whenever possible. This practice is rooted in history and to this very day resorting to courts of law is seen as a last recourse by business elites in the Gulf. It is then easier to understand why the GCC court for the settlement of border disputes between member states was never set up even if it was explicitly envisaged by the Charter of the organization.

During the Iran–Iraq War the organization served an important role in providing diplomatic cover to smaller GCC states that wanted to hedge their bets *vis-à-vis* the two belligerent powers by letting them adopt collectively a far more pro-Iraqi position that they would on a bilateral basis.

Throughout the 1990s the organization has played an important role in spearheading renewed diplomatic efforts in putting the dispute over the islands of Abu Musa and the two Tunbs firmly on the diplomatic agenda of the Gulf. This followed the unilateral rejection by Iran of the pre-existing Memorandum of Understanding (MoU) in 1992. Even in this case the organization was useful as it allowed individual member states to calibrate their diplomatic positions according to whether they were acting on a bilateral or a multilateral basis.

When acting as a locus for settlement of disputes amongst member states and as a single block in trade negotiations the organization has proved less successful than in diplomatic matters. This should not come as a surprise, though, given the sensibility over sovereignty displayed by each of the 'six' and the lack of supranational powers entrusted to the General Secretariat and other institutions. It will be interesting to see if, as political liberalization slowly progresses in individual member states, this reluctance will increase or diminish. The answer to this question will probably verge on whether the political trajectories of individual member states will start diverging widely. If, for example, Kuwait surpasses the tipping point and moves from liberalized autocracy to limited democracy, while other GCC states move more cautiously along the continuum, or even in the opposite direction, we should not expect the GCC Secretariat to be entrusted with more authority.

Such reasoning brings us also to the question of GCC expansion that we see surfacing from time to time as part of debates in the region. The very slow and deliberate, and ultimately stalled, inclusion of Yemen in certain functional committees underlies the difficulty in bringing in new member states that differ markedly at the level of domestic institutions from the six original founders.[7] Having examined how GCC decision-making closely resembles the way decisions are taken at the domestic level in the six member states, it is very difficult to envisage expansion of the GCC in future. In particular, the prospect that Iran and Iraq may one day become members of the organization as it turns into a collective security vehicle is very remote. A shared political culture lies at the basis of this particular sub-regional organization.

Overall, the GCC has proved very useful as a forum for policy coordination by the six member states. Even more importantly it has served as an important functional vehicle to spread best practice within government departments of all six member states or at least to create close functional links between them. Countless meetings at the GCC level have left their marks on the ministries of all the six states. The gamut of issue areas covered by these meetings is impressive and relations between professional counterparts are enhanced on a regular basis.[8]

This contributed decisively to the creation of a *khaliji* persona in international relations. The GCC, as its first Secretary General, Abdullah Bishara, is justifiably proud to point out, has contributed to create the 'Gulf' category in international politics. In other words, the GCC has helped reshape the cognitive boundaries of diplomats and other international relations practitioners.

Therefore, in spite of the institutional setbacks, we can safely conclude that the GCC has had a benign effect on the international relations of the Gulf for much of its history. From a diplomatic point of view it has allowed smaller member states to take diplomatic cover during major crises, and it has constituted a tool for more nuanced stances and multipronged approaches, sending varied messages to different audiences. Furthermore, it has enabled functional cooperation over a wide range of topics and it has led to a number of successes in the economic realm.

However, regime change in Iraq in 2003 and the US–Iran confrontation about the latter's nuclear programme have partially changed the face of international relations in the Gulf. Area specialists too often tend to identify some 'ground rules' and to stick to them.[9] This is a natural reaction to the crude, agenda-driven analysis found in many newspapers and think tank reports. The latter seem to release new overarching theories with uncanny regularity as their purpose is to influence the decision-making process. However, Even area specialists should remain open to the possibility that change actually takes place in security complexes even if in a more nuanced and textured way than partisan analysts purport. Otherwise, the risk of not being able to appropriately redraw our cognitive boundaries so as to account for change remains. Often times, practitioners who have their ears closer to the ground are faster at doing this. The parameters of Gulf security are changing, albeit in a slow, measured fashion.

Recent events in the Gulf and the commotion they have engendered throughout the Middle East, and indeed the world, mean that the GCC will face a number of challenges as it navigates the third decade of its existence. Single GCC states are starting to behave more as individual actors on a global stage. The signing of a bilateral free trade agreement with the United States by Bahrain, the most dependent of the 'six' on Saudi benevolence, is a dramatic departure from notions of deference to Saudi leadership. Even if the military intervention of March 2011 by Saudi and Emirati forces calls into question this renewed agency in the economic field. Qatar is sheltering behind the massive military presence on its territory to conduct a foreign policy that can be characterized as bold and independent. Dubai epitomizes the global city-state and while it still has to act within UAE federal constraints particularly in financial matters, it certainly pays little attention to sub-regional organizations such as the GCC. The rules of what Abdullah Bishara called a 'gentlemen's club' and its ways of doing business seem to be steadily eroding. The notion of Saudi leadership is increasingly defied and disagreements are surfacing in public in a way that would have been unthinkable in the 1980s.

Furthermore, the domestic political trajectories of the single GCC states, which have always been different, are starting to diverge in a fairly dramatic fashion. The five smaller GCC states are liberalizing their political systems, with Kuwait moving quite rapidly along the continuum from liberalized autocracy to constitutional monarchy. They are doing it at different speeds to be sure and in very different ways. Conversely, Saudi Arabia, bigger and more complicated than its neighbours, does not seem to be moving decisively in any particular direction, with a political arena in which traditionalists, Islamists and (far less influential) liberals try to influence the agenda of the royal family. The diverse morphology of the GCC that has always been evident in terms of economics and security is now taking shape even in the political realm.

This widening gap between the political systems of the 'six' has already started to influence the workings of the GCC and it will inevitably do so even more in the future. It will be interesting to see if the organization will be able to find a new equilibrium or whether its role will become increasingly ceremonial as parliaments in some of the member states gain influence and visibility and demand a say in foreign policy decision-making.

At a broader level we are witnessing the hollowing out of the regional dimension in the Gulf as even smaller GCC states start dealing directly with the powers of the day. The two foremost challenges facing the Gulf – the fate of post-Ba'thist Iraq and the confrontation over the Iranian nuclear programme – are truly global in character. This threatens the GCC with the spectre of double redundancy. From the point of view of economic integration it is difficult to envisage Dubai submitting to the constraints of multilateral negotiations as it vigorously pursues its 'developmentalist' policies and strengthens its status as a global city. In defense matters the traditional need to assemble around the core provided by Saudi Arabia, in a true neorealist fashion, always ambivalent at best, is slowly waning. Bilateral basing arrangements and defense treaties with the United States provide all the hard security needed for the smaller GCC states. Domestic reservations, considerable in Saudi Arabia, are a relatively small price to pay for the other five GCC states.

The GCC as an organization will have to react to these challenges by displaying considerable flexibility and ingeniousness if it wants to stay relevant even only as a diplomatic forum. A close examination of the GCC's history and its past role demonstrates also how moot the talk of a new Gulf security architecture is as long as the same key political issues are not solved. As we have seen the GCC has hardly been able to convey a unitary message during its existence. The idea that a security forum patterned after the Organisation for Economic Co-operation and Development (OECD) can be created that encompasses the foremost regional power, Iran, and a renewed Iraq appears remote at best.[10] Briefly, the dilemma of Gulf security can thus be summarized: GCC states will not sit down with Iran to talk seriously about a new security compact without the presence of the United States. Conversely, Iranians demand the withdrawal of all foreign forces before a new security architecture can be agreed upon. This is a basic difference that is too often glossed over by analysts who are eager to see the international relations of the Gulf evolving in a less confrontational direction. The hope is that this study, in addition to assessing the past role of the GCC, has contributed to clarify what are the stark political realities facing the 'six' as they chart their course in the new century.

NOTES

Introduction

1. Crown Prince Abdullah of Saudi Arabia, 30 December 2001.
2. GCC Secretariat, *The Cooperation Council Charter* (Riyadh, GCC Printing Press, 1990). For an English translation, see GCC Secretariat, 'Charter of the GCC', *American–Arab Affairs*, no. 7/Winter (1983–84), pp.157–62.
3. For a solid, theoretically informed discussion of the value of symbols in Arab politics, see Barnett, Michael N., *Dialogues in Arab Politics: Negotiations in Regional Order* (New York, NY, Columbia University Press, 1998), esp. ch.8.
4. For a discussion of this trend, particularly in the field of security, see Barnett, Michael N. and Gause III, F. Gregory, 'Caravans in opposite directions: society, state, and the development of community in the Gulf Cooperation Council', in Adler, Emanuel and Barnett, Michael N. (eds), *Security Communities*. Cambridge Studies in International Relations (Cambridge, Cambridge University Press, 1998).
5. The classic collection of studies on 'new regionalism' is Hettne, Björn, Inotai, Andr and Sunkel, Osvaldo (eds), *Studies in New Regionalism*, Vols I–V (London, MacMillan, 1999–2001). For an interesting collection of case studies and key thematic issues, see also Farrell, Mary, Hettne, Björn and van Langenhove, Luk (eds), *Global Politics of Regionalism: Theory and Practice* (London, Pluto, 2005).
6. Highly critical studies of various aspects of the GCC include Schofield, Richard N., 'Border disputes in the Gulf: past, present, and future', in Sick, Gary G. and Potter, Lawrence G. (eds), *The Persian Gulf at the Millennium: Essays in Politics, Economy, Security, and Religion* (Houndmills, MacMillan, 1997); and Koppers, Simon, *Economic Analysis and Evaluation of the Gulf Cooperation Council (GCC)*. European University Studies: Series V Economics and Management, Vol. 1783 (Frankfurt am Main, Peter Lang, 1995); and, to a lesser extent, Nakhleh, Emile A., *The Gulf Cooperation Council: Policies, Problems and Prospects* (New York, NY, Praeger, 1986). Additionally, many scholars of the Gulf region are implicitly dismissive of the organization. They focus on some of the fields, such as security or economics, that fall within its brief without even mentioning its existence. The influence of the organization on these matters is considered negligible and even the prospect of coordination among its member states is discounted. See, for example, Cordesman, Anthony H., *The Gulf and the West: Strategic Relations and Military Realities* (London, Mansell, 1988); and Cordesman, Anthony H., *After the Storm: The Changing Military Balance in the Middle East* (Boulder, CO, Westview, 1993); or Crystal, Jill, *Oil and Politics in the*

Gulf: Rulers and Merchants in Kuwait and Qatar (Cambridge, Cambridge University Press, 1990). Even more critical and innovative studies of the international politics of the Gulf largely ignore the organization, for example Adib-Moghaddam, Arshin, *The International Politics of the Persian Gulf: A Cultural Genealogy* (London, Routledge, 2006).

7. For example, Peterson, Erik R., *The Gulf Cooperation Council: Search for Unity in a Dynamic Region* (Boulder, CO, Westview, 1988); and Sandwick, John A., *The Gulf Cooperation Council: Moderation and Stability in an Interdependent World* (Boulder, CO, Westview, 1987).
8. For example, Said Zahlan, Rosemarie, *The Making of the Modern Gulf States*, 2nd edn (Reading, Ithaca Press, 1998); or Cordesman: *After the Storm*.
9. For a contrary view on the nature of these organizations, see Peterson: *Gulf Cooperation Council*.
10. Charles Tripp makes this point with regards to all regional experiments in the Middle East in his 'Regional organizations in the Arab Middle East', in Hurrell, Andrew and Fawcett, Louise L'E. (eds), *Regionalism in World Politics: Regional Organization and International Order* (New York, NY, Oxford University Press, 1995), pp.283–309 (p.301).
11. For a good account of regionalism in a theoretical perspective, see Hurrell, Andrew, 'Regionalism in theoretical perspective', in Hurrell, Andrew and Fawcett, Louise L'E. (eds), *Regionalism in World Politics: Regional Organization and International Order* (New York, NY, Oxford University Press, 1995).
12. For such views, see Tripp: 'Regional organizations in the Arab Middle East'; Acharya, Amitav, *The Gulf Cooperation Council and Security: Dilemmas of Dependence 1981–1988* (London, Gulf Centre for Strategic Studies, 1989); and Green, Jerrold D., 'Gulf Security without the Gulf States', *Harvard Journal of World Affairs*, iv/1 (1995), pp.78–89.
13. Barnett and Gause: 'Caravans in opposite directions'.
14. Al-Kuwaiz, Abdullah Ibrahim, 'Economic integration of the Cooperation Council of the Arab States of the Gulf: challenges, achievements and future outlook', in Sandwick, John A. (ed.), *The Gulf Cooperation Council: Moderation and Stability in an Interdependent World* (Boulder, CO, Westview, 1987), pp.71–85 (p.77).
15. Ramazani, R. K., *The Gulf Cooperation Council: Record and Analysis* (Charlottesville, VA, University Press of Virginia, 1988), p.102.
16. Rieger, Hans C., 'Basic issues of ASEAN economic co-operation', in Koppers, Simon (ed.), *Growth Determinants in East and South-East Asian Economies* (Berlin, Duncker & Humblot, 1991), pp.215–38 (p.229).
17. The former Secretary General of the organization, Abdullah Bishara, acknowledged that the Saudi-based force was 'symbolic' in nature; Peterson, J. E., 'The GCC and regional security', in Sandvwick, John A. (ed.), *The Gulf Cooperation Council: Moderation and Stability in an Interdependent World* (Boulder, CO, Westview, 1987), p.197.
18. The best account is Kapiszewski, Andrzej, *Nationals and Expatriates: Population and Labour Dilemmas of the Gulf Cooperation Council States* (Reading, Ithaca Press, 2001). For an interesting argument that links demographic reality and security in the case of the UAE, see also Davidson, Christopher M., *Dubai: The Vulnerability of Success* (New York, NY, Columbia University Press, 2008).

19. For the concept of rentier state and rentier society, see the excellent contributions by Giacomo Luciani and Hazem Beblawi in Luciani, Giacomo (ed.), *The Arab State* (Berkeley, CA, University of California Press, 1990).
20. In March 1991 the six GCC nations, Egypt and Syria formulated the 'Damascus Declaration' that announced plans to establish a regional peace-keeping force. A few months later, Egypt and Syria announced the withdrawal from the project citing disagreements over the size of their forces to be stationed by the two states on the Arabian peninsula and the amount of money they were to receive for such a service. Since then, from time to time, the countries' parties to the declaration have reaffirmed the willingness to provide each other with mutual military support if needed, but no Egyptian or Syrian contingent has been dispatched to the Gulf letalone a joint force being established.
21. Cordesman, Anthony H., 'U.S. forces in the Middle East: resources and capabilities', in Cordesman, Anthony H. (ed.), *Csis Middle East Dynamic Net Assessment* (Boulder, CO, Westview, 1997), p.6.
22. Acharya: *Gulf Cooperation Council and Security*, p.21.
23. Twinam, Joseph W., *The Gulf, Cooperation and the Council* (Washington, DC, Middle East Policy Council, 1992), p.129.

Chapter 1 The Creation of the United Arab Emirates and the First Integration Experiments of the Arab States of the Gulf

1. Ronald H. M. Boyle, British political agent in Doha, Qatar, commenting on the prospects of a Union of Arab Emirates in 1968; Public Records Office/Foreign and Commonwealth Office [hereafter FCO] 8/12.
2. Balfour-Paul, Glen, *The End of Empire in the Middle East* (Cambridge, Cambridge University Press, 1991), p.120. Also interview with Glen Balfour-Paul, Exeter, 7 July 1999. For the original dispatches of Sir William, see FCO 7/12, 8/12. Some of this material has subsequently been discussed, from the point of view of British Imperial history, in Smith, Simon C., *Britain's Revival and Fall in the Gulf: Kuwait, Bahrain, Qatar, and the Trucial States, 1950–71* (New York, NY, RoutledgeCurzon, 2004). For the latter part of the decade, see Al-Saud, Faisal bin Salman, *Iran, Saudi Arabia and the Gulf: Power Politics in Transition 1968–1971* (London, I.B.Tauris, 2003); and for an earlier historical overview of the dealings between the United Kingdom and what would become its protected states in the Gulf, see Al-Qasimi, Muhammad, *The Myth of Arab Piracy in the Gulf*, 2nd edn (London, Routledge, 1988); and Onley, James, *The Arabian Frontier of the British Raj: Merchants, Rulers, and the British in the Nineteenth-Century Gulf* (Oxford, Oxford University Press, 2007). A crucial point of reference remains Lienhardt, Peter and al-Shahi, Ahmed, *Shaikhdoms of Eastern Arabia*. St Antony's Series (Basingstoke, Palgrave, 2001).
3. Saudi Arabia at the time laid claims on about half the territory of present-day Abu Dhabi. Border disputes plague the relations of the Arab monarchies of the Gulf to this day.
4. These were Bahrain, Qatar and the seven Trucial States of Dubai, Abu Dhabi, Sharjah, Ajman, Umm al Qaiwain, Fujairah and Ra's al Khaimah. Oman had a

slightly different legal status but still enjoyed very close ties with Britain which managed its external affairs.

5. The traditional narrative on the establishment of the GCC is found in almost all books dealing with the subject, including: Zahlan, Said, *The Making of the Modern Gulf States*, 2nd edn (Reading, Ithaca Press, 1998); Heard-Bey, Frauke, *From Trucial States to United Arab Emirates: A Society in Transition*, 2nd edn (London, Longman, 1996); Muhammed Morsy, Abdullah, *The United Arab Emirates: A Modern History* (London, Croom Helm, 1978); and Khalifa, Ali, *The United Arab Emirates: Unity in Fragmentation* (Boulder, CO, Westview, 1979). A more nuanced view is exposed by Taryam, Abdullah Omran, *The Establishment of the United Arab Emirates 1950–85* (London, Croom Helm, 1987); and Rumaihi, Muhammd, *Beyond Oil: Unity and Development in the Gulf* (London, Al Saqi, 1986). In the case of Muhammed Morsy the enthusiasm is influenced by a desire to toe the 'official' version of history. The other authors, who are at times highly critical of the ruling families, have been impeded by the lack of access to recently released documentation.

6. Heard-Bey, Frauke, 'The United Arab Emirates: a quarter century of federation', in Hudson, C. Michael (ed.), *Middle East Dilemma: The Politics and Economics of Arab Integration* (London, I.B.Tauris, 1999), pp.144–5.

7. An exception is Muhammed Morsy: *United Arab Emirates*, in which the resistance of the rulers to change is barely mentioned. This is in keeping with the nationalist fervour of the rest of the book which is otherwise valuable for its economic analysis of the modern history of the UAE.

8. For the best accounts of a detailed historical discussion of the development of the federation, see Heard-Bey: *From Trucial States to United Arab Emirates*, pp.336–68; and Taryam: *Establishment of the United Arab Emirates 1950–85*, pp.89–189. See also the excellent Davidson, Christopher M., *The United Arab Emirates: A Study in Survival, The Middle East in the International System* (Boulder, CO, Lynne Rienner, 2005).

9. This speech left no doubt about British intentions in contrast to the ambiguous pronouncements by officials in the preceding months. Up until the Prime Minister's speech it looked like the withdrawal could be confined to Aden and Southern Arabia. For the text of the Prime Minister's announcement, see *Keesing's*, xvi (1967–68), p.224–90.

10. Balfour-Paul: *End of Empire in the Middle East*, pp.121–2. For the record of the process by which the council came about and of all the subsequent meetings, see FCO 8.

11. Taryam: *Establishment of the United Arab Emirates 1950–85*, pp.89–90.

12. Heard-Bey: *From Trucial States to United Arab Emirates*, p.343.

13. For a similar view, see Rumaihi: *Beyond Oil*, p.61.

14. For an exhaustive treatment of the subject, see Chaudry, Kiren Aziz, *The Price of Wealth: Economies and Institutions in the Middle East* (Ithaca, NY, Cornell University Press, 1997).

15. Khalifa: *United Arab Emirates*; Taryam: *Establishment of the United Arab Emirates 1950–85*.

16. Heard-Bey: *From Trucial States to United Arab Emirates*, pp.368–70.

17. On the importance of symbols in the international relations of the Arab Middle East, see Barnett, Michael N., *Dialogues in Arab Politics: Negotiations in Regional Order* (New York, NY, Columbia University Press, 1998).

18. This point is elaborated in Hudson, C. Michael, 'Arab integration: an overview', in Hudson, C. Michael (ed.), *Middle East Dilemma: The Politics and Economics of Arab Integration* (London, I.B.Tauris, 1999), pp.1–33.
19. For example, Mansfield, Edward D. and Milner, Helen V. (eds), *The Political Economy of Regionalism* (New York, NY, Columbia University Press, 1993).
20. Every single 'fact' or assertion in the dispute, apart from the basic ones recounted here, is hotly contested. There are disagreements about the title of ownership, the size and ethnic makeup of the communities settling the islands at any one time, etc. The literature on the subject is quite extensive, even if mostly written in apologetic tones. For a brief overview, see Amirahmadi, Hooshang (ed.), *Small Islands Big Politics: The Tonbs and Abu Musa in the Gulf* (Houndmills, Macmillan, 1996); and Schofield, Richard N., 'Border disputes in the Gulf: past, present, and future', in Sick, Gary G. and Potter, Lawrence G. (eds), *The Persian Gulf at the Millennium: Essays in Politics, Economy, Security, and Religion* (Houndmills, Macmillan, 1997). A much more exhaustive account is Mattair, Thomas R., *The Three Occupied UAE Islands: The Tunbs and Abu Musa* (Abu Dhabi, Emirates Center for Strategic Studies and Research, 2006).
21. Taryam: *Establishment of the United Arab Emirates 1950–85*, pp.188–9.
22. The entire folder relating to the formation of the UAE was declassified in 1999; see FCO 8. Some documents form the basis for Smith: *Britain's Revival and Fall in the Gulf*.
23. Interview with Balfour-Paul. Also FCO 7, 8. Dispatches from the Gulf to London often include firm, if tactful, protests at ministers' interventions by the diplomats posted there.
24. FCO 8/828: Dispatches to Mr. Brown, official at the Foreign Office, of 13 and 28 December 1967.
25. FCO 8/828.
26. This is a reference to the short-lived union between Egypt and Syria.
27. FCO 8/28.
28. For a pessimistic view about the emergence of a cooperative security regime in the Gulf today, see Evron, Yair, 'Towards the emergence of a common security system in the Middle East', in Martin, Leonor G. (ed.), *New Frontiers in Middle East Security* (Houndmills, Macmillan, 1998).
29. The traditional view is summed up by M. E. Yapp who does not mention the influence of Iran, but simply the fact that Bahrain and Qatar 'had acquired identities which they were unwilling to jeopardize'; Yapp, M. E., *The Near East since the First World War* (London, Longman, 1996), pp.205–06.
30. FCO 8/21.
31. FCO 8/21.
32. FCO 8/11.
33. Al-Saud: *Iran, Saudi Arabia and the Gulf*. For a broader overview of the British role in the Gulf throughout history, see Peterson, J. E., 'Britain and the Gulf: at the periphery of Empire', in Potter, Lawrence G. (ed.), *The Persian Gulf in History* (New York, NY, Palgrave, Macmillan, 2009).
34. From this point of view it is striking to note how prescient one of the first accounts of functional integration written shortly before the creation of the GCC proved to be. Tim Niblock rightly stated in 1981 that the vast array of agreements on

cooperation and coordination that had been sealed in the 1970s did not serve the long-term economic and social interests of the population, but rather for local rulers intent on protecting their regimes against internal and external threats. The same can be said for the vast array of GCC initiatives in the decades since the organization was founded, with the notable exception of some economic integration initiatives. For this excellent account, see Niblock, Tim, 'The prospects for integration in the Arab Gulf', in Niblock, Tim (ed.), *Social and Economic Development in the Arab Gulf* (London, Croom Helm, 1981).

35. For a complete collection of the treaties, see Abdulkhalig, Ahmad S. and Alnageeb, Mahmoud H., *Comparative Encyclopedia for Laws, Legislation, and Regulations in Kuwait, Bahrain, Qatar, UAE, and Saudi Arabia* (Kuwait City, Alnageeb Est., 1979). For joint working groups and institutions, see Arab Bureau of Education for the Gulf States, *The Directory of Joint Gulf Organizations and Institutions* (1982).

36. Koppers, Simon, *Economic Analysis and Evaluation of the Gulf Cooperation Council (GCC)*. European University Studies: Series V Economics and Management, Vol. 1783 (Frankfurt am Main, Peter Lang, 1995), p.201.

37. Barnett: *Dialogues in Arab Politics*, p.202.

38. Al-Kuwaiz, Abdullah Ibrahim, 'Economic integration of the Cooperation Council of the Arab States of the Gulf: challenges, achievements and future outlook', in Sandwick, John A. (ed.), *The Gulf Cooperation Council: Moderation and Stability in an Interdependent World* (Boulder, CO, Westview, 1987), pp.71–85 (p.77).

39. I use this term to refer to the future member states of the GCC.

40. For a discussion of normative constraints on the conduct of international relations in the Arab Middle East, see Barnett: *Dialogues in Arab Politics*. The case of the GCC is well discussed by Ramazani, R. K., *The Gulf Cooperation Council: Record and Analysis* (Charlottesville, VA, University Press of Virginia, 1988).

41. For an exhaustive list of these goals, including projects that were initiated after the GCC was formed, see Regional and Country Studies Branch, Division for Industrial Studies, *The Resource Base for Industrialization in the Gulf Co-operation Council Countries: A Framework for Co-operation* (New York, NY, UN Industrial Development Organization, 1983), pp.4–5.

42. Cammett, Melani, 'Defensive integration and late developers: the Gulf Cooperation Council and the Arab Maghreb union', *Global Governance*, v (1999), pp.379–402 (p.387).

43. For an excellent discussion of the water problems of the Gulf and the Middle East in general, see Beaumont, Peter, 'Water and armed conflict in the Middle East – fantasy or reality?', in Gleditsch, N. P. (ed.), *Conflict and the Environment* (Oslo, Kluwer, 1997), pp.355–74.

44. For the entire text of the treaty, see Khalil, Muhammad, *The Arab States and the Arab League: A Documentary Record* (Cairo, League of Arab States, 1962), Vol. 2, pp.99–101.

45. The best source for tracing the development of internal security cooperation is probably *Journal of Gulf and Peninsula Studies* (1975–80). The subject can be glimpsed at in interviews with heads of states and ministers of the Gulf states.

46. Gulf Information and Research Centre, *The GCC* (London, Gulf Information and Research Centre, 1983), p.15.

47. Ministry of Information, *The Way Forward: Cooperation and Unity in the Gulf* (Muscat, Sultanate of Oman, 1985), p.15.

48. Ibid., p.13.

Chapter 2 Creation, Structure and Organization of the GCC

1. First GCC Secretary General Abdullah Bishara, commenting on why he was allowed to serve a third term in spite of the term limits contained in the charter of the organization; author's interview with Abdullah Yacoub Bishara, Kuwait, 15 November 2000.
2. Author's interview with Bishara, 15 November 2000.
3. Heard-Bey, Frauke, *From Trucial States to United Arab Emirates: A Society in Transition*, 2nd edn (London, Longman, 1996), p.383.
4. Ramazani, R. K., *The Gulf Cooperation Council: Record and Analysis* (Charlottesville, VA, University Press of Virginia, 1988), p.6.
5. Dietl, Gulshan, *Through Two Wars and Beyond: A Study of the Gulf Cooperation Council* (New Delhi, Lancers, 1991), p.5.
6. Ibid., p.6.
7. Barnett, Michael N., *Dialogues in Arab Politics: Negotiations in Regional Order* (New York, NY, Columbia University Press, 1998).
8. Chubin, Shahram (ed.), *Security in the Persian Gulf 2: The Role of the Outside Powers* (London, International Institute for Strategic Studies, 1982), p.154.
9. The Baghdad Pact brought together Britain, Iraq, Iran, Turkey and Pakistan; it collapsed in 1958 after the nationalist coup that overthrew the Iraqi monarchy. The organization was renamed the Central Treaty Organization (CENTO). The Iranian revolution of 1979 ended the life of CENTO.
10. 'Minister denies proposal for Strait Alliance', *FBIS-MEA* (4 October 1979).
11. 'Gulf foreign ministers begin meeting in At-Taif', *FBIS-MEA* (17 October 1979).
12. Said Zahlan, Rosemarie, *The Making of the Modern Gulf States*, 2nd edn (Reading, Ithaca Press, 1998), pp.149–50.
13. Author's interviews with: Bishara, Kuwait, 17 November 2000; and Fahim Al-Qasimi, Dubai, 20 April 2002.
14. Government of Bahrain, *Cooperation Council for the Arab States of the Gulf* (Bahrain, Bahrain Government Printing Press, 1983), p.17.
15. Author's interview with Bishara, 17 November 2000.
16. Dunn, Michael, 'The Gulf: Cooperation Council', *Defense and Foreign Affairs Daily*, x/105 (1981), pp.1–2.
17. GCC Secretariat, 'Charter of the GCC', *American–Arab Affairs*, no. 7/Winter (1983–84), pp.157–62.
18. Author's interview with Bishara, 17 November 2000.
19. For example, the European Union relies on an 'institutional triangle' composed of the Commission, the Council and the Parliament, each representing the interests of a different constituency, as well as the Court of Justice and the Court of Auditors which act as independent overseers on its workings.
20. Alswied, Mohammed, *The Gulf Cooperation Council: A Model of a Regional International Regime* (Madison, WI, University of Wisconsin, 1988), p.138.
21. For more on this point and the deliberate ambiguity of the provisional constitution, see Khalifa, Ali, *The United Arab Emirates: Unity in Fragmentation* (Boulder, CO, Westview, 1979), pp.27–35.
22. In 2002 more than 200 employees were Saudi. There were only two female employees.

23. Al-Kuwaiz, Abdullah Ibrahim, 'Economic integration of the Cooperation Council of the Arab States of the Gulf: challenges, achievements and future outlook', in Sandwick, John A. (ed.), *The Gulf Cooperation Council: Moderation and Stability in an Interdependent World* (Boulder, CO, Westview, 1987), pp.71–85 (p.82). The writer was Associate Secretary General for Economic Affairs. See also the author's interview with Bishara, 17 November 2000.
24. For a dismissive view of the organization, see Tripp, Charles, 'Regional organizations in the Arab Middle East', in Hurrell, Andrew and Fawcett, Louise (eds), *Regionalism in World Politics: Regional Organization and International Order* (New York, NY, Oxford University Press, 1995), pp.283–309 (pp.293–5).
25. Interview with former American Assistant Secretary of State Robert Pelletreau, Oxford, 10 October 1999.

Chapter 3 The GCC in Light of International Relations Theory

1. Keohane, Robert O., 'Realism, Neorealism and the study of world politics', in Keohane, Robert O. (ed.), *Neorealism and Its Critics* (New York, NY, Columbia University Press, 1986), p.4.
2. Walt, Stephen, 'International Relations: one world, many theories', *Foreign Policy*, cx (1998), p.1.
3. For example, Fawcett, Louise L'E., 'Regionalism in historical perspective', in Fawcett, Louise L'E. and Hurrell, Andrew (eds), *Regionalism in World Politics: Regional Organization and International Order* (Oxford, Oxford University Press, 1995), p.16.
4. Peterson, Erik R. *The Gulf Cooperation Council: Search for Unity in a Dynamic Region* (Boulder, CO, Westview, 1988), p.174.
5. For a good, systematic treatment conducted from the vantage point of 'foreign policy analysis', see Baabood, Abdulla, 'Dynamics and determinants of the GCC states' foreign policy, with special reference to the EU', in Nonneman, Gerd (ed.), *Analyzing Middle East Foreign Policies and the Relationship with Europe* (New York, NY, Routledge, 2005), pp.145–73.
6. Even the excellent taxonomy developed by Amitav Acharya and Alastair Iain Johnston is not fully capable of capturing the multifaceted nature of the GCC. In particular, the gap between institutionalization and implementation of decision-making has to be explained with reference to the domestic political structures of the member states. However, for an excellent overview of institutional design of regional organizations as well as an exhaustive survey of the literature on regionalism, see Acharya, Amitav and Johnston, Alastair I. (eds), *Crafting Cooperation: Regional International Institutions in Comparative Perspective* (Cambridge, Cambridge University Press, 2007).
7. Cooper, Scott and Taylor, Brock, *Power and Regionalism: Explaining Economic Cooperation in the Persian Gulf* (Provo, UT, Brigham Young University, 2001), p.1.
8. Hurrell, Andrew, 'Regionalism in theoretical perspective', in Hurrell, Andrew and Fawcett, Louise L'E. (eds), *Regionalism in World Politics: Regional Organization and International Order* (Oxford, Oxford University Press, 1995), p.39.
9. Nye, Joseph S., *International Regionalism* (Boston, MA, Little Brown, 1968), p.vii.
10. Fawcett: 'Regionalism in historical perspective', pp.12–15.

11. Wallace, William, 'Regionalism in Europe', in Hurrell, Andrew and Fawcett, Louise L'E. (eds), *Regionalism in World Politics* (Oxford, Oxford University Press, 1995), p.202.
12. Author's interview with Abdullah Yacoub Bishara, Kuwait, 17 November 2000.
13. Allison, Graham T., *Essence of Decision: Explaining the Cuban Missile Crisis* (Boston, MA, Little Brown, 1971). For the preponderance of realism among scholars, see Viotti, Paul R. and Kauppi, Mark V., *International Relations Theory: Realism, Pluralism, Globalism, and Beyond*, 3rd edn (Boston, MA, Allyn & Bacon, 1999), pp.82–3; and Art, Robert J. and Jervis, Robert, *International Politics: Enduring Concepts and Contemporary Issues*, 5th edn (New York, NY, Longman, 2000).
14. Mearsheimer, John J., *The Tragedy of Great Power Politics* (New York, NY, Norton, 2001), pp.22–7.
15. Art, Robert J. and Jervis, Robert, *International Politics: Enduring Concepts and Contemporary Issues*, 4th edn (New York, NY, HarperCollins College Publ., 1996).
16. Waltz, Kenneth N., *Theory of International Politics* (New York, NY, McGraw-Hill, 1979).
17. For the importance of regime threats outside the major industrialized democracies in determining alliance patterns, see David, Steven R., 'Explaining Third World alignment', *World Politics: Quarterly Journal of International Relations*, xliii/2 (1991), pp.233–56. For a brilliant and innovative discussion of the influence of the state formation on international relations in the Arab Middle East, see Lawson, Fred H., *Constructing International Relations in the Arab World* (Stanford, CA, Stanford University Press 2006).
18. Lepgold, Joseph and Nincic, Miroslav, *Beyond the Ivory Tower: International Relations Theory and the Issue of Policy Relevance* (New York, NY, Columbia University Press, 2001), pp.142–8.
19. Ibid., p.146.
20. Ibid., p.143.
21. Wæver, Ole, 'Introduction', in Neumann, Iver B. and Wæver, Ole (eds), *The Future of International Relations: Masters in the Making?* New International Relations (London, Routledge, 1997).
22. Waever, Ole, 'The rise and fall of the inter-paradigm debate', in Smith, Steve, Booth, Ken and Zalewski, Marysia (eds), *International Theory: Positivism and Beyond* (Cambridge, Cambridge University Press, 1996), pp.163–4.
23. Ayoob, Mohammed, 'Subaltern Realism: International Relations Theory meets the Third World', in Neuman, Stephanie G. (ed.), *International Relations Theory and the Third World* (Basingstoke, Macmillan, 1998), p.37.
24. For a good review of the literature, see Oye, Kenneth A., 'Explaining cooperation under anarchy: hypotheses and strategies', *World Politics: Quarterly Journal of International Relations* xxxviii/1 (1985), pp.1–24.
25. Author's interview with Abdullah Ibrahim Al-Kuwaiz, London, 16 November 1998. For a very good discussion of the economic challenges facing the six member states, see also Kapiszewski, Andrzej, *Nationals and Expatriates: Population and Labour Dilemmas of the Gulf Cooperation Council States* (Reading, Ithaca Press, 2001).
26. For example, see his classic work: Deutsch, Karl, *Political Community in the North Atlantic Area: International Organization in Light of Historical Experience* (Princeton, NJ, Princeton University Press, 1957).

27. A good example of how one of Deutsch's central concepts has been elaborated in a contemporary light is Adler, Emanuel and Barnett, Michael N., *Security Communities*. Cambridge Studies in International Relations (Cambridge, Cambridge University Press, 1998).
28. Rose, Gideon, 'Neoclassical Realism and theories of foreign policy', *World Politics*, Fall (October)/51 (1998), pp.3–4.
29. Ibid., p.3.
30. Walt, Stephen, *The Origins of Alliances* (Ithaca, NY, Cornell University Press, 1987).
31. Barnett, Michael N., *Dialogues in Arab Politics: Negotiations in Regional Order* (New York, NY, Columbia University Press, 1998).
32. For example, see the excellent Adler and Barnett: *Security Communities*.
33. Wendt, Alexander, 'Constructing international politics', *International Security*, xx/1 (1995), pp.71–81.
34. Morgenthau, Hans J., *Politics among Nations: The Struggle for Power and Peace* (New York, NY, Knopf, 1949); even more relevant is Morgenthau, Hans J., 'Alliances in theory and practice', in Wolfers, Arnold, (ed.), *Alliance Policy in the Cold War* (Baltimore, MD, Johns Hopkins Press, 1959); as well as Niebuhr, Rienhold, 'The illusion of world government', *Foreign Affairs*, xxvii/3 (1949), pp.379–88; and Kennan, George F., *The Cloud of Danger: Current Realities of American Foreign Policy* (Boston, MA, Little Brown, 1977).
35. Schweller, Randall L., 'Bandwagoning for profit: bringing the revisionist state back in', *International Security*, xix/1 (1994), pp.72–107.
36. Schweller, Randall L. and Priess, David, 'A tale of two realisms: expanding the institutions debate', *Mershon International Studies Review*, xli/1 (1997), pp.1–32.
37. Author's interview with Bishara.
38. Gause III, F. Gregory, 'Balancing what? Threat perception and alliance choice in the Gulf' Security Studies 13, no. 2 (Winter 2003/2004): 273–305; for a similar view, see also Vasquez, John A., 'The Realist paradigm and degenerative versus progressive research programs: an appraisal of neotraditional research on Waltz's balancing proposition', *American Political Science Review*, xci/4 (1997), pp.899–912.
39. Lecture by Joseph Nye, Oxford, 21 January 2003.
40. For the concept of 'coup-proof', see Vasquez: 'Realist paradigm and degenerative versus progressive research programs'.
41. Author's interview with Colonel Savino Onelli, Italian Military Attaché, Kuwait, 15 November 2000. The programme included a wholesale overhaul of ordnance and military platforms.
42. For the most comprehensive account of his thesis, see Barnett: *Dialogues in Arab Politics*.
43. Gause: 'Balancing what?', p.2.
44. For a similar view, see Barnett, Michael N. and Gause III, F. Gregory, 'Caravans in opposite directions: society, state, and the development of community in the Gulf Cooperation Council', in Adler, Emanuel and Barnett, Michael N. (eds), *Security Communities* (Cambridge, Cambridge University Press, 1998), pp.161–97 (pp.166–8).
45. Whose announcement is found in Ajami, Fouad, 'The end of Pan-Arabism', *Foreign Affairs*, lvii/2 (1978/79), pp.355–73.
46. Barnett, Michael N., 'Sovereignty, nationalism, and regional order in the Arab states system', *International Organization*, il/3 (1995), pp.479–510.

47. For example, Sultan Al-Qasimi, 'Introduction', in Ramazani, R. K., *The Gulf Cooperation Council: Record and Analysis* (Charlottesville, VA, University Press of Virginia, 1988).
48. Walt: *Origins of Alliances*.
49. David: 'Explaining Third World alignment'.
50. For a discussion of the role cultural theories can play in supplementing existing theories of International Relations, see Desch, Michael C., 'Culture clash: assessing the importance of ideas in security studies', *International Security*, xxiii/1 (1998), pp.141–70.
51. Hurrell: 'Regionalism in theoretical perspective', p.39.
52. Ibid., pp.39–40.
53. For example, see the classic Ayubi, Nazih N. M., *Over-Stating the Arab State: Politics and Society in the Middle East* (London, I.B.Tauris, 1995).
54. For two dismissive critiques of the GCC achievements in this field, see Aarts, Paul, *Dilemmas of Regional Cooperation in the Middle East*. Lancaster Papers No. 4 (Lancaster, Department of Politics and International Relations, Lancaster University, 1999), pp.8–9; and Al-Hamad, Turki, 'Will the Gulf monarchies work together?', *Middle East Quarterly*, iv/1 (1997).
55. Author's interview with Abdulaziz Sultan, Chairman of KEO Consulting, Kuwait Coordinator of the Development Forum, and Leader of the National Democratic Movement, Kuwait, 11 November 2000.
56. Hurrell: 'Regionalism in theoretical perspective', p.41.
57. See the archive of articles appearing in the British, French and American press relating to the Arab world collected by the Association for Arab–British Understanding and housed at the Gulf Documentation Center, University of Exeter, Exeter.
58. For example, Al-Isa, Shamlan Yusif and Al-Manufi, Kamal, *Trends in Kuwaiti Public Opinion Regarding the Gulf Cooperation Council* (Kuwait, Department of Political Science, University of Kuwait, 1985).
59. Hurrell: 'Regionalism in theoretical perspective', p.42.
60. Ibid., pp.44–5.
61. Lepgold and Nincic: *Beyond the Ivory Tower*, p.139.
62. Nye, Joseph S., 'Comparative regional integration: concept and measurement', *International Organization*, Fall/22 (1968), p.858.

Chapter 4 GCC Economic Integration: Disappointing Regionalism and Encouraging Regionalisation

1. Author's interviews with: Abdullah Ibrahim Al-Kuwaiz, London, 16 November 1998; and Abdullah Yacoub Bishara, Kuwait, 17 November 2000. The latter was particularly apologetic about the lack of progress in this field.
2. For the view that joint development projects are what really matters, see Al-Kuwaiz, Abdullah Ibrahim, 'Economic integration of the Cooperation Council of the Arab States of the Gulf: challenges, achievements and future outlook', in Sandwick, John A. (ed.), *The Gulf Cooperation Council: Moderation and Stability in an Interdependent World* (Boulder, CO, Westview, 1987), pp.71–85.

3. The expression is coined by Gary Sick in his 'The coming crisis in the Persian Gulf', in Sick, Gary and Potter, Lawrence G. (eds), *The Persian Gulf at the Millennium: Essays in Politics, Economy, Security, and Religion* (Basingstoke, Macmillan, 1997). Sick focuses more on the political situation, but in this crisis the realms of politics and economic are intertwined.
4. For an excellent treatment, see Hertog, Steffen, 'The GCC and Arab economic integration: a new paradigm', *Middle East Policy*, xiv/1 (2007), pp.52–69.
5. For a modified version of this concept, see Wyatt-Walter, Andrew, 'Regionalism, globalization, and world economic order', in Hurrell, Andrew and Fawcett, Louise (eds), *Regionalism in World Politics: Regional Organization and International Order* (Oxford, Oxford University Press, 1995), p.77. Wyatt-Walter, though, distinguishes solely between conscious economic policies and economic outcomes, whereas I am more interested in noting the burgeoning ties between professional organizations and non-governmental organizations (NGOs) in the six GCC states.
6. See the series of final reports of the 'Development Forum' and various documents issued by Chambers of Commerce throughout the member states.
7. Interview with Abdulaziz Sultan, Chairman of Keo Consulting, Kuwait, coordinator of the Development Forum, and leader of the Kuwait National Democratic movement, Kuwait City, 13 November 2000.
8. Balassa, Bela, *The Theory of Economic Integration* (London, Allen & Unwin, 1961). For articles by GCC officials utilizing this categorization, see Bishara, Abdullah Yacoub, 'The Gulf Cooperation Council: achievements and challenges', *American–Arab Affairs*, no. 7/Winter (1983–84), pp.40–4; and Al-Kuwaiz, 'Economic integration of the Cooperation Council of the Arab States of the Gulf', pp.71–85; in addition to various issues of *Al-Taawun* ('Cooperation'), journal of the GCC General Secretariat.
9. Figures are contested and opaque. The best treatment of the subject is Kapiszewski, Andrzej, *Nationals and Expatriates: Population and Labour Dilemmas of the Gulf Cooperation Council States* (Reading, Ithaca Press, 2001); but see also Peterson, Erik R., *The Gulf Cooperation Council: Search for Unity in a Dynamic Region* (Boulder, CO, Westview, 1988); and Koppers, Simon, *Economic Analysis and Evaluation of the Gulf Cooperation Council (GCC)*. European University Studies: Series V Economics and Management, Vol. 1783 (Frankfurt am Main, Peter Lang, 1995); as well as the statistical reports of individual countries. Bahrain and Qatar have the lowest number of expatriates in the workforce (but still well over 60%), whereas in the United Arab Emirates, where statistics are considered reliable, over 90% of the workforce is expatriate.
10. Interview with Abdullah Ibrahim Al-Kuwaiz; also Al-Kuwaiz: 'Economic Integration of the Cooperation Council of the Arab States of the Gulf'.
11. Rieger, Hans C., 'Basic issues of ASEAN economic co-operation', in Koppers, Simon (ed.), *Growth Determinants in East and South-East Asian Economies* (Berlin, Duncker & Humblot, 1991), pp.215–38 (p.229). For a similar line of argument, see Koppers: *Economic Analysis and Evaluation of the Gulf Cooperation Council (GCC)*, pp.74–7.
12. For a realistic assessment of the efforts at the indigenization of the workforce in the six GCC states, see Kapiszewski: *Nationals and Expatriates*, pp.69–87.
13. Koppers: *Economic Analysis and Evaluation of the Gulf Cooperation Council (GCC)*, p.75. See also the excellent Niblock, Tim, *The Political Economy of Saudi Arabia* (London, Routledge, 2007); and Davidson, Christopher M., *Dubai: The Vulnerability of Success* (New York, NY, Columbia University Press, 2008).

14. Dietl, Gulshan, *Through Two Wars and Beyond: A Study of the Gulf Cooperation Council* (New Delhi, Lancers, 1991), p.212.
15. Interview with Abdullah Ibrahim Al-Kuwaiz.
16. Bishara: 'Gulf Cooperation Council: achievements and challenges'.
17. Nakhleh, Emile A., *The Gulf Cooperation Council: Policies, Problems and Prospects* (New York, NY, Praeger, 1986), p.26.
18. GCC Secretariat, *The Unified Economic Agreement* (Riyadh, GCC Printing Press, 1981).
19. Nakhleh: *Gulf Cooperation Council*, p.27.
20. For a recent review by the office of the US Trade Representative of the wide array of non-tariff barriers still facing businesses that want to operate within the GCC, see http://www.ustr.gov/assets/Document_Library/Reports_Publications/2004/2004_National_Trade_Estimate/2004_NTE_Report/asset_upload_file226_4769.pdf (January 2007).
21. For a complete list of the teething problems, see Koppers: *Economic Analysis and Evaluation of the Gulf Cooperation Council (GCC)*, pp.99–102; and more recent issues of the *Middle East Economic Digest*.
22. Koppers: *Economic Analysis and Evaluation of the Gulf Cooperation Council (GCC)*, p.103.
23. Interviews conducted with foreign diplomats in Kuwait, 1999; and European Union officials in Brussels and South Korea, 2004.
24. Interview with Dr Abdel Aziz Abu Hamad Aluwasheig, Director of the GCC Economic Integration Department, Venice, November 2008.
25. Written remarks to the *Gulf 2000* academic listserv, 26 March 2005.
26. The security implications of these new bilateral FTAs have been the subject of a masterly and yet unpublished presentation by Professor Fred Lawson at the Middle East Studies Association (MESA) meeting in Montreal, 2007.
27. For the Annual Report for 2007, see http://www.gic.com.kw/ (January 2009).
28. For an overview of the funding of the GIC, see Al-Fayez, Khaled, 'The Gulf Investment Corporation', *American–Arab Affairs* no. 11/Winter (1984–85).
29. Koppers: *Economic Analysis and Evaluation of the Gulf Cooperation Council (GCC)*, p.160; GIC reports.
30. For a list of all participated companies, see http://www.gulfinvestmentcorp.com/history.htm also (January 2007).
31. Koppers: *Economic Analysis and Evaluation of the Gulf Cooperation Council (GCC)*, p.160.
32. For an overview of the GOIC, see http://www.goic.org.qa/; but for an analysis on the part of one of its former Secretary Generals who does not shy away from examining the difficulties faced by the organization, see Al-Jafary, Abdul Rahman, 'Investment opportunities in the Gulf: manufacturing industry joint venture opportunities', paper presented at the 2nd GCC–EU Industrial Conference, Doha, Qatar, 1992.
33. For a brief description, see Ramazani, R. K., *The Gulf Cooperation Council: Record and Analysis* (Charlottesville, VA, University Press of Virginia, 1988), p.205.
34. Peterson, *The Gulf Cooperation Council*, pp.152–3.
35. See http://www.ustr.gov/reports/nte/2000/contents.html (January 2007).
36. See http://www.europarl.eu.int/factsheets/6_3_9_en.htm (January 2007).

37. *BP Statistical Review of World Energy 2003*. Available http://www.bp.com/files/16/bp_stats_history_1611.xls (January 2007).
38. Luciani, Giacomo (ed.), *The Arab State* (Berkeley, CA, University of California Press, 1990).
39. Sick: 'Coming of the crisis in the Persian Gulf'; but for a detailed analysis of the structural problems of GCC economies, see also Kapiszewski: *Nationals and Expatriates*.
40. Niblock, Tim, 'The prospects for integration in the Arab Gulf', in Niblock, Tim (ed.), *Social and Economic Development in the Arab Gulf* (London, Croom Helm, 1981).
41. The partial exception being Dubai and Bahrain, where the fact that oil has all but run out has forced the authorities to foster a more business-friendly environment. This may indeed constitute the pathway to sustainable reform. Also in Oman the percentage of expatriates in the workforce is a little less than in the other GCC states (but still well over 60%).

Chapter 5   GCC Defense Cooperation: Beyond Symbolism?

1. First GCC Secretary General Abdullah Bishara, September 1986.
2. US Secretary of Defense Dick Cheney, May 1991.
3. For the useful analytical distinction between Gulf dynastic monarchies and other Middle East monarchies, see Herb, Michael, *All in the Family: Absolutism, Revolution, and Democracy in the Middle Eastern Monarchies*. SUNY Series in Middle Eastern Studies (Albany, NY, State University of New York Press, 1999). The differences are also highlighted by Kostiner, Joseph, *Middle East Monarchies: The Challenge of Modernity* (Boulder, CO, Lynne Rienner, 2000).
4. Tow develops his criteria in Tow, William T., *Subregional Security Cooperation in the Third World* (Boulder, CO, Lynne Rienner, 1990). In spite of the now outdated references to the Cold War this is still the most lucid theoretical treatment of Subregional Security Organizations. The fact that the GCC is treated as such in this and in other works of International Relations indicates how external observers always considered security to be the central focus of the organization.
5. The definition is found in Shlaim, Avi, *War and Peace in the Middle East: A Concise History*, Revd Edn (New York, NY, Penguin, 1995).
6. I am indebted to Philip Robins for this image.
7. A different conceptualization is contained in Bill, James A., 'The geometry of instability in the Gulf: the rectangle of tension', in Al-Suwaidi, Jamal S. (ed.), *Iran and the Gulf: A Search for Stability* (Abu Dhabi, Emirates Center for Strategic Studies and Research, 1996). In my opinion, *contra* Bill, while the United States is an essential actor in the Gulf it cannot (yet) be considered a local actor. In spite of its intervention in Iraq, the United States does not interfere in the domestic politics of the GCC states and Iran as much as Britain used to do during its long spell as a hegemonic power.
8. The other two are Turkey and Egypt.
9. For a good overview of the military effects of the Iran–Iraq War on GCC countries, see Potter, Lawrence G. and Sick, Gary (eds), *Iran, Iraq, and the Legacies of War* (New York, NY, Palgrave Macmillan, 2004).

10. For a comprehensive treatment of the disputes surrounding the Shatt al-Arab, see Schofield, Richard N., 'Position, function, and symbol: the Shatt al-Arab dispute in perspective', in Potter, Lawrence G. and Sick, Gary (eds), *Iran, Iraq, and the Legacies of War* (New York, NY, Palgrave Macmillan, 2004).
11. Conferences and workshops on the possibility of establishing a collective security system abound, but technical discussions are to no avail until the United States and Iran can sit at the same table.
12. For example, Cordesman, Anthony H., *The Gulf and the West: Strategic Relations and Military Realities* (London, Mansell, 1988); or the more recent Cordesman, Anthony H., *Kuwait, Csis Middle East Dynamic Net Assessment* (Boulder, CO, Westview, 1997); or for a European view, see Guazzone, Laura, 'Gulf Cooperation Council: the security policies', *Survival*, 30/2 (1988). Colonel Giuseppe Di Miceli, Italian Military Attaché in Kuwait – in an author's interview, Kuwait, 12 November 2000 – colourfully described the situation as 'trying to defend San Marino from an Italian attack', with reference to the landlocked microstate situated in Central Italy.
13. For an excellent treatment of American deployments in the region during the 1990s, see Cordesman, Anthony H., 'U.S. forces in the Middle East: resources and capabilities', in Cordesman, Anthony H., *CSIS Middle East Dynamic Net Assessment* (Boulder, CO, Westview, 1997). For a more up-to-date account focusing on Saudi Arabia, see Cordesman, Anthony H., *Saudi Arabia Enters the Twenty-First Century: The Military and International Security Dimensions* (Westport, CT, Praeger, 2003).
14. The establishment of the EuroGolfe network of scholars in 2002 was financed by two French arms manufacturers, amongst others. In the United States the National Council of US–Arab relations, active in the fields of elite networking and public diplomacy, is largely sponsored by American defense contractors.
15. For a rather impatient view of the GCC military achievements, see Cordesman, *Saudi Arabia Enters the Twenty-First Century*, pp.66–7.
16. This issue was perceptively highlighted by Laura Guazzone in the 1980s; Guazzone, 'Gulf Cooperation Council', pp.142–3. The following 20 years have fully validated her insight.
17. Author's interview with Di Miceli; also Cordesman, *Saudi Arabia Enters the Twenty-First Century*, p.66.
18. Cordesman, *Saudi Arabia Enters the Twenty-First Century*, p.66.
19. Peterson, Erik R., *The Gulf Cooperation Council: Search for Unity in a Dynamic Region* (Boulder, CO, Westview, 1988), p.205.
20. Guazzone, 'Gulf Cooperation Council', p.143.
21. Quoted in Peterson, *Gulf Cooperation Council*, p.205.
22. An examination of the final communiqués and statements of the meetings of the Supreme Council gives an idea of the insistence with which this notion is propounded by the organization.
23. For the reasons why the GCC does not constitute a security community, see Barnett, Michael N. and Gause III, F. Gregory, 'Caravans in opposite directions: society, state, and the development of community in the Gulf Cooperation Council', in Adler, Emanuel and Barnett, Michael N. (eds), *Security Communities* (Cambridge, Cambridge University Press, 1998), pp.161–97. Karl Deutsch defines a pluralistic security community as one in which states become integrated to a point at which they have a sense of community, which, in turn, creates assurances that they will

settle their differences short of war; Deutsch, Karl, *Political Community in the North Atlantic Area: International Organization in Light of Historical Experience* (Princeton, NJ, Princeton University Press, 1957).

24. One of the more amusing proofs of the success of these symbolic actions has been the call for a dissolution of the GCC on the part of a hostile author. Simon Henderson, who has written an account of Gulf security for the Washington Institute of Near East Policy, calls for the dissolution of the organization on the grounds that it provides a dangerous counterbalance to the American presence in the Gulf(!); Henderson, Simon, *The New Pillar: Conservative Arab Gulf States and U.S. Strategy.* Policy Paper No. 58 (Washington, DC, Washington Institute for Near East Policy, 2003).
25. Dietl, Gulshan, *Through Two Wars and Beyond: A Study of the Gulf Cooperation Council* (New Delhi, Lancers, 1991), pp.171–2.
26. For this and other factors that prevent the GCC from evolving into a fully fledged security community, see Barnett and Gause, 'Caravans in opposite directions'.
27. For example, I asked Prince Turki bin Faisal, who headed Saudi intelligence for more than 20 years and who was then Ambassador to London – in an interview in Oxford, 18 November 2003 – to tell me what were his thoughts about the organization. He replied, 'The GCC? You will have to tell me because I do not know anything about it.' He then went on to emphasize how little interaction both his offices had with the organization.
28. *Al-Mustaqbal* (23 January 1982); see also Chapter 2.
29. For the concept of 'external manipulative mobilization', see Hameed, Mazher A., *Arabia Imperilled: The Security Imperatives of the Arab Gulf States* (Washington, DC, Middle East Assessments Group, 1986). See also the brief discussion in Guazzone, 'Gulf Cooperation Council', pp.136–8.
30. For the Kuwaiti accomodationist policy towards Iran and the Soviet bloc during the 1980s, see Assiri, Abdhul Ridha, *Kuwait's Foreign Policy: City-State in World Politics* (Boulder, CO, Westview, 1990). At the time Kuwait seemed the GCC state more mistrustful of Saudi hegemony, a role now played by Qatar.
31. Author's interview with Abdullah Yacoub Bishara, Kuwait, 17 November 2000.
32. For the evolution of political discourse in Kuwait, see Tétreault, Mary Ann, *Stories of Democracy: Politics and Society in Contemporary Kuwait* (New York, NY, Columbia University Press, 2000).
33. Tow, *Subregional Security Cooperation in the Third World*, p.9.
34. For the conventional wisdom about the difference in threat perception among the six GCC states, see Rabi, Uzi, 'The GCC: the endless quest for regional security', paper presented at the MESA Meeting, San Francisco, CA, USA, 2004; or Ramazani, R. K., *The Gulf Cooperation Council: Record and Analysis* (Charlottesville, VA, University Press of Virginia, 1988). In fact, GCC states all recognize the fact that preserving their external security will necessitate American physical presence in the Gulf for the foreseeable future.
35. A note of caution is in order here. It is in fact remarkable how widespread is the feeling among the Iraqi population, including notable members of the former opposition to Saddam Hussein, that Kuwait is but an appendix of Iraq. At the very least there is a widespread consensus in Iraq that their access to the Gulf should be broadened. For a comprehensive treatment of Iraqi political culture giving

rise to these feelings, see Tripp, Charles, *A History of Iraq* (Cambridge, Cambridge University Press, 2000).
36. Author's interview with former Assistant Secretary of State Robert Pelletreau, Oxford, 4 December 1999.

Chapter 6   GCC Diplomatic Coordination: The Limited Role of Institutions

1. Attributed to Otto von Bismarck.
2. For a full explanation of this scholarly method, see Finnemore, Martha, *The Purpose of Intervention: Changing Beliefs About the Use of Force*. Cornell Studies in Security Affairs (Ithaca, NY, Cornell University Press, 2003), p.13. She takes inspiration from Ruggie, John G., *Constructing the World Polity: Essays on International Institutionalization*, The New International Relations (London, Routledge, 1998); and Peirce, Charles S. and Buchler, Justus, *The Philosophy of Peirce: Selected Writings* (New York, NY, AMS Press, 1978).
3. Peterson, Erik R., *The Gulf Cooperation Council: Search for Unity in a Dynamic Region* (Boulder, CO, Westview, 1988), p.138.
4. GCC Secretariat, *Rules of Procedures Commission for the Settlement of Disputes* (Riyadh, GCC Printing Press, 1985).
5. For elucidation on the administrative culture prevailing in some of the GCC member states, see Davidson, Christopher M., *The United Arab Emirates: A Study in Survival*, The Middle East in the International System (Boulder, CO, Lynne Rienner, 2005); and Tétreault, Mary A., *Stories of Democracy: Politics and Society in Contemporary Kuwait* (New York, NY, Columbia University Press, 2000). An illuminating case study of a major government organization is also Tétreault, Mary A., *The Kuwait Petroleum Corporation and the Economics of the New World Order* (Westport, CT, Quorum, 1995). Finally, for a look at another international organization, see Tétreault, Mary A., *The Organization of Arab Petroleum Exporting Countries: History, Policies, and Prospects*. Contributions in Economics and Economic History No. 40 (Westport, CT, Greenwood, 1981).
6. Baabood, Abdulla and Edwards, Geoffrey, 'Reinforcing ambivalence: the interaction of Gulf States and the European Union', paper presented at the Eighth Mediterranean Social and Political Research Meeting, European University Institute, Montecatini, 2007.
7. For example, Gause III, F. Gregory, *Oil Monarchies: Domestic Security Challenges in the Arab Gulf States* (New York, NY, Council on Foreign Relations Press, 1994); Peterson: *Gulf Cooperation Council*; and Nakhleh, Emile A., *The Gulf Cooperation Council: Policies, Problems and Prospects* (New York, NY, Praeger, 1986). For a more nuanced and comprehensive treatment, see Nonneman, Gerd, 'The Gulf states and the Iran–Iraq War: pattern shifts and continuities', in Potter, Lawrence G. and Sick, Gary (eds), *Iran, Iraq, and the Legacies of War* (New York, NY, Palgrave Macmillan, 2004). For general histories of the Iran–Iraq War, see Chubin, Shahram and Tripp, Charles, *Iran and Iraq at War* (London, I.B.Tauris, 1988); and Karsh, Efraim, *The Iran–Iraq War, 1980–1988*, Essential Histories (Oxford, Osprey, 2002). Even more readable is Hiro, Dilip, *The Longest War: The Iran–Iraq Military Conflict* (London,

Paladin, 1990). A good bibliographic guide is Gardner, J. Anthony, *The Iraq–Iran War: A Bibliography* (Boston, MA, G. K. Hall, 1988).

8. For a more comprehensive account of the balance of power dynamics in the Gulf in the last two centuries, see Legrenzi, Matteo, 'Iraq, Iran e Arabia Saudita come triangolo scaleno: per una storia degli equilibri di potenza nella regione del Golfo', in Nordio, M., Torri, M. and Vercellin, G. (eds), *Grande Medio Oriente* (Milan, Bruno Mondadori, 2006).

9. See the long-running discussion on the topic in the *Gulf 2000* academic list. Available https://www1.columbia.edu/sec/cu/sipa/GULF2000/index.html (after registration).

10. For two excellent accounts of this aspect of the conflict, see Navias, Martin S. and Hooton, E. R., *Tanker Wars: The Assault on Merchant Shipping During the Iran–Iraq Conflict, 1980–1988* (London, I.B.Tauris, 1996); and El-Shazly, Nadia El-Sayed, *The Gulf Tanker War: Iran and Iraq's Maritime Swordplay* (New York, NY, St Martin's, 1998).

11. For an interesting account of how the decision of Ayatollah Khomeini took by surprise even his own lieutenants, see Milani, Mohsen M., *The Making of Iran's Islamic Revolution* (Boulder, CO, Westview, 1994), pp.214–15.

12. For an excellent account of events leading up to the downing of the Iranian airliner, see Dotterway, K. A., *Systematic Analysis of Complex Dynamic Systems: The Case of the USS Vincennes* (Monterey, CA, Naval Postgraduate School, 1992).

13. For an exhaustive discussion of the issue from an Iranian point of view, see http://www.sharghnewspaper.com/830630/societ.htm#s112668 (in Farsi); or the discussion on the *Gulf 2000* academic list in September 2004 at https://www1.columbia.edu/sec/cu/sipa/GULF2000/ (after registration).

14. Nonneman: 'Gulf states and the Iran–Iraq War', p.168.

15. Ibid., p.169. For a military analysis of the significance of the Strait of Hormuz, see also Cordesman, Anthony H., *Bahrain, Oman, Qatar, and the UAE: Challenges of Security, CSIS Middle East Dynamic Assessment* (Boulder, CO, Westview, 1997). In particular, it is debatable whether Iran nowadays could be contained as effectively as it was during the war. The procurement of Chinese Silkworm missiles seems to have added to the insidiousness of the Iranian military in the Gulf. These same missiles, undoubtedly supplied by Iran, were utilized to great effect by Hezbollah in its 2006 conflict with Israel against its navy.

16. Nonneman, Gerd, *Iraq, the Gulf States & the War* (London: Ithaca, 1986), pp.22–3.

17. For an English text of the communiqué, see Peterson: *Gulf Cooperation Council*, p.286; for the Arabic text, see Government of Bahrain, *Cooperation Council for the Arab States of the Gulf* (Bahrain, Bahrain Government Printing Press, 1983).

18. Nonneman: 'Gulf states and the Iran–Iraq War', p.180.

19. Ibid., p.178; also Cordesman, Anthony H., *The Iran–Iraq War and Western Security 1984–87: Strategic Implications and Policy Options* (London, Jane's, 1987). For a more technical, military analysis, see Karsh, Efraim, *The Iran–Iraq War, a Military Analysis*. Adelphi Papers No. 220 (London, International Institute for Strategic Studies, 1987). For a more polemical stance on this issue, see Cass, Stephen J. R., *The US Takes Sides: US Policy Towards Iraq During the Iran–Iraq War* (Oxford, University of Oxford, 1994).

20. Security Council Resolution 552 (1984) of 1 June 1984.

21. Nonneman, 'Gulf states and the Iran–Iraq War', p.179.
22. Nonneman: *Iraq, the Gulf States & the War*, pp.102–04.
23. For a list of most of the communiqués, see http://www.gcc-sg.org/. The remaining ones are available in printed form at the GCC Secretariat.
24. Some of the closing statements of the GCC Supreme Council since 1981 are now available at http://www.gcc-sg.org/closingsessions.html (January 2008).
25. For an English translation of the Supreme Council communiqués throughout this period, see also Peterson: *Gulf Cooperation Council*, pp.286–309.
26. Nonneman: 'Gulf states and the Iran–Iraq War', pp.180–2.
27. Nonneman: *Iraq, the Gulf States & the War*.
28. See English translations of the closing statements of the Supreme Council available at: http://www.gcc-sg.org/eng/indexcb9a.html?action=Sec-Show&ID=5 (June 2011).
29. See English translations of the closing statements of the Supreme Council available at: http://www.gcc-sg.org/eng/indexcb9a.html?action=Sec-Show&ID=5 (June 2011).
30. Nonneman: 'Gulf states and the Iran–Iraq War', p.185.
31. Mattair, Thomas R., *The Three Occupied UAE Islands: The Tunbs and Abu Musa* (Abu Dhabi, Emirates Center for Strategic Studies and Research, 2006), p.18. For an account that is more sympathetic to the Iranian position, see Amirahmadi, Hooshang (ed.), *Small Islands Big Politics: The Tonbs and Abu Musa in the Gulf* (Houndmills, MacMillan, 1996). Also Schofield, Richard N., 'Border disputes in the Gulf: past, present, and future', in Sick, Gary G. and Potter, Lawrence G. (eds), *The Persian Gulf at the Millennium: Essays in Politics, Economy, Security, and Religion* (Houndmills, MacMillan, 1997).
32. Cordesman: *Bahrain, Oman, Qatar, and the UAE*, pp.298–9.
33. Mattair: *Three Occupied UAE Islands*, p.286.
34. Ibid., p.287.
35. The Secretariat General of The Cooperation Council for the Arab States of the Gulf, *Closing Statements of the Sessions of the Supreme Council: Sessions 1–18* (Riyadh, 1998), p.108.
36. Ibid., p.124.
37. For an exhaustive analysis of the Memorandum of Understanding, see Schofield, Richard N., *Unfinished Business: Iran, the Uae, Abu Musa and the Tunbs* (London, Royal Institute of International Affairs, 2003).
38. Mattair: *Three Occupied UAE Islands*, p.290.
39. Ibid., p.292.
40. Ibid., p.300.
41. Ibid., p.315.
42. The 'rules of shaikhly exchange' is a particularly felicitous expression that encapsulates the habits of political mediation in the Gulf. It can be traced back to Nonneman. See exchange on the *Gulf 2000* academic list available at https://www1.columbia.edu/sec/cu/sipa/GULF2000/ (after registration).
43. For a very good overview of border disputes in the Gulf, see Schofield, 'Border disputes in the Gulf'.
44. For an illuminating discussion, see Said Zahlan, Rosemarie, *The Making of the Modern Gulf States*, 2nd edn (Reading, Ithaca Press, 1998).
45. Al-Makhawi, Rashid, *The Gulf Cooperation Council: A Study in Integration* (Salford, University of Salford, 1990), p.129. The dispute is discussed in detail by Said

Zahlan: *Making of the Modern Gulf States*, and it gave rise to a wide literature: for example, Cordesman: *Bahrain, Oman, Qatar, and the UAE*; and Joffé, George, 'Arab frontiered disputes: the consequences for Arab security', *Geopolitics and International Boundaries* i/2 (1996). The most monumental account is that based on the documents presented by Bahrain to the ICJ: Al-Arayed, Jawad S., *A Line in the Sea: The Qatar v. Bahrain Border Dispute in the World Court* (Berkeley, CA, North Atlantic, 2003). Here the topic will be tackled only in relation to the GCC (in)action on the issue.
46. Al-Arayed: *Line in the Sea*, p.326.
47. For a complete list of the five principles, see Government of Bahrain, *Case Concerning Maritime Delimitation and Territorial Questions between Qatar and Bahrain (Qatar Vs. Bahrain). Counter-Memorial Submitted by the State of Bahrain. Questions of Jurisdiction and Admissibility* (Manama, 1992). This is also found in a more readable form in Al-Arayed: *Line in the Sea*.
48. Al-Arayed: *Line in the Sea*, p.326.
49. Priess, David, *Alliance Durability: Why Breaking Up Is Hard to Do* (Durham, NC, Duke University, 2000), p.237.
50. Al-Arayed: *Line in the Sea*, p.328.
51. Nonneman, Gerd, 'EU–GCC relations: dynamics, perspectives, and the issue of political reform', *Journal of Social Affairs* xxiii/92 (2006), p.14.
52. Baabood, Abdulla, 'Dynamics and determinants of the GCC states' foreign policy, with special reference to the EU', in Nonneman, Gerd (ed.), *Analyzing Middle East Foreign Policies and the Relationship with Europe* (New York, NY, Routledge, 2005), pp.145–73 (p.164).
53. For some recent examples of communiqués, see http://www.eu2005.lu/en/actualites/communiques/2005/04/05uegolfe/0504uegolfe.pdf; and http://www.consilium.europa.eu/ueDocs/cms_Data/docs/pressdata/en/er/89619.pdf (both January 2008). For a more general account of the reasons for the lack of credibility of the European Union in the Gulf in defense matters, see Baabood and Edwards: 'Reinforcing ambivalence'.
54. Baabood and Edwards: 'Reinforcing ambivalence', p.6.
55. Nonneman, 'EU–GCC relations', p.13. For a supplemental discussion of the effects of the FTA on GCC economic integration, see Chapter 4.
56. Nonneman: 'EU–GCC relations', p.18.
57. Ibid., p.19.
58. For the problems encountered by the European Union, see ibid.; for the similar ill-fated attempts by NATO, which are in fact made easier by the exclusion of Saudi Arabia, see Chapter 8.

Chapter 7   The GCC, Iran and Nuclear Proliferation in the Gulf

1. Egyptian diplomat, London, April 2008, Personal communication.
2. For the final communiqué, see http://www.spa.gov.sa/English/ContentPage.php?cid = 34&id = 10654; and on the GCC website at http://www.gcc-sg.org/home_e.htm (August 2007).

3. As judged by the commentary it elicited in publications such as *WMD Insights*, *Carnegie Proliferation Bulletin*, and *Foreign Policy*.
4. For a fascinating discussion of what constitutes a security complex, see the classic Buzan, Barry, *People, States and Fear: An Agenda for International Security in the Post-Cold War Era*, 2nd edn (London, Harvester Wheatsheaf, 1991). For a detailed discussion of the interrelation between regions and security in a post-bipolar era, see Buzan, Barry and Wæver, Ole, *Regions and Powers: The Structure of International Security*. Studies in International Relations No. 91 (Cambridge, Cambridge University Press, 2003).
5. See King Abdallah of Jordan's Sh'iah crescent remark (*Washington Post*, December 2004); and Saud al-Faisal at the Council on Foreign Relations, September 2005. Available http://www.cfr.org/publication/8908/fight_against_extremism_and_the_search_for_peace_rush_transcript_federal_news_service_inc.html (August 2007).
6. Remarks by Ambassador Richard LeBaron, Mubarak Al Abdullah Joint Command and Staff College, Kuwait, 25 May 2005. Available http://kuwait.usembassy.gov/may_25_2005.html (August 2007).
7. 'Kuwaiti speaker criticizes US ambassador over remarks on Iran', Xinhua World News (5 June 2005). Available http://english.people.com.cn/200506/05/eng20050605_188579.html (August 2007).
8. 'GCC wary of Iran nuclear activities', UPI (3 January 2005). Available http://www.washtimes.com/upi-breaking/20050103-101602-5134r.htm (August 2007).
9. 'Saudis warn Iran that its nuclear plan risks disaster', *The Times* (16 January 2006). Available http://www.timesonline.co.uk/article/0,,251-1988111,00.html (August 2007).
10. 'Region could be first victim of Iran's nuke programme', *Gulf News* (4 March 2006). Available http://archive.gulfnews.com/articles/06/04/03/10030372.html (August 2007).
11. For an example of the latest, see Henderson, Simon, *The New Pillar: Conservative Arab Gulf States and U.S. Strategy*. Policy Paper No. 58 (Washington, DC, Washington Institute for Near East Policy, 2003).
12. For Iran's role in Iraq, see *Iran in Iraq: How Much Influence?* Middle East Report No. 38, 21 March (International Crisis Group, 2005). Available http://www.crisisgroup.org/home/index.cfm?id = 3395&l = 1 (January 2008).
13. Saud al-Faisal at the Council on Foreign Relations, September 2005. Available http://www.cfr.org/publication/8908/fight_against_extremism_and_the_search_for_peace_rush_transcript_federal_news_service_inc.html (January 2008).
14. Mokhtari, Fariborz, 'No one will scratch my back: Iranian security perceptions in historical context', *Middle East Policy* Spring (2005).
15. Okruhlik, Gwenn, 'Saudi Arabian–Iranian relations: external rapprochement and internal consolidation', *Middle East Policy* ii/Summer (2003).
16. 'Arab attitudes toward political and social issues, foreign policy and the media' (October 2005). Available http://www.bsos.umd.edu/SADAT/PUB/Arab-attitudes-2005.htm (August 2007).
17. Telhami, Shibley, 'Seeing Iran through an American prism', *The Baltimore Sun* (14 May 2006). Available http://www.brookings.edu/views/op-ed/telhami/20060514.htm (August 2007).
18. Arab attitudes toward political and social issues, foreign policy and the media'.

19. BBC interview with Saud al-Faisal, December 2005. Available http://news.bbc.co.uk/2/hi/middle_east/4615832.stmxvii (August 2007).
20. Ibid.
21. Leverett, Flynt, 'The Gulf between US', *The New York Times* (24 January 2006). Available http://www.nytimes.com/2006/01/24/opinion/24leverett.html?ex = 1295758800&en = 8861b5fd24f73a32&ei = 5088&partner = rssnyt&emc = rss (August 2007).
22. Ideas for US-centred or indigenous security arrangements in the Gulf have proliferated in recent years. While commendable, they all fail to appreciate the Gulf states' lack of options *vis-à-vis* Iran, and the fact that they are stuck with the United States.
23. 'Iran, Qatar leaders argue over Gulf name', Associated Press (3 May 2006). Available http://news.yahoo.com/s/ap/20060503/ap_on_re_mi_ea/iran_qatar_diplomatic;_ylt = Ar_a4NQhJR0ZBdD76Rnw94hvaA8F;_ylu = X3oDMTA5aHJvMDdwB-X3oDMTA5aHJvMDdwBHNlYwN5bmNhdA (August 2007).
24. 'Gulf states caught in Iran vortex', Associated Press (23 May 2006). Available http://timesofindia.indiatimes.com/articleshow/1549151.cmsxxii (August 2007).
25. 'Qatar pours cold water on Gulf initiative on Iran', Agence France Presse (25 May 2006). Available http://www.khaleejtimes.com/DisplayArticleNew.asp?xfile = data/middleeast/2006/May/middleeast_May60.2.xml&section = middleeast&col = col = (August 2007).
26. Al-Homayed, Tariq, 'Iran ... "I cry out in the Gulf"', Asharq Alawsat (13 April 2006). Available http://aawsat.com/english/news.asp?section = 2&id = 4523 (August 2007).
27. 'Iran seeks to calm GCC states about its nuclear activities', *Daily Star* (8 May 2006). Available http://www.dailystar.com.lb/article.asp?edition_id = 10&categ_id = 2&article_id = 24238 (January 2007).
28. Interview with a senior US analyst, Washington, DC, September 2005.
29. Quinlivan, James T., 'Coup-proofing: its practice and consequences in the Middle East', *International Security* xxiv/2 (1999), pp.131–65.
30. For an overview of the GCC–Iran military balance, see 'IISS Military Balance' at http://www.iiss.org/publications/the-military-balance; and Cordesman, Anthony, 'The Middle East military balance: definition, regional developments and trends' (23 March 2005). Available http://www.csis.org/media/csis/pubs/050323_memilbaldefine%5B1%5D.pdf (August 2007).
31. Laipson, Ellen, 'The absence of a U.S. policy towards Iran and its consequences', speech given at the American Academy of Diplomacy, 27 May 2004. Available http://www.stimson.org/pub.cfm?id = 118 (August 2007).
32. Bill, James A., *The Eagle and the Lion: The Tragedy of American–Iranian Relations* (London, Yale University Press, 1988), p.203; also Gasiorowski, Mark J., *U.S. Foreign Policy and the Shah: Building a Client State in Iran* (Ithaca, NY, Cornell University Press, 1991), p.100; and Palmer, Michael A., *Guardians of the Gulf: A History of America's Expanding Role in the Persian Gulf, 1833–1992* (New York, NY, Free Press, 1992), pp.86–8.
33. *Bahrain: Key Issues for US Policy*. CRS Report, 24 March 2005. Available http://fpc.state.gov/documents/organization/46433.pdf (August 2007). See also Chapters 2 and 6.

Notes

34. For a recent essay summarizing the views of multiple studies, see Kapoor, Sh. R. K., *The Economics of Nuclear Power: Is Nuclear the Socially Optimal Technology?* Available http://weber.ucsd.edu/~vcrawfor/Kapoor06Essay.pdf/. For the bright prospects of five out of six GCC members in the hydrocarbon sector, see the annual *EIA International Energy Outlook* at http://www.eia.doe.gov/oiaf/ieo/oil.html (August 2007).
35. For an insightful analysis of the importance of these deals to both parties, see Gause III, F. Gregory, 'Saudi Arabia and the proposed arms sale', testimony given before the House Committee on Foreign Affairs, 18 September 2007. Available http://foreignaffairs.house.gov/110/gau091807.htm (January 2008).
36. For a perceptive analysis, see Evron, Yair, *Israel's Nuclear Dilemma* (London, Routledge, 1994).
37. For an in-depth analysis of the success and failure of different NWFZ projects, see Thakur, Ramesh C., *Nuclear Weapons-Free Zones* (Houndmills, Macmillan, 1998).
38. For a very useful summary of the state of compliance with WMD agreements around the world, see Findlay, Trevor, Asplund, Erik, Persbo, Andreas and Woodward, Angela, *Wmd Verification & Compliance: The State of Play. A Study for the Weapons of Mass Destruction Commission (WMDC)* (Stockholm, Weapons of Mass Destruction Commission, 2004).
39. The classic reference handbook for all data on the subject is Diehl, Sarah J. and Moltz, James C., *Nuclear Weapons and Nonproliferation: A Reference Handbook*. Contemporary World Issues (Santa Barbara, CA, ABC-CLIO, 2007).
40. For the classic elaboration on the subject, see Wendt, Alexander, *Social Theory of International Politics* (Cambridge, Cambridge University Press, 1999). For a theoretical discussion, see also Chapter 3.
41. For a comprehensive treatment of the subject, at a much rosier time in history, see Mi'Ari, Mahmoud, 'Attitudes of Palestinians toward normalization with Israel', *Journal of Peace Research* xxxvi/3 (1999), pp.339–48.
42. For a rather more optimistic review of the same topic, see Johnson, Rebecca, 'Rethinking security interests for a nuclear-weapon-free zone in the Middle East', *Disarmament Diplomacy* no. 86/Autumn (2007).
43. The literature on this topic is vast, but for a good overall account, see Israël Shahak, Israël, *Open Secrets: Israeli Foreign and Nuclear Policies* (London, Pluto, 1997). From the time this book was published attitudes in Israel have stiffened considerably.
44. On the collapse of the Arms Control and Regional Security (ACRS) Working Group and the topic of Track II diplomacy in the region, see Saddam Hussein, Agha, Khalidi, Ahmad, Feldman, Shai and Schiff, Zeev, *Track-II Diplomacy: Lessons from the Middle East*. BCSIA Studies in International Security (Cambridge, MA, MIT Press, 2003). The conceptualization of nuclear weapons as the ultimate trump card in regional politics is fruitfully discussed by Solingen, Etel, *Nuclear Logics: Contrasting Paths in East Asia and the Middle East*. Studies in International History and Politics (Princeton, NJ, Princeton University Press, 2007).
45. For a spirited discussion of the resistance engendered by such programmes, see Rao, Rahul, 'The Empire writes back (to Michael Ignatieff)', *Millennium* xxiii/1 (2004), pp.145–66.

Chapter 8   The GCC, NATO and the Gulf Security Complex

1. NATO Rear Admiral, Oxford, November 2006, Personal Communication.
2. The original idea for this chapter stemmed from a workshop on Security Sector Reform in the Gulf held in at the Stimson Center, Washington, DC. The author would like to thank all the participants, in particular Ellen Laipson and Emile El-Hokayem. For the report of the workshop, which is slightly more optimistic about the prospect of the NATO enterprise, see at http://www.stimson.org/pub.cfm?id=323 (January 2007). For an earlier version of my argument, see Legrenzi, Matteo, 'NATO in the Gulf: who is doing whom a favor?', *Middle East Policy* xiv/1 (2007).
3. Article 5 famously states that 'The parties agree that an armed attack against one or more of them in Europe or North America shall be considered an attack against them all [...].' It forms the bedrock of the NATO system of collective self-defense.
4. For a brief overview of the Greater Middle East Initiative, see United States Congress, Senate Committee on Foreign Relations, *The Greater Middle East Initiative: Sea Island and Beyond: Hearing before the Committee on Foreign Relations, United States Senate, One Hundred Eighth Congress, Second Session, June 2, 2004*. iii, 79 (Washington, DC, US Government Printing Office (GPO), 2004). A first critical assessment is Carothers, Thomas and Ottaway, Marina, 'Greater Middle East initiative: off to a false start', in *Policy Brief*, 7 (Washington, DC, Carnegie Endowment for International Peace, 2004). For a fuller overview of all these programmes, see Ottaway, Marina and Choucair-Vizoso, Julia, *Beyond the Facade: Political Reform in the Arab World* (Washington, DC, Carnegie Endowment for International Peace, 2008).
5. For an overview of the MEPI, see http://www.state.gov/r/pa/scp/2005/49757.htm (January 2008).
6. Interviews with NATO officials during the 'Which Future for NATO's Mediterranean Dialogue and Istanbul Cooperation Initiative?' seminar, Rome, Italy, 6–8 May 2008.
7. For the 28 June 2004 text of the policy initiative, see 'Istanbul Cooperation Initiative'. Available http://www.nato.int/docu/comm/2004/06-istanbul/docu-cooperation.htm (January 2008). Note in particular the constant reference to the PfP programme as an antecedent.
8. For a brief outline of the PfP programme, see http://www.nato.int/issues/pfp/index.html/. The initiative was also extended to countries that were neutral during the Cold War such as Switzerland and Sweden; for the complete list, see http://www.nato.int/pfp/sig-cntr.htm (both January 2008). For a scholarly evaluation of the programme, see Spillmann, Kurt R. and Wenger, Andreas, *Towards the 21st Century: Trends in Post-Cold War International Security Policy* (Bern, Peter Lang, 1999); for a technical analysis of some of the achievements, see Rush, Robert S., Epley, William W. and Center of Military History, *Multinational Operations, Alliances, and International Military Cooperation: Past and Future*. Proceedings of the 5th Workshop of the Partnership for Peace Consortium's Military History Working Group, Vienna, Austria, 4–8 April 2005. Cmh Publ. No. 70-101-1 (Washington, DC: Center for Military History, US Army, 2006).
9. Reuters (22 January 2007).

10. For a list of all NATO commitments as well as the most up-to-date enunciation of ICI objectives, see the speech by NATO Secretary General Jaap de Hoop Scheffer at the NATO–Kuwait Public Diplomacy Conference, 12 December 2006, at http://www.nato.int/docu/speech/2006/s061212a.htm (January 2007).
11. Among many contributions on the subject, see, for example, Sadiki, Larbi, *The Search for Arab Democracy: Discourses and Counter-Discourses* (New York, NY, Columbia University Press, 2004).
12. For a comprehensive if somewhat romanticized account of this episode, see Trofimov, Yaroslav, *The Siege of Mecca: The Forgotten Uprising in Islam's Holiest Shrine and the Birth of Al Qaeda* (New York, NY, Doubleday, 2007).
13. A number of public gatherings have been organized so far in the Gulf to publicize the ICI initiative with policy-makers and local elites.
14. Monarchical regimes were overthrown by army coups in Libya, Egypt and Iraq, and the army played a crucial role in the political developments of other states such as Algeria, Syria and Yemen.
15. For a good treatment of the almost symbiotic relationship between the Hashemite royal family and the military in Jordan, see the relevant chapter in Massad, Joseph A., *Colonial Effects: The Making of National Identity in Jordan* (New York, NY, Columbia University Press, 2001). For a more mainstream account of the origins of the relationship, see Vatikiotis, P. J., *Politics and the Military in Jordan, A Study of the Arab Legion, 1921–1957* (London, Cass, 1967).
16. For a classical overview of how Arab armies operate, see Pollack, Kenneth M., *Arabs at War: Military Effectiveness, 1948–1991*. Studies in War, Society, and the Military (Lincoln, NE, University of Nebraska Press, 2002).
17. I thank my friend Dr Steffen Hertog for this particular insight. For a good work highlighting the different trajectory of Oman before the coming to power of Sultan Qabus, see Rabi, Uzi, *The Emergence of States in a Tribal Society: Oman under Sa'id Bin Taymur, 1932–1970* (Brighton, Sussex Academic, 2006). For an illuminating, detailed treatment of Oman's counterinsurgency operations and the structure of its security apparatus, see Peterson, John, *Oman's Insurgencies: The Sultanate's Struggle for Supremacy* (London, Saqi, 2007). Very useful for a general overview is also Anthony, John D., Peterson, J. E. and Abelson, Donald S., *Historical and Cultural Dictionary of the Sultanate of Oman and the Emirates of Eastern Arabia* (Metuchen, NJ, Scarecrow, 1976).
18. For an illuminating discussion of the genesis and role of Jordan's national security establishment, see Tal, Lawrence, *Politics, the Military and National Security in Jordan 1955–1967* (New York, NY, Palgrave, 2002), pp.1–19. See also the relevant sections in Robins, Philip, *A History of Jordan* (Cambridge, Cambridge University Press, 2004).
19. Bryden, Alan and Hanggi, Heiner, *Understanding and Supporting Security Sector Reform* (London, UK Department for International Development, n.d.); for a wealth of related material, see also the website of the Centre for Security Sector Management (CSSM). Available http://ssronline.org/.
20. See the proceedings of 'NATO's Evolving Role in the Middle East: The Gulf Dimension', Washington, DC, USA, 3 June 2005, in particular the speech of De Hoop Scheffer. Available http://www.stimson.org/swa/?SN=SW20050608841 (January 2007).

21. See the 28 June 2004 text of the 'Istanbul Cooperation Initiative'. Eventual NATO membership has been explicitly ruled out by the NATO Policy Council, the highest political body within the alliance.
22. For a proud history of this 'precedent setting' project, see the Vinnell Corporation website. Available http://www.vinnell.com/ (January 2007).
23. See, for example, the controversy regarding the Al-Yamamah (The Dove) arms deal. This is one of the few cases in which the specific amount of 'commissions' (around £5.2 million per Tornado combat aircraft) has become public because of a clerical error at the British Ministry of Defense; Leigh, Davis and Evans, Rob, 'The secret Whitehall telegram that reveals the truth behind controversial Saudi arms deal', The Guardian (28 October 2006). Available http://politics.guardian.co.uk/foi/story/0,,1933764,00.html (accessed January 2007). The subsequent decision to call off a Serious Fraud Office prosecution, followed by the Saudi decision to renew the multi-billion pound deal, has given rise to a spirited debate in Britain. It was followed by a formal Organisation for Economic Co-operation and Development (OECD) reproach for having contravened an Anti-Bribery Convention that had been signed in the UK; BBC News, 'OECD "concerns" over Saudi probe', BBC News (18 January 2007). Available http://news.bbc.co.uk/go/pr/fr/-/2/hi/uk_news/politics/6275199.stm (January 2007). Indeed, as a former Conservative Minister Ian Gilmour promptly remarked, 'You either got the business and bribed, or you didn't bribe and didn't get the business [...].' It is highly questionable whether the word 'bribe' is appropriate given the institutional framework of Saudi Arabia. The Saudi authorities were fully behind the deal. However, the sheer amount of hypocrisy surrounding the whole episode makes it interesting.
24. Jourde, Cédric, 'Constructing representations of the "Global War on Terror" in the Islamic Republic of Mauritania', *Journal of Contemporary African Studies* 25/1 (2007), pp.77–100.
25. See, for example, 'NATO's Mediterranean Dialogue and Istanbul Cooperation Initiative'. Available http://www.nato.int/med-dial/qa.htm; or recent speeches by Nicola De Santis, NATO official in charge of the ICI public diplomacy component.
26. Remarks made off the record during the 'Which Future for NATO's Mediterranean Dialogue and Istanbul Cooperation Initiative?' seminar.
27. Remarks delivered in November 2006.

Conclusion

1. For an excellent overview of this literature and an interesting agenda for future research, see Acharya, Amitav and Johnston, Alastair I. (eds), *Crafting Cooperation: Regional International Institutions in Comparative Perspective* (Cambridge, Cambridge University Press, 2007).
2. See the classic Fawcett, Louise L'E. and Hurrell, Andrew, *Regionalism in World Politics: Regional Organization and International Order* (Oxford, Oxford University Press, 1995). For a volume focusing on the Middle East, see Hudson, C. Michael, 'Arab integration: an overview', in Hudson, C. Michael (ed.), *Middle East Dilemma: The Politics and Economics of Arab Integration* (London, I.B.Tauris, 1999), pp.1–33. For a more recent contribution that also concentrates on the Middle East, see Legrenzi, Matteo and

Harders, Cilja (eds), *Beyond Regionalism? Regionalism, Regionalization and Regional Integration in the Middle East. International Political Economy* (London, Ashgate, 2007).
3. See the literature on 'new regionalism best exemplified by Hettne, Björn, Inotai, Andr and Sunkel, Osvaldo (eds), *Studies in New Regionalism*, Vols I–V (London, MacMillan, 1999–2001). See also the series of policy-relevant reports and volumes emanating from the United Nations University-Comparative Regional Integration Studies (UNU-CRIS) based in Bruges, Belgium. Available http://www.cris.unu.edu/.
4. For the most exhaustive account, see Davidson, Christopher M., *The United Arab Emirates: A Study in Survival, The Middle East in the International System* (Boulder, CO, Lynne Rienner, 2005).
5. Gerd Nonneman used this expression in debates on the topic in the *Gulf 2000* academic list; see also Chapter 6.
6. Niblock, Tim, *Saudi Arabia: Power, Legitimacy and Survival, The Contemporary Middle East* (London, Routledge, 2006).
7. In December 2001 Yemen was allowed to join the health, labour and social ministerial councils.
8. For a complete list of these meetings, see the monthly bulletin *GCC News*; for thematic studies the best source is *Al-Ta'wun* (Cooperation) magazine. Both publications are issued by the Secretariat General.
9. Good examples are: Brown, Carl, *International Politics and the Middle East: Old Rules, Dangerous Game* (Princeton, NJ, Princeton University Press, 1984); and more recently Brown, Carl, *Diplomacy in the Middle East, the International Relations of Regional and Outside Powers* (London, I.B.Tauris, 2004), where the Middle East is explicitly hailed as a unique sub-system in International Relations where states answer to different, unique rules. The case for a more historical approach with regards to the Arab–Israeli dispute is made, for example, by Shlaim, Avi, 'The rise and fall of the Oslo Peace Process', in Fawcett, Louise L'E. (ed.), *International Relations of the Middle East* (Oxford, Oxford University Press, 2005).
10. The desirability of an all-encompassing security architecture has long been recognized. However, the political obstacles have always been daunting. In his excellent overview of the GCC as part of a larger study, Philip Robins stressed the need for a 'new multilateral framework embracing the whole of the Gulf'. Two decades later the framework is still desirable but the political obstacles are, if anything, more daunting; Robins, Philip, *The Future of the Gulf: Politics and Oil in the 1990s, The Energy and Environmental Programme* (London, Royal Institute of International Affairs, 1989), p.78.

APPENDIX

FORMS OF COOPERATION AMONG GULF ARAB STATES, 1971–80

Date	Countries involved	Host Country	Description
Bilateral Cooperation			
June 1973	UAE and Qatar	Both Countries	Series of economic agreements regarding free movements of capital and workers
June 1973	Kuwait and Bahrain	Kuwait	Agreements and cooperation on economics, media and education
November 1976	Kuwait and UAE	Kuwait	Cooperation in the economic sphere
Ministerial Meetings			
October 1975	Bahrain, Kuwait, Oman, Qatar, Saudi Arabia and UAE (Future GCC states)	Saudi Arabia (Riyadh)	Education ministers
January 1976	Bahrain, Kuwait, Oman, Qatar, Saudi Arabia, UAE (Future GCC states) **and Iraq**	UAE (Abu Dhabi)	Information ministers

Date	Countries involved	Host Country	Description
February 1976	Future GCC states and Iraq	Saudi Arabia (Riyadh)	Industry ministers
February 1976	Future GCC states and Iraq	Saudi Arabia (Riyadh)	Agricultural ministers
October 1977	Future GCC states and Iraq	Saudi Arabia (Riyadh)	Information ministers
October 1977	Future GCC states and Iraq	Iraq (Baghdad)	Trade and finance ministers
February 1978	Future GCC states and Iraq	Saudi Arabia (Riyadh)	Social affairs and labour ministers
1979	Future GCC states and Iraq	Bahrain	Information ministers
January 1979	Future GCC states and Iraq	Saudi Arabia (Riyadh)	Trade and finance ministers
January 1979	Future GCC states and Iraq	Saudi Arabia (Riyadh)	Planning ministers
1980	Future GCC states and Iraq	Qatar	Information ministers
1980	Future GCC states and Iraq	Qatar	Planning ministers
Joint Working Organizations			
October 1975	Bahrain, Kuwait, Oman, Qatar, Saudi Arabia, UAE **and Iraq**	Headquarters Riyadh	The Gulf States Arab Education Office
January 1976	Future GCC states and Iraq	Headquarters Kuwait	The Joint Institution for the Production of Programs
February 1976	Future GCC states and Iraq	Headquarters Qatar (Doha)	The Gulf Organization for Industrial investments
June 1976	Future GCC states and Iraq	Headquarters UAE (Abu Dhabi)	Conference for the Coordination of Television
September 1977	Future GCC states and Iraq	Headquarters Saudi Arabia (Riyadh)	Gulf Postal Authority
October 1977	Future GCC states and Iraq	Headquarters Bahrain	The Gulf News Agency, created as result of meeting of information ministers in Riyadh

Date	States	Headquarters	Organization
April 1978	Future GCC states and Iraq	Headquarters Kuwait	Arab Center for Educational Research
October 1979	Future GCC states and Iraq	Headquarters UAE (Abu Dhabi)	Union of the Chambers of Commerce and Industry in the Gulf States
February 1980	Future GCC states and Iraq	Headquarters Iraq (Baghdad)	Center for the Documentation of Information in the Gulf
March 1980	Future GCC states except Oman and UAE and Iraq	Bahrain (Manama)	University of the Gulf Joint Public Economic Institutions

Joint Companies

Date	States	Headquarters	Company
1974	Bahrain, Oman, Qatar and UAE		Gulf Air
December 1974	All future GCC states (except Oman) and Iraq	Bahrain	Arab Shipbuilding and Repair Yard Company
November 1975	All future GCC states (except Oman) and Iraq	Kuwait	Arab Petroleum Investment Corporation
December 1975	All future GCC states (except UAE) and Iraq	Bahrain	Gulf International Bank
January 1976	All future GCC states (except Oman) and Iraq	Kuwait	Arab Maritime Company
June 1976	Kuwait and Saudi Arabia	Saudi Arabia	Saudi-Kuwaiti Cement Company
October 1976	All future GCC states and Iraq	Saudi Arabia (Damman)	Gulf Ports Union
August 1977	Bahrain and Saudi Arabia	Saudi Arabia	Saudi-Bahraini Cement Company
February 1979	Kuwait, Qatar and Saudi Arabia	Kuwait	Joint Company for Maritime Transport
May 1980	Kuwait, Qatar and Saudi Arabia	Bahrain	Gulf Petrochemical Industries Company

Note: GCC, Gulf Cooperation Council; UAE, United Arab Emirates.

BIBLIOGRAPHY

Selected interviews

Al-Khorafi, Mohammed Jassim, Speaker of the Kuwaiti Parliament, Kuwait, 5 December 2000.

Al-Kuwaiz, Abdullah Ibrahim, Associate Secretary General for Economic Affairs in London, London, 16 November 1998.

Al-Qasimi, Fahim, Dubai, 20 April 2002.

Al-Saud, Prince Turki Al-Faisal, Oxford, 18 November 2003.

Aluwaisheg, Abdel Aziz Abu Hamad, Venice, 17 October 2008.

Balfour-Paul, Glen Exeter, Former British Political Agent in the Gulf, 7 July 1999.

Bishara, Abdullah Yacoub, First Secretary General of the GCC, multiple interviews, Kuwait, November and December 2000.

Di Miceli, Giuseppe, Army Colonel and Italian Military Attaché, Kuwait, 15 November 2000.

Onelli, Savino, Colonel, Italian Center for Strategic Studies, Florence, 10 March 2002.

Pelletreau, Robert, Former Assistant Secretary of State, United States of America, Oxford, 10 October 1999.

Sultan, Abdulaziz, Chairman of KEO Consulting, Kuwait Coordinator of the Development Forum and Leader of the National Democratic Movement, Kuwait, 11 November 2000.

Primary and secondary sources

These are only the sources actually quoted in the body of the work.

Aarts, Paul, *Dilemmas of Regional Cooperation in the Middle East*. Lancaster Papers No. 4 (Lancaster, Department of Politics and International Relations, Lancaster University, 1999).

Abdulkhalig, Ahmad S. and Alnageeb, Mahmoud H., *Comparative Encyclopedia for Laws, Legislation, and Regulations in Kuwait, Bahrain, Qatar, UAE, and Saudi Arabia* (Kuwait City, Alnageeb Est., 1979).

Acharya, Amitav, *The Gulf Cooperation Council and Security: Dilemmas of Dependence 1981–1988* (London, Gulf Centre for Strategic Studies, 1989).

Acharya, Amitav and Johnston, Alastair I. (eds), *Crafting Cooperation: Regional International Institutions in Comparative Perspective* (Cambridge, Cambridge University Press, 2007).

Adib-Moghaddam, Arshin, *The International Politics of the Persian Gulf: A Cultural Genealogy* (London, Routledge, 2006).

Adler, Emanuel and Barnett, Michael N., *Security Communities*. Studies in International Relations (Cambridge, Cambridge University Press, 1998).

Ajami, Fouad, 'The end of Pan-Arabism', *Foreign Affairs*, lvii/2 (1978/79), pp.355–73.

Al-Arayed, Jawad S., *A Line in the Sea: The Qatar v. Bahrain Border Dispute in the World Court* (Berkeley, CA, North Atlantic, 2003).

Al-Fayez, Khaled, 'The Gulf Investment Corporation', *American–Arab Affairs* no. 11/ Winter (1984–85).

Al-Hamad, Turki, 'Will the Gulf monarchies work together?', *Middle East Quarterly*, iv/1 (1997).

Al-Isa, Shamlan Y. and Al-Manufi, Kamal, *Trends in Kuwaiti Public Opinion Regarding the Gulf Cooperation Council* (Kuwait, Department of Political Science, University of Kuwait, 1985).

Al-Jafary, Abdul R., 'Investment opportunities in the Gulf: manufacturing industry joint venture opportunities', paper presented at the 2nd GCC–EU Industrial Conference, Doha, Qatar, 1992.

Al-Kuwaiz, Abdullah I., 'Economic integration of the Cooperation Council of the Arab States of the Gulf: challenges, achievements and future outlook', in Sandwick, John A. (ed.), *The Gulf Cooperation Council: Moderation and Stability in an Interdependent World* (Boulder, CO, Westview, 1987), pp.71–85.

Al-Makhawi, Rashid, *The Gulf Cooperation Council: A Study in Integration* (Salford, University of Salford, 1990).

Al-Qasimi, Muhammad, *The Myth of Arab Piracy in the Gulf*, 2nd edn (London, Routledge, 1988).

Al-Saud, Faisal bin Salman, *Iran, Saudi Arabia and the Gulf: Power Politics in Transition 1968–1971* (London, I.B.Tauris, 2003).

Allison, Graham T., *Essence of Decision: Explaining the Cuban Missile Crisis* (Boston, MA, Little Brown, 1971).

Alswied, Mohammed, *The Gulf Cooperation Council: A Model of a Regional International Regime* (Madison, WI, University of Wisconsin, 1988).

Amirahmadi, Hooshang (ed.), *Small Islands Big Politics: The Tonbs and Abu Musa in the Gulf* (Houndmills, MacMillan, 1996).

Anthony, John D., Peterson, J. E. and Abelson, Donald S., *Historical and Cultural Dictionary of the Sultanate of Oman and the Emirates of Eastern Arabia* (Metuchen, NJ, Scarecrow, 1976).

Arab Bureau of Education for the Gulf States, *The Directory of Joint Gulf Organizations and Institutions* (1982).

Art, Robert J. and Jervis, Robert, *International Politics: Enduring Concepts and Contemporary Issues*, 4th edn (New York, NY, HarperCollins College, 1996).
Art, Robert J. and Jervis, Robert, *International Politics: Enduring Concepts and Contemporary Issues*, 5th edn (New York, NY, Longman, 2000).
Assiri, Abdhul R., *Kuwait's Foreign Policy: City-State in World Politics* (Boulder, CO, Westview, 1990).
Ayoob, Mohammed, 'Subaltern Realism: International Relations theory meets the Third World', in Neuman, Stephanie G. (ed.), *International Relations Theory and the Third World* (Basingstoke, Macmillan, 1998).
Ayubi, Nazih N. M., *Over-Stating the Arab State: Politics and Society in the Middle East* (London, Tauris, 1995).
Baabood, Abdulla, 'Dynamics and determinants of the GCC states' foreign policy, with special reference to the EU', in Nonneman, Gerd (ed.), *Analyzing Middle East Foreign Policies and the Relationship with Europe* (New York, NY, Routledge, 2005), pp.145–73.
Baabood, Abdulla and Edwards, Geoffrey, 'Reinforcing ambivalence: the interaction of Gulf States and the European Union', paper presented at the Eighth Mediterranean Social and Political Research Meeting, European University Institute, Montecatini, 2007.
Balassa, Bela, *The Theory of Economic Integration* (London, Allen & Unwin, 1961).
Balfour-Paul, Glen, *The End of Empire in the Middle East* (Cambridge, Cambridge University Press, 1991).
Barnett, Michael N., *Dialogues in Arab Politics: Negotiations in Regional Order* (New York, NY, Columbia University Press, 1998).
Barnett, Michael N., 'Sovereignty, nationalism, and regional order in the Arab states system', *International Organization*, il/3 (1995), pp.479–510.
Barnett, Michael N. and Gause III, F. Gregory, 'Caravans in opposite directions: society, state, and the development of community in the Gulf Cooperation Council', in Adler, Emanuel and Barnett, Michael N. (eds), *Security Communities* (Cambridge, Cambridge University Press, 1998), pp.161–97.
Beaumont, Peter, 'Water and armed conflict in the Middle East – fantasy or reality?', in Gleditsch, N. P. (ed.), *Conflict and the Environment* (Oslo, Kluwer, 1997), pp.355–74.
Bill, James A., *The Eagle and the Lion: The Tragedy of American–Iranian Relations* (London, Yale University Press, 1988).
Bill, James A., 'The geometry of instability in the Gulf: the rectangle of tension', in Al-Suwaidi, Jamal S. (ed.), *Iran and the Gulf: A Search for Stability* (Abu Dhabi, Emirates Center for Strategic Studies and Research, 1996).
Bishara, Abdullah Y., 'The Gulf Cooperation Council: achievements and challenges', *American–Arab Affairs* Winter/7 (1983–84), pp.40–4.
Brown, Carl, *Diplomacy in the Middle East, the International Relations of Regional and Outside Powers* (London, I.B.Tauris, 2004).
Brown, Carl, *International Politics and the Middle East: Old Rules, Dangerous Game* (Princeton, NJ, Princeton University Press, 1984).

Buzan, Barry, *People, States and Fear: An Agenda for International Security in the Post-Cold War Era*, 2nd edn (London, Harvester Wheatsheaf, 1991).

Buzan, Barry and Wæver, Ole, *Regions and Powers: The Structure of International Security*. Studies in International Relations No. 91 (Cambridge, Cambridge University Press, 2003).

Cammett, Melani, 'Defensive integration and late developers: the Gulf Cooperation Council and the Arab Maghreb Union', *Global Governance* 5 (1999), pp.379–402.

Carothers, Thomas and Ottaway, Marina, 'Greater Middle East initiative: off to a false start', in *Policy Brief*, 7 (Washington, DC, Carnegie Endowment for International Peace, 2004).

Cass, Stephen J. R., *The US Takes Sides: US Policy Towards Iraq During the Iran–Iraq War* (Oxford, University of Oxford, 1994).

Chaudry, Kiren A., *The Price of Wealth: Economies and Institutions in the Middle East* (Ithaca, NY, Cornell University Press, 1997).

Chubin, Shahram (ed.), *Security in the Persian Gulf 2: The Role of the Outside Powers* (London, International Institute for Strategic Studies, 1982).

Chubin, Shahram and Tripp, Charles, *Iran and Iraq at War* (London, I.B.Tauris, 1988).

Cooper, Scott and Taylor, Brock, *Power and Regionalism: Explaining Economic Cooperation in the Persian Gulf* (Provo, UT, Brigham Young University, 2001).

Cordesman, Anthony H., *After the Storm: The Changing Military Balance in the Middle East* (Boulder, CO, Westview, 1993).

Cordesman, Anthony H., *Bahrain, Oman, Qatar, and the UAE: Challenges of Security, Csis Middle East Dynamic Assessment* (Boulder, CO, Westview, 1997).

Cordesman, Anthony H., *Kuwait, Csis Middle East Dynamic Net Assessment* (Boulder, CO, Westview, 1997).

Cordesman, Anthony H., *Saudi Arabia Enters the Twenty-First Century: The Military and International Security Dimensions* (Westport, CT, Praeger, 2003).

Cordesman, Anthony H., *The Gulf and the West: Strategic Relations and Military Realities* (London, Mansell, 1988).

Cordesman, Anthony H., *The Iran–Iraq War and Western Security 1984–87: Strategic Implications and Policy Options* (London, Jane's, 1987).

Cordesman, Anthony H., 'U.S. forces in the Middle East: resources and capabilities', in Cordesman, Anthony H. (ed.), *Csis Middle East Dynamic Net Assessment* (Boulder, CO, Westview, 1997).

Crystal, Jill, *Oil and Politics in the Gulf: Rulers and Merchants in Kuwait and Qatar* (Cambridge, Cambridge University Press, 1990).

David, Steven R., 'Explaining Third World alignment', *World Politics: Quarterly Journal of International Relations* xliii/2 (1991), pp.233–56.

Davidson, Christopher M., *Dubai: The Vulnerability of Success* (New York, NY, Columbia University Press, 2008).

Davidson, Christopher M., *The United Arab Emirates: A Study in Survival*, The Middle East in the International System (Boulder, CO, Lynne Rienner, 2005).

Desch, Michael C., 'Culture clash: assessing the importance of ideas in security studies', *International Security* xxiii/1 (1998), pp.141–70.

Deutsch, Karl, *Political Community in the North Atlantic Area: International Organization in Light of Historical Experience* (Princeton, NJ, Princeton University Press, 1957).

Diehl, Sarah J. and Moltz, James C., *Nuclear Weapons and Nonproliferation: A Reference Handbook*. Contemporary World Issues (Santa Barbara, CA, ABC-CLIO, 2007).

Dietl, Gulshan, *Through Two Wars and Beyond: A Study of the Gulf Cooperation Council* (New Delhi, Lancers, 1991).

Dotterway, K. A., *Systematic Analysis of Complex Dynamic Systems: The Case of the USS Vincennes* (Monterey, CA, Naval Postgraduate School, 1992).

Dunn, Michael, 'The Gulf: Cooperation Council', *Defense and Foreign Affairs Daily* x/105 (1981), pp.1–2.

El-Shazly, Nadia El-Sayed, *The Gulf Tanker War: Iran and Iraq's Maritime Swordplay* (New York, NY, St. Martin's, 1998).

Evron, Yair, 'Towards the emergence of a common security system in the Middle East', in Martin, Leonor G. (ed.), *New Frontiers in Middle East Security* (Houndmills, MacMillan, 1998).

Evron, Yair, *Israel's Nuclear Dilemma* (London, Routledge, 1994).

Farrell, Mary, Hettne, Björn and van Langenhove, Luk (eds), *Global Politics of Regionalism: Theory and Practice* (London, Pluto, 2005).

Fawcett, Louise, 'Regionalism in historical perspective', in Fawcett, Louise and Hurrell, Andrew (eds), *Regionalism in World Politics: Regional Organization and International Order* (Oxford, Oxford University Press, 1995).

Fawcett, Louise and Hurrell, Andrew, *Regionalism in World Politics: Regional Organization and International Order* (Oxford, Oxford University Press, 1995).

Findlay, Trevor, Asplund, Erik, Persbo, Andreas and Woodward, Angela, *Wmd Verification & Compliance: The State of Play. A Study for the Weapons of Mass Destruction Commission (WMDC)* (Stockholm, Weapons of Mass Destruction Commission, 2004).

Finnemore, Martha, *The Purpose of Intervention: Changing Beliefs About the Use of Force*. Cornell Studies in Security Affairs (Ithaca, NY, Cornell University Press, 2003).

Gardner, J. Anthony, *The Iraq–Iran War: A Bibliography* (Boston, MA, G. K. Hall, 1988).

Gasiorowski, Mark J., *U.S. Foreign Policy and the Shah: Building a Client State in Iran* (Ithaca, NY, Cornell University Press, 1991).

Gause III, F. Gregory, 'Balancing what? Threat perception and alliance choice in the Gulf' Security Studies 13, no. 2 (Winter 2003/2004): 273–305.

Gause III, F. Gregory, *Oil Monarchies: Domestic Security Challenges in the Arab Gulf States* (New York, NY, Council on Foreign Relations Press, 1994).

GCC Secretariat, 'Charter of the GCC', *American–Arab Affairs*, no. 7/Winter (1983–84), pp.157–62.

GCC Secretariat, *Rules of Procedures Commission for the Settlement of Disputes* (Riyadh, GCC Printing Press, 1985).

GCC Secretariat, *The Cooperation Council Charter* (Riyadh, GCC Printing Press, 1990).

GCC Secretariat, *The Unified Economic Agreement* (Riyadh, GCC Printing Press, 1981).

Government of Bahrain, *Case Concerning Maritime Delimitation and Territorial Questions between Qatar and Bahrain (Qatar Vs. Bahrain). Counter-Memorial Submitted by the State of Bahrain. Questions of Jurisdiction and Admissibility* (Manama, 1992).

Government of Bahrain, *Cooperation Council for the Arab States of the Gulf* (Bahrain, Bahrain Government Printing Press, 1983).

Green, Jerrold D., 'Gulf security without the Gulf states', *Harvard Journal of World Affairs* iv/1 (1995), pp.78–89.

Guazzone, Laura, 'Gulf Cooperation Council: the security policies', *Survival* xxx/2 (1988).

Gulf Information and Research Centre, *The GCC* (London, Gulf Information and Research Centre, 1983).

Hameed, Mazher A., *Arabia Imperilled: The Security Imperatives of the Arab Gulf States* (Washington, DC, Middle East Assessments Group, 1986).

Heard-Bey, Frauke, 'The United Arab Emirates: a quarter century of federation', in Hudson, C. Michael (ed.), *Middle Dilemma: The Politics and Economics of Arab Integration* (London, I.B.Tauris, 1999), pp.128–50.

Heard-Bey, Frauke, *From Trucial States to United Arab Emirates: A Society in Transition*, 2nd edn (London, Longman, 1996).

Henderson, Simon, *The New Pillar: Conservative Arab Gulf States and U.S. Strategy*. Policy Paper No. 58 (Washington, DC, Washington Institute for Near East Policy, 2003).

Herb, Michael, *All in the Family: Absolutism, Revolution, and Democracy in the Middle Eastern Monarchies*. SUNY Series in Middle Eastern Studies (Albany, NY, State University of New York Press, 1999).

Hertog, Steffen, 'The GCC and Arab economic integration: a new paradigm', *Middle East Policy* xiv/1 (2007), pp.52–69.

Hettne, Björn, Inotai, Andr and Sunkel, Osvaldo (eds), *Studies in New Regionalism*, Vols I–V (London, MacMillan, 1999–2001).

Hiro, Dilip, *The Longest War: The Iran–Iraq Military Conflict* (London, Paladin, 1990).

Hudson, C. Michael, 'Arab integration: an overview', in Hudson, C. Michael (ed.), *Middle East Dilemma: The Politics and Economics of Arab Integration* (London, I.B.Tauris, 1999), pp.1–33.

Hurrell, Andrew, 'Regionalism in theoretical perspective', in Hurrell, Andrew and Fawcett, Louise (eds), *Regionalism in World Politics: Regional Organization and International Order* (Oxford, Oxford University Press, 1995).

Hussein, Agha, Khalidi, Ahmad, Feldman, Shai and Schiff, Zeev, *Track-II Diplomacy: Lessons from the Middle East*. BCSIA Studies in International Security (Cambridge, MA, MIT Press, 2003).

Joffé, George, 'Arab frontiered disputes: the consequences for Arab security', *Geopolitics and International Boundaries* i/2 (1996).

Johnson, Rebecca, 'Rethinking security interests for a nuclear-weapon-free zone in the Middle East', *Disarmament Diplomacy* no. 86/Autumn (2007).

Jourde, Cédric, 'Constructing representations of the "Global War on Terror" in the Islamic Republic of Mauritania', *Journal of Contemporary African Studies* xxv/1 (2007), pp.77–100.

Kapiszewski, Andrzej, *Nationals and Expatriates: Population and Labour Dilemmas of the Gulf Cooperation Council States* (Reading, Ithaca Press, 2001).

Karsh, Efraim, *The Iran–Iraq War, 1980–1988, Essential Histories* (Oxford, Osprey, 2002).

Karsh, Efraim, *The Iran–Iraq War, a Military Analysis*. Adelphi Papers No. 220 (London, International Institute for Strategic Studies, 1987).

Kennan, George F., *The Cloud of Danger: Current Realities of American Foreign Policy* (Boston, MA, Little Brown, 1977).

Keohane, Robert O., 'Realism, Neorealism and the study of world politics', in Keohane, Robert O. (ed.), *Neorealism and Its Critics* (New York, NY, Columbia University Press, 1986).

Khalifa, Ali, *The United Arab Emirates: Unity in Fragmentation* (Boulder, CO, Westview, 1979).

Khalil, Muhammad, *The Arab States and the Arab League: A Documentary Record*, Vol. 2 (Cairo, League of Arab States, 1962).

Koppers, Simon, *Economic Analysis and Evaluation of the Gulf Cooperation Council (GCC)*. European University Studies: Series V Economics and Management, Vol. 1783. Frankfurt am Main: Peter Lang, 1995).

Kostiner, Joseph, *Middle East Monarchies: The Challenge of Modernity* (Boulder, CO, Lynne Rienner, 2000).

Lawson, Fred H., *Constructing International Relations in the Arab World* (Stanford, CA, Stanford University Press, 2006).

Legrenzi, Matteo and Harders, Cilja (eds), *Beyond Regionalism? Regionalism, Regionalization and Regional Integration in the Middle East. International Political Economy* (London, Ashgate, 2007).

Legrenzi, Matteo, 'Iraq, Iran e Arabia Saudita come triangolo scaleno: per una storia degli equilibri di potenza nella regione del Golfo', in Nordio, M., Torri, M. and Vercellin, G. (eds), *Grande Medio Oriente* (Milan, Bruno Mondadori, 2006).

Legrenzi, Matteo, 'NATO in the Gulf: who is doing whom a favor?', *Middle East Policy* xiv/1 (2007).

Lepgold, Joseph and Nincic, Miroslav, *Beyond the Ivory Tower: International Relations Theory and the Issue of Policy Relevance* (New York, NY, Columbia University Press, 2001).

Lienhardt, Peter and al-Shahi, Ahmed, *Shaikhdoms of Eastern Arabia*. St. Antony's Series (Basingstoke, Palgrave, 2001).

Luciani, Giacomo (ed.), *The Arab State* (Berkeley, CA, University of California Press, 1990).

Mansfield, Edward D. and Milner, Helen V. (eds), *The Political Economy of Regionalism* (New York, NY, Columbia University Press, 1993).

Massad, Joseph A., *Colonial Effects: The Making of National Identity in Jordan* (New York, NY, Columbia University Press, 2001).

Mattair, Thomas R., *The Three Occupied UAE Islands: The Tunbs and Abu Musa* (Abu Dhabi, Emirates Center for Strategic Studies and Research, 2006).

Mearsheimer, John J., *The Tragedy of Great Power Politics* (New York, NY, Norton, 2001).

Mi'Ari, Mahmoud, 'Attitudes of Palestinians toward normalization with Israel', *Journal of Peace Research* xxxvi/3 (1999), pp.339–48.

Milani, Mohsen M., *The Making of Iran's Islamic Revolution* (Boulder, CO, Westview, 1994), pp.214–15.

Ministry of Information, *The Way Forward: Cooperation and Unity in the Gulf* (Muscat, Sultanate of Oman, 1985).

Mokhtari, Fariborz, 'No one will scratch my back: Iranian security perceptions in historical context', *Middle East Policy* Spring (2005).

Morgenthau, Hans J., 'Alliances in theory and practice', in Wolfers, Arnold (ed.), *Alliance Policy in the Cold War* (Baltimore, MD, Johns Hopkins University Press, 1959).

Morgenthau, Hans J., *Politics among Nations: The Struggle for Power and Peace* (New York, NY, Knopf, 1949).

Muhammed Morsy, Abdullah, *The United Arab Emirates: A Modern History* (London, Croom Helm, 1978).

Nakhleh, Emile A., *The Gulf Cooperation Council: Policies, Problems and Prospects* (New York, NY, Praeger, 1986).

Navias, Martin S. and Hooton, E. R., *Tanker Wars: The Assault on Merchant Shipping During the Iran–Iraq Conflict, 1980–1988* (London, I.B.Tauris, 1996).

Niblock, Tim, *Saudi Arabia: Power, Legitimacy and Survival*, The Contemporary Middle East (London, Routledge, 2006).

Niblock, Tim, *The Political Economy of Saudi Arabia* (London, Routledge, 2007).

Niblock, Tim, 'The prospects for integration in the Arab Gulf', in Niblock, Tim (ed.), *Social and Economic Development in the Arab Gulf* (London, Croom Helm, 1981).

Niebuhr, Rienhold, 'The illusion of world government', *Foreign Affairs* xxvii/3 (1949), pp.379–88.

Nonneman, Gerd, 'EU–GCC relations: dynamics, perspectives, and the issue of political reform', *Journal of Social Affairs* xxiii/92 (2006).

Nonneman, Gerd, *Iraq, the Gulf States & the War* (London, Ithaca Press, 1986).

Nonneman, Gerd, 'The Gulf states and the Iran–Iraq War: pattern shifts and continuities', in Potter, Lawrence G. and Sick, Gary (eds), *Iran, Iraq, and the Legacies of War* (New York, NY, Palgrave Macmillan, 2004).

Nye, Joseph S., 'Comparative regional integration: concept and measurement', *International Organization* 22/Fall (1968).

Nye, Joseph S., *International Regionalism* (Boston, MA, Little Brown, 1968).

Okruhlik, Gwenn, 'Saudi Arabian–Iranian relations: external rapprochement and internal consolidation', *Middle East Policy* ii/Summer (2003).

Onley, James. *The Arabian Frontier of the British Raj: Merchants, Rulers, and the British in the Nineteenth-Century Gulf* (Oxford, Oxford University Press, 2007).

Ottaway, Marina and Choucair-Vizoso, Julia, *Beyond the Facade: Political Reform in the Arab World* (Washington, DC: Carnegie Endowment for International Peace, 2008).

Oye, Kenneth A, 'Explaining cooperation under anarchy: hypotheses and strategies', *World Politics: Quarterly Journal of International Relations* xxxviii/1 (1985), pp.1–24.

Palmer, Michael A., *Guardians of the Gulf: A History of America's Expanding Role in the Persian Gulf, 1833–1992* (New York, NY, Free Press, 1992).

Peirce, Charles S. and Buchler, Justus, *The Philosophy of Peirce: Selected Writings* (New York, NY, AMS Press, 1978).

Peterson, Erik R., *The Gulf Cooperation Council: Search for Unity in a Dynamic Region* (Boulder, CO, Westview, 1988).

Peterson, J. E., 'Britain and the Gulf: at the periphery of Empire', in Potter, Lawrence G. (ed.), *The Persian Gulf in History* (New York, NY, Palgrave, Macmillan, 2009).

Peterson, J. E., 'The GCC and regional security', in Sandwick, John A. (ed.), *The Gulf Cooperation Council: Moderation and Stability in an Interdependent World* (Boulder, CO, Westview, 1987).

Peterson, John, *Oman's Insurgencies: The Sultanate's Struggle for Supremacy* (London, Saqi, 2007).

Pollack, Kenneth M., *Arabs at War: Military Effectiveness, 1948–1991*. Studies in War, Society, and the Military (Lincoln, NE, University of Nebraska Press, 2002).

Potter, Lawrence G. and Sick, Gary, *Iran, Iraq, and the Legacies of War* (New York, NY, Palgrave Macmillan, 2004).

Priess, David, *Alliance Durability: Why Breaking Up Is Hard to Do* (Durham, NC, Duke University, 2000).

Quinlivan, James T., 'Coup-proofing: its practice and consequences in the Middle East', *International Security* xxiv/2 (1999), pp.131–65.

Rabi, Uzi, *The Emergence of States in a Tribal Society: Oman under Sa'id Bin Taymur, 1932–1970* (Brighton: Sussex Academic, 2006).

Rabi, Uzi, 'The GCC: the endless quest for regional security', paper presented at the MESA Meeting, San Francisco, CA, USA, 2004.

Ramazani, R. K., *The Gulf Cooperation Council: Record and Analysis* (Charlottesville, VA, University Press of Virginia, 1988).

Rao, Rahul, 'The Empire writes back (to Michael Ignatieff)', *Millennium* xxiii/1 (2004), pp.145–66.

Regional and Country Studies Branch, Division for Industrial Studies, *The Resource Base for Industrialization in the Gulf Co-operation Council Countries: A Framework for Co-operation* (New York, NY, UN Industrial Development Organization, 1983).

Rieger, Hans Christoph, 'Basic Issues of ASEAN Economic Co-operation', in Koppers, Simon (ed.), *Growth Determinants in East and South-East Asian Economies* (Berlin, Duncker & Humblot, 1991), pp.215–38.

Robins, Philip, *A History of Jordan* (Cambridge, Cambridge University Press, 2004).

Robins, Philip, *The Future of the Gulf: Politics and Oil in the 1990s*, The Energy and Environmental Programme (London, Royal Institute of International Affairs, 1989).

Rose, Gideon, 'Neoclassical Realism and theories of foreign policy', *World Politics*, October/51 (1998), pp.144–72.

Ruggie, John G., *Constructing the World Polity: Essays on International Institutionalization*, The New International Relations (London, Routledge, 1998).

Rumaihi, Muhammd, *Beyond Oil: Unity and Development in the Gulf* (London, Al Saqi, 1986).

Rush, Robert S., Epley, William W. and Center of Military History, *Multinational Operations, Alliances, and International Military Cooperation: Past and Future*. Proceedings of the 5th Workshop of the Partnership for Peace Consortium's Military History Working Group, Vienna, Austria, 4–8 April 2005. Cmh Publ. No. 70-101-1 (Washington, DC: Center for Military History, US Army, 2006).

Sadiki, Larbi, *The Search for Arab Democracy: Discourses and Counter-Discourses* (New York, NY, Columbia University Press, 2004).

Said Zahlan, Rosemarie, *The Making of the Modern Gulf States*, 2nd edn (Reading, Ithaca Press, 1998).

Sandwick, John A., *The Gulf Cooperation Council: Moderation and Stability in an Interdependent World* (Boulder, CO, Westview, 1987).

Schofield, Richard N., 'Border disputes in the Gulf: past, present, and future', in Sick, Gary G. and Potter, Lawrence G. (eds), *The Persian Gulf at the Millennium: Essays in Politics, Economy, Security, and Religion* (Houndmills, MacMillan, 1997).

Schofield, Richard N., 'Position, function, and symbol: the Shatt Al-Arab dispute in perspective', in Potter, Lawrence G. and Sick, Gary (eds), *Iran, Iraq, and the Legacies of War* (New York, NY, Palgrave Macmillan, 2004).

Schofield, Richard N., *Unfinished Business: Iran, the Uae, Abu Musa and the Tunbs* (London, Royal Institute of International Affairs, 2003).

Schweller, Randall L., 'Bandwagoning for profit: bringing the revisionist state back in', *International Security* xix/1 (1994), pp.72–107.

Schweller, Randall L. and David Priess, 'A tale of two realisms: expanding the institutions debate', *Mershon International Studies Review* xli/1 (1997), pp.1–32.

Shahak, Israël, *Open Secrets: Israeli Foreign and Nuclear Policies* (London, Pluto, 1997).

Shlaim, Avi, 'The rise and fall of the Oslo Peace Process', in Fawcett, Louise (ed.), *International Relations of the Middle East* (Oxford, Oxford University Press, 2005).

Shlaim, Avi, *War and Peace in the Middle East: A Concise History*. Revd edn (New York, NY, Penguin, 1995).

Sick, Gary, 'The coming crisis in the Persian Gulf', in Sick, Gary and Potter, Lawrence G. (eds), *The Persian Gulf at the Millennium: Essays in Politics, Economy, Security, and Religion* (Basingstoke, Macmillan, 1997).

Smith, Simon C., *Britain's Revival and Fall in the Gulf: Kuwait, Bahrain, Qatar, and the Trucial States, 1950–71* (New York, NY, RoutledgeCurzon, 2004).

Solingen, Etel, *Nuclear Logics: Contrasting Paths in East Asia and the Middle East*. Studies in International History and Politics (Princeton, NJ, Princeton University Press, 2007).

Spillmann, Kurt R. and Wenger, Andreas, *Towards the 21st Century: Trends in Post-Cold War International Security Policy* (Bern, Peter Lang, 1999).

Sultan Al-Qasimi, 'Introduction', in Ramazani, R. K., *The Gulf Cooperation Council: Record and Analysis* (Charlottesville, VA, University Press of Virginia, 1988)

Tal, Lawrence, *Politics, the Military and National Security in Jordan 1955–1967* (New York, NY, Palgrave, 2002).

Taryam, Abdullah O., *The Establishment of the United Arab Emirates 1950–85* (London, Croom Helm, 1987).

Tétreault, Mary A., *Stories of Democracy: Politics and Society in Contemporary Kuwait* (New York, NY, Columbia University Press, 2000).

Tétreault, Mary A., *The Kuwait Petroleum Corporation and the Economics of the New World Order* (Westport, CT, Quorum, 1995).

Tétreault, Mary A., *The Organization of Arab Petroleum Exporting Countries: History, Policies, and Prospects*. Contributions in Economics and Economic History No. 40 (Westport, CT, Greenwood, 1981).

Thakur, Ramesh C., *Nuclear Weapons-Free Zones* (Houndmills, Macmillan, 1998).

The Secretariat General of The Cooperation Council for the Arab States of the Gulf, *Closing Statements of the Sessions of the Supreme Council: Sessions 1–18* (Riyadh, 1998).

Tow, William T. *Subregional Security Cooperation in the Third World* (Boulder, CO, Lynne Rienner, 1990).

Tripp, Charles, 'Regional organizations in the Arab Middle East', in Hurrell, Andrew and Fawcett, Louise (eds), *Regionalism in World Politics: Regional Organization and International Order* (New York, NY, Oxford University Press, 1995), pp.283–309.

Tripp, Charles, *A History of Iraq* (Cambridge, Cambridge University Press, 2000).

Trofimov, Yaroslav, *The Siege of Mecca: The Forgotten Uprising in Islam's Holiest Shrine and the Birth of Al Qaeda* (New York, NY, Doubleday, 2007).

Twinam, Joseph W., *The Gulf, Cooperation and the Council* (Washington, DC, Middle East Policy Council, 1992).

United States Congress, Senate Committee on Foreign Relations, *The Greater Middle East Initiative: Sea Island and Beyond: Hearing before the Committee on Foreign Relations, United States Senate, One Hundred Eighth Congress, Second Session, June 2, 2004.* (Washington, DC, US Government Printing Office (GPO), 2004).

Vasquez, John A., 'The Realist paradigm and degenerative versus progressive research programs: an appraisal of neotraditional research on Waltz's balancing proposition', *American Political Science Review* xci/4 (1997), pp.899–912.

Vatikiotis, P. J., *Politics and the Military in Jordan, A Study of the Arab Legion, 1921–1957* (London, Cass, 1967).

Viotti, Paul R. and Kauppi, Mark V., *International Relations Theory: Realism, Pluralism, Globalism, and Beyond*. 3rd edn (Boston, MA, Allyn & Bacon, 1999).

Wæver, Ole, 'Introduction', in Neumann, Iver B. and Wæver, Ole (eds), *The Future of International Relations: Masters in the Making?* (London, Routledge, 1997).

Waever, Ole, 'The rise and fall of the inter-paradigm debate', in Smith, Steve, Booth, Ken and Zalewski, Marysia (eds), *International Theory: Positivism and Beyond* (Cambridge, Cambridge University Press, 1996).

Wallace, William, 'Regionalism in Europe', in Hurrell, Andrew and Fawcett, Louise (eds), *Regionalism in World Politics* (Oxford, Oxford University Press, 1995).

Walt, Stephen, 'International relations: one world, many theories', *Foreign Policy* 110 (1998), pp.29.

Walt, Stephen, *The Origins of Alliances* (Ithaca, NY, Cornell University Press, 1987).

Waltz, Kenneth N., *Theory of International Politics* (New York, NY, McGraw-Hill, 1979).

Wendt, Alexander, 'Constructing international politics', *International Security* xx/1 (1995), pp.71–81.

Wendt, Alexander, *Social Theory of International Politics* (Cambridge, Cambridge University Press, 1999).

Wyatt-Walter, Andrew, 'Regionalism, globalization, and world economic order', in Hurrell, Andrew and Fawcett, Louise (eds), *Regionalism in World Politics: Regional Organization and International Order* (Oxford, Oxford University Press, 1995).

Yapp, M. E., *The Near East Since the First World War* (London, Longman, 1996).

INDEX

A
Adler, Emanuel, 47
al-Abbas, Bandar, 75
al-Faisal, Saud, 95, 116
al-Faisal, Turki, 117
Al-Hujailan, Jamil Ibrahim, Shaikh, 104
Al-Khalifa, Khalifa bin Salman, Shaikh, 80
Al-Kharafi, Jassem, 116
Al-Maskari, Saif, 102
Al-Qasimi, Fahim bin Sultan, Shaikh, 103
Al Qasimi, Saqr bin Muhammad, Shaikh, 15
Al Sabah, Jabar, Shaikh, 24
Al Sabah, Saad, Shaikh, 24
Allison, Graham, 43
Arab Deterrent Force, 29
Arab National Charter, 29
Arab nationalism, centrist conception of, 49, 50
Arms Control and Regional Security (ACRS), 134
Association of Southeast Asian Nations (ASEAN), 61
Attiya, Abdel Rahman, 116
Ayoob, Mohammed, 46

B
Ba'athist regime, 28, 48
Bahrain-Qatar disputes, the, 104–107
Barnett, Michael, 29, 47

Bentham, Jeremy, 45
Bishara, Abdullah Yacoub, 43, 78, 81, 98, 106, 117, 153, 154

C
Camp David accords, 29
Common market, 61
Complete economic integration, 61
Comprehensive Test Ban Treaty (CTBT), 135
Cordesman, Anthony, 77
Crawford, Stewart, 18
Crucé, Émeric, 45
Customs union, 61, 64–66

D
David, Steven, 51
Détente, short-term, 123

E
Economic citizenship, 58–60
Economic integration, 21
   customs union, 61, 64–66
   free trade area, 60–61, 63–64
   joint industrial projects, 66
   obstacles and perspectives, 70–72
   oil policies, 69–70
   regionalism, 58–60
Economic union, 61
European Union–GCC Cooperation Agreement, 108

F
Free trade agreements (FTA), 66
Free trade area, 60–61, 63–64

G
Gause, Gregory, 48
GCC Specification and Measures Organization (GSMO), 69
Great Mosque of Mecca, 30
Grotius, Hugo, 45
Gulf Cooperation Council (GCC), 12
  Abu Musa and Tunb, 99–104
  Ba'athist regime, 28
  Bahrain-Qatar disputes, the, 104–107
  charter, analysis of, 34
  Commission for the Settlement of Disputes, 35
  customs union, 61, 64–66
    free trade area, 60–61, 63–64
    joint industrial projects, 66
    obstacles and perspectives, 70–72
    oil policies, 69–70
    regionalism, 58–60
  diplomacy in, 88–89
  economic integration
  European Union negotiations, 107–110
  external defense, 76–79
  first phase, conflict of, 93–94
  first summit, in Abu Dhabi, 33
  functional cooperation, 20–25
  incentives, issue of, 143–144
  internal security, 79–84
  International relations theory, regionalism concept
    Ba'athist regime, 48
    idealism, 45
    khaliji (Gulf) identity, 50, 51, 54
    neofunctionalism, 45
    neoliberal institutionalism, 44–46
    neoliberalism, 46
    neorealism, 44
    Pan-Arabism, 50, 51
    regional awareness, 46
  Iran–Iraq War, the, 27, 28, 31, 89–92
  Iranian nuclear challenge, 115–116
  Iranian revolution, 27
  NATO, 139–140
    experience, Eastern Europe, 144
    Istanbul Cooperation Initiative, 140–143
  negotiating with Iran, costs of, 120–124
  nuclear Iran *vs.* Iraq, 116–120
  nuclear option, 130–132
  outside powers role, UAE formation, 17–20
  power, realities of, 74–76
  preamble and 22 articles, 33
  second phase, conflict of, 94–96
  security conditions, 27–39
  security sector, 144–147
  showdown, implications of, 124–127
  third phase, conflict of, 96–99
  threat perceptions, 127–130
  'turning east' policy of, 151
  United Arab Emirates (UAE), precursor of, 12–13
  WMD proliferation, 132–135
Gulf International Bank (GIB), 67
Gulf Investment Corporation (GIC), 22, 67, 68
Gulf Organization for Industrial Consulting (GOIC), 68

H
Haas, Ernst, 45
Hamad, Emir, 123
Hammadi, Saadoun, 29
Hertog, Steffen, 58
Hurrell, Andrew, 52, 55
Hussein, Saddam, 29, 90, 93, 95, 115, 127, 130, 143

I
Ibrahim, Ezzat, 29
Idealism, 45

International Court of Justice (ICJ), 102, 103
International Monetary Fund (IMF), 35
International relations theory, regionalism concept
   Ba'athist regime, 48
   idealism, 45
   khaliji (Gulf) identity, 50, 51, 54
   neofunctionalism, 45
   neoliberal institutionalism, 44–46
   neoliberalism, 46
   neorealism, 44
   Pan-Arabism, 50, 51
   regional awareness, 46
Iran–Iraq War, 27, 28, 31, 48, 75, 89–92, 97, 118
Iranian Revolutionary Guard Corps, 100, 101
Islamic Conference Organization (ICO), 94

J
Joint industrial projects, 66

K
Kant, Immanuel, 45
khaliji (Gulf) identity, 50, 51, 54
Khomeini, Ayatollah, 27, 92, 118, 129
Kuwait National Democratic movement, 60

L
League of Arab States (LAS), 20–21, 22
   Cultural Treaty of, 22
   Charter of, 20, 21
LeBaron, Richard, 116
Lepgold, Joseph, 55
Luce, William, 11–12
Luciani, Giacomo, 69

M
Mattair, Thomas, 99
Mearsheimer, John, 42
Memorandum of Understanding (MoU), 152

Mill, John Stuart, 45
Moussa, Amr, 120
Muscat conference, 24, 25

N
Narrative explanatory protocol, 87
Nasserism, 11
NATO Istanbul Cooperation Initiative (NATO ICI), 140–143, 146–148
Neoclassical Realism, 47
Neoclassical Realist approach, 42
Neofunctionalism, 45
Neoliberal Institutionalism, 44–46
Neoliberalism, 46
Neorealism, 45, 46
Niblock, Tim, 71, 151
Nincic, Miroslav, 55
Nonneman, Gerd, 92
North American Free Trade Agreement (NAFTA), 22
North Atlantic Treaty Organization (NATO), 39, 77, 104
Nuclear Non-Proliferation Treaty, 119
Nuclear weapons-free zones (NWFZs), 132, 134
Nye, Joseph, 42, 48, 56

O
Oil policies, 69–70
Omani proposal, 29–30
Omnia munda mundis, 143
Operation Desert Storm, 100, 101
Organisation for Economic Co-operation and Development (OECD), 155
Organization of Arab Petroleum Exporting Countries (OAPEC), 34, 70
Organization of the Petroleum Exporting Countries (OPEC), 34, 70, 131

P
Pan-Arabism, 50, 51
Pelletreau, Robert, 51

Peninsula Shield Force, 78
Peninsula Solidarity Project, 11–12
Peterson, Erik, 88
Prima facie, 132
Prima facie trivial gestures, 15

Q
Qabus, Sultan, 24

R
Ra's al Khaimah, 15–17
Reagan, Ronald, 90
Regional awareness, 46
Regionalism, definition of, 43
Regionalization, 52
Rieger, Hans Christoph, 61
Rizzo, Alessandro Minuto, 141
Rowhani, Hassan, 116
Rushdie, Salman, 129

S
Saudi Basic Industries Corporation (SABIC), 58
Saudi International Bank (SIB), 67, 68
Scheffer, Jaap de Hoop, 144
Security and Extradition treaty, 23
Security Sector Reform (SSR), 140
Seznec, Jean-François, 66
Shlaim, Avi, 74
Status quo ante, 102, 103, 106
Sub-regional integration, 44, 47

Sui generis federation, 12
Sultan, Abdulaziz, 60

T
Tow, William, 74, 82
Transnationalism, 149

U
Unified Economic Agreement (UEA), 20, 63
United Nations Security Council Resolution 598, 96–98

V
Velayati, Ali-Akbar, 95

W
Waever, Ole, 46
Walt, Stephen, 47, 51
Waltz, Kenneth, 44
Weapons of Mass Destruction (WMD) proliferation, 114, 115, 132–135
Weapons of Mass Destruction Free Zone (WMDFZ), 133, 134
Weir, Michael, 19
Wendt, Alexander, 47
Wiggin, C. D., 19
Wilkinson, John, 107
Wilson, Harold, 14

Z
Zayid, Shaikh, 32
Zoellick, Robert, 66

www.ingramcontent.com/pod-product-compliance
Lightning Source LLC
Chambersburg PA
CBHW061445300426
44114CB00014B/1841